Hirschberg has laid out and estal
easy-to-read how-to-do-it book -
next great feature screenplay – frc
buffs eager for a fun, inspiring read.

.....ა ເວ just plain cinema

— Geoff Silverman, Literary Manager, Rain
Management, Santa Monica; Former Executive for
Brett Ratner, Brandon Tartikoff, and David Gerber

Create great characters and viewers will follow your story anywhere! This
insider's guide shows exactly how to do that, using current examples, numerous
excerpts, and advice from top screenwriters. A must read!

— Evan Smith, Author, *Writing Television Sitcoms*

Hirschberg's been there and done that. That's why this original contribution
to the screenwriter's craft is not only a "how to" and a "how not to," but also
a treasury of authentic and revealing insights into the construction of many of
the cinema's most memorable characters. Hirschberg clearly loves these characters and delights in searching for the secret that has brought them to life.

— David Feldshuh, Artistic Director, Schwartz Center for
the Performing Arts, Cornell University; Author, *Miss
Evers' Boys* (Pulitzer Prize nomination; winner of five
Emmys for HBO)

Hirschberg's *Reflections of the Shadow* is a smart, witty, and eclectically engaging
book that's full of great information and cogent observations. Furthermore,
it's wonderfully useful in that it can just as easily be used in a screenwriting
class as in a popular culture or a film and TV studies course, making it one of
the best books on narrative currently available.

— Robert C. Sickels, Editor, *The Business of Entertainment*;
Professor of American Film & Popular Culture,
Whitman College

Fresh and powerful. You will look at the fascinating mystery that is the good
guy/bad guy divide in all new ways, and get clues to clarify and enhance this
dynamic in your story, thanks to Jeff's book.

— Blake Snyder, Author, *Save the Cat!*®

Yes, Jeffrey Hirschberg's wonderful *Reflections of the Shadow* will definitely
help screenwriters create more fascinating villains and heroes. But for movie
addicts like me, it's just plain fun to read!

— Betty Jo Tucker, Editor and lead Film Critic, ReelTalk
Movie Reviews; Author of *Confessions of a Movie Addict*
and *Susan Sarandon: A True Maverick*

Hirschberg, an accomplished screenwriter at the core, compellingly "shows"
what other screenwriting books only begin to "tell." There is no "same old,
same old" in this indispensable approach to understanding the most essential
elements underlying this craft.

— Michael Schoonmaker, Chairman, Department of
Television-Radio-Film, The Newhouse School of
Syracuse University

Too many people write too many books in which they take a few of their favorite movies and try to impose on them the rules of screenwriting. Jeffrey Hirschberg is far more ambitious. He has taken a large number of films that are generally acknowledged to be the most successful American popular films, and he has analyzed them in depth, looking for the common principles that have led to the creation of memorable heroes and villains.

> — Howard Suber, Author, *The Power of Film*; Founding
> Chair, UCLA Film and Television Producers Program

Reflections of the Shadow not only breaks down classic movie good guys and bad guys, using script excerpts to illustrate exactly how they work, it also offers specific and practical exercises to help you build the same qualities into your own characters. Using this book almost feels like cheating, but, hey — if it gets your script sold, by all means, cheat away.

> — Chad Gervich, Author, *Small Screen, Big Picture: A
> Writer's Guide to the TV Business*; TV Writer/Producer,
> *Reality Binge, Foody Call, Speeders*

Hirschberg has done the impossible, filling a niche with his new, easy-to-digest guide for creating memorable characters. This book takes a rightful place among my "go-to" screenwriting guides that I always peruse before undertaking a new project. I can easily recommend it to newbies when they ask what books on screenwriting stand out among the masses. I will tell them there is a new screenwriting hero — Jeff Hirschberg!"

> — Lon Diamond, Co-Executive Producer and Creator,
> *Parker Lewis Can't Lose*; Consulting Producer, *The Tick*
> and *One Tree Hill*

Hirschberg's book will prove to be an indispensable tool to all emerging screenwriters. His Eleven "Laws" of Great Storytelling should be the final checklist every screenwriter consults before deeming his or her script "finished and ready" to be sent out into the world.

> — Marc Lapadula, Chairman, Yale University Screen-
> writing Program; Founder of the screenwriting
> programs at the University of Pennsylvania and Johns
> Hopkins University

It was nice to read in book form all the lessons I've learned from Jeff over the years when he would look at my rough drafts. With fun-to-read real life examples instead of just the typical abstract theory, this book is for everyone who wants to make their heroes and villains stand out from the crowd.

> — Matthew Berry, Story Editor, *Married With Children*;
> Co-writer, *Crocodile Dundee in Los Angeles*

REFLECTIONS
of the SHADOW
CREATING MEMORABLE HEROES AND VILLAINS FOR FILM AND TV

JEFFREY HIRSCHBERG

Published by Michael Wiese Productions
3940 Laurel Canyon Blvd. # 1111
Studio City, CA 91604
tel. 818.379.8799
fax 818.986.3408
mw@mwp.com
www.mwp.com

Cover Design: MWP
Interior Book Design: Gina Mansfield Design
Editor: Gary Sunshine

Printed by McNaughton & Gunn, Inc., Saline, Michigan
Manufactured in the United States of America

© 2009 Jeffrey Hirschberg

Library of Congress Cataloging-in-Publication Data

Hirschberg, Jeffrey, 1976–
  Reflections of the Shadow : creating memorable heroes and villains for
film and TV / Jeffrey Hirschberg.
       p. cm.
  Includes bibliographical references.
  ISBN 978-1-932907-61-2
1. Motion picture authorship. 2. Television authorship. 3. Heroes in
motion pictures. 4. Villains in motion pictures. 5. Heroes on television.
6. Villains on television. I. Title.
  PN1996.H57 2009
  808.2'3--dc22
                                        2009009674

for Michael Nozik

❦

A hero in his own right…

Why Should You Buy This Book?

The short answer is: because I need to put three kids through college. But, I'm sure you don't care about the mountain of expenses my wife and I will be facing with our kids' post-secondary education.

To paraphrase the immortal words of Donna Summer, you work hard for your money, and want to make sure the purchase of this book is a worthwhile investment in your life as a writer or film aficionado. But, are you the right audience?

Hollywood executives are obsessed with the subject of audience – specifically with the question, "Who is going to see this movie?" As they should be. After all, when the average studio film costs over $100 million (including prints and advertising), the person writing the check has every right to understand the audience the film is intended to attract.

Books are not too different. Publishers also want to know who will be interested in purchasing their product. Regarding this book, I would consider taking the plunge if you fall into one of the following categories:

: If you are a new or experienced screenwriter, producer, director, or studio executive, you will find value in the analysis of twenty memorable heroes and villains, interviews with screenwriters, and advice on creating unforgettable characters. Ideally, my hope is this book will play a small role in helping you write or discover the next global blockbuster (and if it happens to win a few awards along the way, all the better). A lofty goal, but hey, this is Hollywood, right?

If you are a film enthusiast, *Reflections of the Shadow* will enrich your viewing experience and help you apply a more critical eye to watching movies and television. For instance, you will be able to impress your friends with witty observations like, "Notice how the hero transforms from reactive to active at the midpoint of Act Two."

This book is different from others in its class because it is the perfect companion to many of the successful screenwriting and film-making books currently in the marketplace. Many of these books focus on story, structure, or "writing the screenplay that sells" – far fewer help writers create memorable heroes and villains. So, no matter what film books occupy your library, *Reflections of the Shadow* is an ideal complement.

But, is it for everybody? As much as I would like to think this topic garners interest from "kids from one to ninety-two," the truth is that *Reflections of the Shadow* is for those of you who bought advance IMAX tickets for *The Dark Knight*, gathered friends together to watch the season finale of *Lost*, and still get a chill every time Dorothy transforms from black and white into glorious color....

Acknowledgments

While my name may be the only one on the cover of *Reflections of the Shadow*, this book's gestation from idea to published tome had many cooks in the proverbial kitchen.

To my publisher, Michael Wiese Productions, and specifically Michael Wiese, Ken Lee, Gary Sunshine, and Gina Mansfield. Without them, I would have a really long and lonely Microsoft Word document sitting on my hard drive.

To Brett Kinsler, who initially helped me with a Jung-influenced title – including the concept of a "shadow." When I pitched the concept to David Koepp during our interview, he immediately reminded me of Belloq's brilliant speech in *Raiders of the Lost Ark*. Belloq (the film's villain) tells Indiana Jones (the film's hero), "I am a shadowy reflection of you. It would take only a nudge to make you like me. To push you out of the light." So, thank you, David, for transforming a kernel of an idea into a popcorn of a book title.

To my students, from whom I learn as much as I teach.

To my parents, who now have something to show every person who walks through their front door.

At last, this book – like any of my creative endeavors – is developed for, with, and because of the four people with whom I cohabitate. Without my wife Cindy and sons Marty, Nathan, and Justin (and how can I forget our little Al, the Havanese named after Alfred Hitchcock?), I doubt I would have ever written a solitary word – my true source for creative inspiration, indeed.

Table of Contents

Foreword

Back in the 1970s I had a brainstorm: Since I was already making so little money as a freelance magazine writer, it would be a career move to make even *more* less money as a freelance screenwriter! The only problem was, I could not lay my hands on a screenwriting manual. In that benighted, pre-Amazon era, I ended up having to take the train from Philadelphia to what was probably the only film-oriented bookstore on the Eastern seaboard, Manhattan's Cinemabilia, where I purchased the single volume they carried – itself a reprint from the '40s.

Today, of course, there are hundreds of "how to write a screenplay" books – but the one you are presently holding may be all you will need. In *Reflections of the Shadow*, Jeffrey Hirschberg has written the Swiss Army knife of screenplay texts. Taking his cues from not only Aristotle and Tolstoy, but the Metropolitan Museum of Art's Philippe de Montebello as well, Jeffrey uses guided "walking tours" to lead the reader through the corridors of well-known films, illuminating critical elements, turning points, and key plot revelations. The result is new insight into audience favorites, demonstrating that films coming from literally the opposite ends of the movie universe such as *Wall Street*, *Toy Story*, and *Star Wars* share structural and conceptual architecture, and – even more importantly – that the characters inhabiting those films' screenplays share the same psychological DNA.

Alfred Hitchcock once famously advised that any key piece of exposition the audience needed to know had to be stated three times. The first of Jeffrey's Eleven "Laws" of Great Storytelling is his own spin on Hitchcock's adage, and, in the spirit of the Master, I recommend that the entire list be *read* at least three times, and committed to memory. In short, whether you are an avid filmgoer, filmmaker, student, or teacher of film (or merely dreaming of doing one of the above), this is your book.

However, in the remote chance that you there pondering the purchase of this volume are, say, a business major who, as a result of some synergy-free, misguided media-merger-to-come will someday be sitting across from me in a Hollywood meeting, I'm begging you: *Please*, buy this book, and spare me yet another session with somebody who doesn't know the difference between Joseph Campbell and Campbell's soup, or who can't see that Gordon Gekko is worse than Darth Vader (and why), or cannot grasp that "protagonist" does not, in fact, always mean "the good guy." To you, Sir or Madame, I humbly plead, *buy this book*: If as Jeffrey reminds us, every hero's journey is a voyage to self-discovery, then *Reflections of the Shadow* can be your map to knowing what the hell you're talking about should I ever meet you. My peace of mind and your future are both in your hands, so stop reading this page and go to the cashier; this isn't a library, kid.

Steven E. de Souza
Screenwriter, *Die Hard, 48 Hrs., Lara Croft Tomb Raider: Cradle of Life*
Los Angeles, California
February 2009

Prelude

Why do heroes and villains in American cinema do what they do? What motivates them to risk their well-being to achieve goals that are often selfless and seemingly unattainable? Ever since the origins of storytelling, there have been heroes and villains captivating audiences and making people like you and me wish we were alongside them in their grandest pursuits.

The intention of this book is to provide insights into select film heroes and villains and the universal qualities they possess.

It is the thoughtful and prudent writer who looks to the past to examine characters who have stood the test of time and, in doing so, is able to create memorable heroes and villains who share similar traits, yet have an undeniable sense of uniqueness and individuality.

But first, my motivation for delving into such a topic.

A long time ago in a galaxy far, far away...

Actually, it was May 25, 1977, in Rochester, New York – and we knew our lives were about to change forever.

To be sure, there were other big movie openings. I vaguely remembered *Jaws* (1975) two years earlier (and subsequently began a ban on swimming that remains to this day); thanks to *Network* (1976), my friends and I were fond of chanting, "I'm as mad as hell, and I'm not gonna take this anymore!" (it would be another thirteen years until I actually saw the film); and *Logan's Run* (1976) was a recent hit (thankfully, I wasn't going to turn thirty for a *million* years).

But on this day, something special was in the air. Doug Ring, Mike Nozik, and I had the eerie sense history would be made.

After a precarious trek down French Road with our three-speed Schwinns, we landed at the Pittsford Plaza Cinema, secured our bikes with the most primitive of locks, and took our place in line.

Then we waited, and waited... and waited.

I cannot recall the exact conversation, but I feel fairly confident it was not about Laura Tipton's sudden metamorphosis into womanhood, the stark injustice of Mr. Felipe's latest Spanish test, or Bob Backlund's recent ascension within the World Wrestling Federation. No, we had only one thing on our minds on that humid day in Rochester – today was finally the day we were going to see *Star Wars* (1977).

When we settled into the vast theater filled to the brim, something very strange occurred. Something for which there was no precedent. Something so against our very fiber, we never could explain it. At that moment, waiting for the film to begin, we ate our popcorn with mechanic precision – and did not say a word to one another.

It was nothing less than a dead, catatonic gaze at the screen – not unlike Randle P. McMurphy at the end of *One Flew Over the Cuckoo's Nest* (1975) or Jack Torrance during most of *The Shining* (1980) (both unforgettably played by Jack Nicholson).

The truth is we did not speak because at the ripe age of ten, we could not verbalize what was going through our minds. We could not talk about the sense of anticipation running through our veins. All we could do was occasionally glance at one another, deliver a subtle nod, then avert our collective stares back to the screen.

After we listened to Muzak for what seemed like an eternity, the theater suddenly went dark. I had been in movie theaters many times before, but this time was different. I clutched my popcorn as tightly as I could – as if the rotund carton would somehow be my companion for what was about to transpire. The majestic 20th Century-Fox logo and accompanying rhythmic snare drum illuminated the theater, preparing each and every one of us for the grandeur soon to come. I took a deep breath, delivered a final glimpse at Doug and Mike, and then... the John Williams score reverberated through my body like a jolt of electricity. The *Star Wars* logo brandished itself in giant, lustrous white letters, then faded into oblivion. The crowd cheered, I raised my arms in some sort of perceived victory, and the carton of popcorn fell through my knees and smashed onto the floor. Except for the single piece I embraced in my hand, I never looked down to investigate the fate of the carton – my eyes refused to leave the screen.

As the rolling prelude began, I noticed the lone piece of popcorn cradled in my hand and instinctively tossed it into my mouth. Maybe it was that John Williams score again, but going to the movies never tasted so good.

About four and a half minutes into the film, an unforgettable moment occurred. First, there was the ominous music… then the faint image of a sturdy, soaring black figure draped in a flowing cape… then a cacophony of pure white smoke. Finally, there was the breathing. Deep breathing. The kind of breaths one would only hear via a scuba mask in the depths of the ocean.

But, there was no water to be found. No, this intimidating series of inhaled and exhaled breaths emanated from none other than the film's evil incarnate: Darth Vader.

He had no dialogue during those first few moments on screen. No matter. We were immediately drawn to his overt malevolence, towering stature, and command of all others on the screen. Put simply, we could not wait to see him again. We took the bait and were hooked – and it was this story's villain who was doing the fishing.

At the time, I had no idea I would follow this saga for the next six years. In fact, it would not be until *Return of the Jedi* (1983) when Vader's character arc would become complete. Near death, in the arms of Skywalker, Vader speaks to his one-time nemesis – not as a foe, but as a father (from a screenplay by Lawrence Kasdan and George Lucas, based on a story by George Lucas).

```
                    DARTH VADER
         Luke, help me take this mask off.


                        LUKE
              But you'll die.
```

```
          DARTH VADER
Nothing can stop that now. Just
for once, let me look on you
with my own eyes. Now go, my son.
Leave me.

          LUKE
No, you're coming with me. I
will not leave you here. I've
got to save you.

          DARTH VADER
You already have, Luke. You
were right. You were right about
me. Tell your sister — you were
right.
```

It is only at this point that Vader is finally aware of his shortcomings as a human being and a paternal figure. That this epiphany comes at the concluding moments of his life makes this timeless villain far more ironic and tragic than the audience could ever have imagined.

For the majority of the initial *Star Wars* trilogy, Skywalker saw Darth Vader as the personification of pure evil, intent on achieving ultimate power and the destruction of all that was good. In the end, however, Skywalker sees Vader as a sympathetic old man who ultimately is able to look deep within himself, with Vader finally concluding that Skywalker's journey was indeed virtuous and just.

Speaking of Skywalker, something spectacular happened about thirty minutes into the film. I cannot place the exact moment, nor can I attribute this phenomenon to a specific exchange of dialogue, a furtive glance between characters, or a moment of stunning visuals. At some point toward the end of Act One, it was no longer Luke Skywalker discovering his destiny and ultimately destroying the Evil Empire. It wasn't even the childlike Mark Hamill playing a role. Up on the screen, it was me. The rarest of cinematic magical moments took place in the middle of that theater on May 25, 1977.

For 121 minutes, I was a hero.

No one was going to stop me from blowing that Death Star to bits. Not Darth Vader, not the Emperor, and certainly not my own insecurities. I would risk it all and never look back. It didn't matter that when the lights went up, I was the same gawky ten-year-old I was two hours earlier. What mattered was that for the briefest of moments, I saw myself as a true hero and began to realize what was possible. After all, if Skywalker could save the world, maybe I could ace my next spelling test.

CUT TO: *Twenty-Eight Years Later*

It was the winter of 2005 and the sixteen inches of snow that blanketed Rochester the night before precluded my sons Marty and Nathan (seven and five, respectively) and me from doing anything except staying inside and keeping warm. I'm not sure what motivated me to reach for my VHS copy of *Star Wars* on that Saturday afternoon (perhaps it was my very own Obi-Wan Kenobi tucked away in my subconscious), but something inside said it was time for my boys to partake in the same experience I had enjoyed back in 1977. While my head told me my thirty-two inch Sony Wega television and accompanying Bose Wave radio would not deliver quite the visceral punch of that theater in Rochester, my heart nonetheless told me it didn't matter.

I gave little warning to the lads as to what they were about to see — just that I wanted to show them "a cool movie." So, I closed every shade in the room and, to my wife's dismay, cranked up the volume. Then, I just watched them watch the story unfold.

It was better than the movie itself.

part 1

Exploring Memorable Heroes and Villains

chapter 1

The Incomplete Hero:
Why Do Heroes Do What They Do?

"A hero is someone who has given his or her life to something bigger than oneself."

– Joseph Campbell

.Defining the Hero

```
          RENAULT
     What in heaven's name brought
     you to Casablanca?

          RICK
     My health. I came to
     Casablanca for the waters.

          RENAULT
     The waters? What waters?
     We're in the desert.

          RICK
     I was misinformed.
```

Luke Skywalker is far from the only hero depicted in film. In 2003, the American Film Institute (AFI) issued its list, *100 Years... 100 Heroes & Villains* (Gregory Peck's unforgettable portrayal of Atticus Finch in *To Kill a Mockingbird* (1962) received the most votes in the "Hero" category). The AFI uses the following definition for a "hero":

"For voting purposes, a 'hero' was defined as a character(s) who prevails in extreme circumstances and dramatizes a sense of morality, courage, and purpose. Though they may be ambiguous or flawed, they often sacrifice themselves to show humanity at its best."

While this description embraces many of a hero's traits, it does not adequately encompass the importance of the hero's goal, nor does it place enough emphasis on the obstacles a hero must overcome in order to achieve said goal. So, for the purposes of this discussion, we will use the following definition I have utilized throughout my eighteen years of screenwriting:

"A hero is someone who accomplishes a clear goal for a greater good by overcoming obstacles with the help of a mentor at significant risk to the hero's livelihood."

Ever since Achilles' exploits in *The Iliad*, heroes have been a staple in Western literature and, subsequently, in modern American cinema. They capture our imagination, send our pulse through the roof, and bring us to the edge of our seat – helping us see ourselves in them – and helping us see the potential in all of us.

The goals of this chapter are: 1) to explore the motivations behind cinematic heroism (Why do heroes do what they do?); and 2) to explore the commonalities among popular American cinematic heroes, focusing on two classic Hollywood good guys: Rick Blaine in *Casablanca* (1942) and Rocky Balboa in *Rocky* (1976).

I also will demonstrate that creating an effective hero in American cinema is one of the most critical goals a screenwriter or director should have in order to connect with the audience – just as important as the film's structure, genre, or core concept.

As Shakespeare might have said if he were a screenwriter, "The hero's the thing."

Why Do Heroes Do What They Do?

> ADRIAN
>
> Why do you wanna fight?
>
> ROCKY
>
> Because I can't sing or dance.

While Joseph Campbell's 1972 book, *The Hero With a Thousand Faces* and Christopher Vogler's *The Writer's Journey: Mythic Structure for Writers* (3rd ed., 2007) focus on the journey of the hero, a more fundamental question remains: What motivates the hero to embark on the journey in the first place? In other words, why do heroes do what they do?

A simple question, but far from an easy answer.

According to S. Mackey-Ellis in her book *The Hero and the Perennial Journey Home in American Film* (2001), central to the hero's motivation is his desire to return home. She exemplifies this concept by analyzing Odysseus' journey in *The Odyssey*. She writes:

> "This circular or mandalic pattern is most clearly articulated in Homer's *Odyssey* where Odysseus (literally 'the traveler'), after leaving Ithaca to fight the Trojan War, both wittingly and unwittingly travels for another ten years before finally arriving home. Along the way he and his shipmates encounter numerous challenges that ultimately result in Odysseus' edification and growth. He alone of all his companions, however, does not succumb to the appeals of the unconscious, and thus returns to Ithaca where he must battle the numerous suitors for his wife's hand who have moved in and polluted his hearth and home" (4).

Just in case you haven't read *The Odyssey* since high school, there are several relevant examples of a hero's desire to go home in film. For instance, Mackey-Ellis continues by suggesting that several preeminent American films released in the 1930s and 1940s, including *Gone with the*

Wind (1939), *The Wizard of Oz* (1939), and *It's a Wonderful Life* (1946), draw on the "universal quest for home" (126).

As we will discuss later in the book, the "universal quest for home" also has manifested itself in contemporary movies. For example, in *Gladiator* (2000), General Maximus is clear and consistent in communicating his goal throughout the film — he wants to go home.

That many Hollywood heroes embark on a journey to find their literal or figurative home is readily apparent. However, the primary motivation for many of these heroes, it is argued, lies within the heroes themselves and their desire to feel complete.

For example, Table 1 features a sample of heroes who appeared in the top ten on AFI's list of *100 Years... 100 Heroes & Villains:*

Table 1: Anatomy of a Hero

Hero	Goal	Obstacle(s)	Risk
Atticus Finch *To Kill a Mockingbird* (1962)	: To acquit Tom Robinson	: The town : Racism	: His career and reputation : His own life and the life of his family
Indiana Jones *Raiders of the Lost Ark* (1981)	: To obtain the Ark of the Covenant	: The Nazis : The environment	: His own life : The lives of his comrades
James Bond *Dr. No* (1962)	: To thwart Dr. No's plan for world domination	: Dr. No and his henchmen : Time	: His own life : The lives of countless others
Rick Blaine *Casablanca* (1942)	: To reunite with Ilsa : To ensure Ilsa's happiness : To save Ilsa	: Ilsa's marriage to Victor : The Nazis	: His heart : His own life
Clarice Starling *The Silence of the Lambs* (1991)	: To catch "Buffalo Bill"	: Hannibal Lecter : Buffalo Bill : Her own past	: Her own life : Her job
Rocky Balboa *Rocky* (1976)	: To go the distance with Apollo Creed : To win Adrian's heart	: Apollo Creed : His own physical limitations : His own insecurities	: His health : His pride : His heart
Ellen Ripley *Aliens* (1986)	: To destroy The Alien : To survive	: The Alien : The environment	: Her own life
T.E. Lawrence *Lawrence of Arabia* (1962)	: To defeat the Turks	: The Turks	: His own life

Interestingly, of the heroes listed above, seven out of eight risked their own lives to achieve their goals. That is an indication of the types of heroes who are most appealing to audiences – those who "risk it all." Stakes as dramatic as the loss of one's life tend to be universal in nature, and therefore increase the ability of a film's hero to connect with an audience.

Heroes Are Completely Incomplete

While the specific motivations of the heroes in Table 1 vary, there is a common personality trait we see over and over in American film: The hero feels "completely incomplete" and must fill a void. Whether this feeling of incompleteness is unconscious or conscious is not as relevant as the end result — that many heroes begin with something of significance missing in their lives and end with a feeling of completeness.

Sigourney Weaver's performance in *Aliens* (1986) as the tough-as-nails Ellen Ripley is an example of a hero yearning to be complete (more on this unforgettable hero in Chapter Three). In this case, her incompleteness takes a bifurcated form: part desire to bring her experience with The Alien to closure (her experience depicted in the first film continues to monopolize her dreams), and part desire to act on her maternal instincts. In *Projecting the Shadow: The Cyborg Hero in American Film* (1995), J. H. Rushing and T. S. Frentz describe the extent to which Ellen must journey in order to defeat her monstrous adversary. They write:

> "… The heroine must first become a hardened warrior. That is, she must become what she fights, a technologized hunter possessed by an egoic perfectionism that fuels an almost demonic drive to destroy her nemesis, even if that obsession means the ruin of herself and those around her" (214).

It is precisely Ellen's "obsession" that allows her to fill the void The Alien has created within her. In addition, the fact that The Alien is female and laying eggs — effectively creating an entire population of like creatures — brings out Ellen's maternal instincts in protecting Rebecca 'Newt' Jorden, a young girl stranded on the precarious planet. It is this life and death encounter that elucidates these instincts and thus helps complete a persona that was theretofore without purpose.

Accomplishing a Clear Goal for a Greater Good

```
            ILSA
You're saying this only to
make me go.


            RICK
I'm saying it because it's true.
Inside of us, we both know you
belong with Victor. You're part
of his work, the thing that keeps
him going. If that plane leaves
the ground and you're not with
him, you'll regret it. Maybe not
today. Maybe not tomorrow, but
soon and for the rest of your life.
```

What is it about film heroes that draw us in? Why do we root for them... clench our fists in anticipation of their perilous predicaments... sit up straight in our seat, assuming our posture will aid them in achieving their goals... and close our eyes, as if our limited vision will guide our heroes to victory? Perhaps it is a film's ability to allow viewers to see themselves as heroes − an occurrence that typically commences when a hero begins her journey.

Campbell (1972) writes of "The Call to Adventure," where the hero is summoned to take part in a journey. He states:

> "But whether small or great, and no matter what the stage or grade of life, the call rings up the curtain, always, on a mystery of transfiguration − a rite, or moment, of spiritual passage, which when complete, amounts to a dying and a birth. The familiar life horizon has been outgrown; the old concepts, ideals, and emotional patterns no longer fit; the time for the passing of a threshold is at hand" (51).

Vogler (2007) adds: "The Call to Adventure can often be unsettling and disorienting to the hero" (102). That is precisely the case with Ellen Ripley in *Aliens*, as she is called once again to confront her greatest fears in battling The Alien. To say this adventure is "unsettling and disorienting" to her is an understatement. She is about to embark on a journey of unconscionable peril and is understandably reluctant to begin. It is this impending danger and her initial unwillingness to participate that helps the audience connect with her, and feel empathy for her.

Let's face it: Heroes are reluctant because they are often rational – and most rational people do not willingly enter into potentially perilous situations on a whim.

As we see with many "incomplete" heroes in movies, Campbell's "threshold" often outwardly takes the form of obtaining a tangible goal or defeating a villain. Inwardly, however, the hero's villain is often herself – thus the need to feel complete.

Rick Blaine and Rocky Balboa

On the surface, Rick Blaine (Humphrey Bogart) and Rocky Balboa (Sylvester Stallone) could not be more dissimilar. They are of different eras, different demographics, and from different backgrounds. One could even argue the films in question – *Casablanca* and *Rocky* – attract a completely different audience. That stated, both films have proven to be enormously successful. *Casablanca* was nominated for eight Academy Awards, winning three (Best Picture, Best Director, and Best Screenplay). *Rocky* won the Golden Globe for Best Motion Picture – Drama and was nominated for ten Academy Awards, winning three (Best Picture, Best Director, and Best Film Editing). In addition, both Humphrey Bogart and Sylvester Stallone earned Best Actor in a Leading Role Academy Award nominations for their heroic portrayals of Rick Blaine and Rocky Balboa, respectively.

Beyond the Hollywood accolades these two films garnered is a more important commonality of their two heroes – their desire to achieve a clear goal for a greater good. In *Rocky*, Rocky Balboa's external goal is readily apparent and accessible to the audience – to go the distance with Apollo Creed. The goal is made that much more poignant since the public wants Apollo defeated by our heroic underdog – thus increasing the pressure (and the stakes) for Balboa to emerge victorious.

Balboa's internal goal – to win Adrian's heart – is a fundamentally more arduous objective to achieve. In his core, Balboa understands the harder he pushes himself physically, the more likely he will achieve success in his bout with Apollo Creed. There is a quantitative nature to his quest. But, love is another story. Balboa also understands no matter how valiant his pursuit of Adrian, there are many indefinable factors out of his control – factors that will in no way guarantee his success. It is the very qualitative nature of this goal that makes Balboa's heart that much more vulnerable than the rest of his body.

Sometimes, a hero's goal can evolve. In *Casablanca*, Rick Blaine's initial goal is to reunite with his lost love, Ilsa (Ingrid Bergman). When he discovers she is married to Victor Laszlo (Paul Henreid), however, his goal becomes completely selfless – to ensure Ilsa's happiness. Blaine's motivation is that of a classic hero. In allowing Ilsa and Victor to board the plane in the final scene, he is accomplishing his ultimate goal – ensuring the woman he loves will be happy forever. And, he is motivated by the common good – so Victor may continue his revolutionary efforts against the Nazis.

The irony of Blaine's final act cannot be overstated. In Act One of the film, he is fond of saying, "I stick my neck out for nobody." It is not until Act Three – specifically the final scene – when we see the true metamorphosis of his character. It is at this moment when Blaine, in fact, does the one thing he promised he would never do – stick his neck out by concocting a plot to save the woman he loves while leaving himself behind.

Overcoming Obstacles With the Help of a Mentor

```
            ROCKY
Ah come on, Adrian, it's true.
I was nobody. But that don't
matter either, you know? Cause
I was thinkin', it really don't
matter if I lose this fight. It
really don't matter if this guy
opens my head, either. Cause all
I wanna do is go the distance...
```

Timeless heroes in American film simply can't overcome the internal and external obstacles they face on their own. They need help, and assistance often comes in the form of a mentor, a friend, or even a stranger who can act as a catalyst. As J. L. Henderson writes in *Ancient Myths and Modern Man* (1964):

> "In many of these stories the early weakness of the hero
> is balanced by the appearance of strong 'tutelary' figures
> – or guardians – who enable him to perform the super-
> human tasks that he cannot accomplish unaided" (101).

One of the most prominent and influential cinematic tutelary figures in the last thirty years is *Star Wars'* Yoda. Rushing and Frentz (1995) describe him as having "the holy man's qualities of patience, discipline, indifference to material wealth, willingness to suffer, intro-spection, and higher consciousness" (2).

Regarding the mentor's ability to influence heroes, Vogler (2007) writes, "Mentors in stories act mainly on the mind of the hero, chang-ing her consciousness or redirecting her will" (121). Like most heroes in film, Balboa needs assistance from other characters to overcome his inner demons. Ultimately, it is Balboa's manager, Mickey, who inspires him to fill his void of insecurity and achieve his ultimate goal, thus becoming Balboa's "Yoda" – his "tutelary" motivator.

To be sure, Balboa has both internal and external obstacles to overcome. Internally, he is plagued with self-doubt. For much of the film, he thinks he is nothing more than "just a bum." Overcoming this inherent lack of self-worth is critical for him to achieve his goal – especially in light of the fact his opponent – Apollo Creed – is any-thing but lacking in confidence. As with most heroes, the likelihood of Balboa achieving his goal without the tutelage of his mentor is, at best, uncertain.

In *Casablanca*, the character of Rick Blaine is more of a conundrum. Like Winston Churchill's assessment of Russia, Blaine is a "riddle, wrapped in a mystery, inside an enigma." Yet, it is his self-centered neutrality we find most intriguing. When he says, "I stick my neck out for nobody," he means it. In Act One of the film, Ugarte, one of

Blaine's regulars, entrusts him to hold invaluable Letters of Transit. Blaine obliges, but when Ugarte is arrested moments later, Blaine refuses to help him. Soon thereafter, Ugarte is arrested and Blaine offers no regret.

This selfish – or "incomplete" – aspect of Blaine's character cannot change without the help of his "tutelary" motivator, Ilsa, in that it is his love for her that allows him to become selfless – risking his own life while saving her at the end of the film. As Henderson (1964) writes:

> "... The essential function of the heroic myth is the development of the individual's ego-consciousness – his awareness of his own strengths and weaknesses – in a manner that will equip him for the arduous tasks with which life confronts him" (101).

With both Rocky Balboa and Rick Blaine, their transformation to become "complete" is a journey of self-awareness – a journey that, if executed effectively alongside a mentor, brings a willing audience along for the ride.

Risking His/Her Livelihood

```
              RICK
    Last night we said a great many
    things. You said I was to do the
    thinking for both of us. Well,
    I've done a lot of it since then,
    and it all adds up to one thing:
    You're getting on that plane with
    Victor where you belong.
```

Heroes are no more than mere mortals if they do not risk their livelihood. In the case of Rocky Balboa, one can argue he is a character with nothing to lose, so the risk is minimal. One can approach his journey, however, in another way. It is true, Balboa has little in his life in terms of material goods or familial support, so in that sense, he has little to lose. However, should his trek be unsuccessful – should he not achieve his goal – he will have nothing left and in his mind, forever be "a bum," successfully fulfilling his self-prophecy.

Moreover, if he doesn't achieve his goal of winning Adrian's heart, his soul will surely forever feel "incomplete." So, the risk to Balboa is real and significant. His sheer perseverance to stay the course inspires the audience to root for him to achieve his external goal (going the distance with Apollo Creed) and his internal goal (gaining the confidence to win Adrian's heart).

Rick Blaine also risks a broken heart with his desire to reunite with Ilsa. Unlike Balboa, however, he also risks his life by devising a plot to fool the Nazis – a scheme that will surely guarantee his being on the run for the rest of his days. It is the moment when Blaine decides to plot against the Nazis in order to save Ilsa when he finally becomes "complete" – a satisfying denouement to his character's arc.

As he holds her in his arms, we can feel something of significance going through Blaine's mind: He has reached an epiphany that will forever change the course of his life.

We, of course, do not experience the extent of his true selflessness until the very end of the film and it is at that point when we see his void has been filled – by insisting she board the plane with Victor, he has risked his life to save the woman he loves – knowing he will never see her again.

Heroes are a complicated lot. On the one hand, they often are intro-duced as selfish, self-absorbed characters who loathe the idea of sac-rificing themselves for the sake of others. But, as with so many of the films that have stood the test of time, the heroes we remember best are the ones who do just that.

Storytellers who have given us classic films like the ones that appear on AFI's *100 Years... 100 Heroes & Villains* list understand that creating a compelling and memorable hero is precisely the element that brings the film together and provides a sense of timelessness all filmmakers hope to achieve.

Heroes like Rick Blaine and Rocky Balboa have captivated audiences for as long as storytelling has existed. That they often sacrifice themselves in order to feel "complete" can be a conscious or unconscious act. Nevertheless, it is their steadfastness toward achieving a clear goal for the common good by overcoming obstacles with the help of a mentor, while risking their own livelihood, that enthralls our collective imagination, allowing us to see the hero in all of us.

exercises

(*Note:* These exercises are interchangeable with the villain exercises at the end of Chapter Two.)

1. Re-watch your three favorite films, paying special attention to the heroes. Take notes during your viewings and determine their motivations for heroism.

2. Watch three trailers from upcoming films. What can you ascertain about each movie's hero? Are their goals clearly stated?

3. Write down three favorite novels and see if the heroes fit within the definition offered at the beginning of the chapter: "A hero is someone who accomplishes a clear goal for a greater good by overcoming obstacles with the help of a mentor at significant risk to the hero's livelihood."

chapter 2

The Villain as Outsider:
Why Do Villains Do What They Do?

"The more successful the villain, the more successful the picture"

– Alfred Hitchcock

Introduction

Why do villains in film do what they do? What motivates them to shun the mores of society in order to achieve goals that typically are contrary to what most would consider good and just?

There is little doubt that audiences have always been enthralled with villains. Yet, those same audiences consistently root for heroes to defeat the most boisterous bad guys. Why? Is it possible we only like our villains as appetizers, but by the end of the meal, crave a heroic dessert?

The idea of crafting memorable villains has relevance in the milieus of film criticism and screenwriting. The thoughtful critic and prudent writer looks to the past to examine characters who have stood the test of time, and in doing so, is able to create memorable villains who often share similar traits, yet have an undeniable sense of uniqueness and individuality.

While much has been written about cinematic heroism, there has been far less of a discussion on villains in film. "Although the hero archetype has been explored in-depth," writes Michaela Meyer in "Utilizing Mythic Criticism in Contemporary Narrative Culture" (*Communication Quarterly*, 51.4), "other prominent archetypal forms such as the shadow, trickster, or sage are under-explored and under-theorized" (520).

The goals of this chapter are: 1) to explore the motivations behind cinematic villainy (Why do villains do what they do?); and 2) to explore the commonalities among popular American cinematic villains, focusing on two classic Hollywood baddies: Alex Forrest in *Fatal Attraction* (1987) and Gordon Gekko in *Wall Street* (1987).

Defining the Villain

As mentioned in the Prelude, while Darth Vader is widely considered one of the iconic villains in American cinema, he has had more than his share of competition for evil. In the American Film Institute (AFI) list, *100 Years... 100 Heroes & Villains*, Anthony Hopkins' portrayal of Dr. Hannibal Lecter in *The Silence of the Lambs* (1991) received the most votes in the "Villain" category. The AFI uses the following definition for a "Villain":

> "For voting purposes, a 'villain' was defined as a character(s) whose wickedness of mind, selfishness of character, and will to power are sometimes masked by beauty and nobility, while others may rage unmasked. They can be horribly evil or grandiosely funny, but are ultimately tragic."

While the above definition can apply to many villains in film, it is ultimately limiting in that it neglects to address the facet of motivation. To that end, for the purposes of this discussion, we will use the following definition I have utilized throughout my career:

> "Externally, a villain is someone who strives to achieve a goal without regard to the welfare of the other characters or norms of society. Internally, however, the villain is an outsider yearning for legitimacy – desperately wanting to be a part of the same society that will forever shun him/her."

Even though villains' motivations are bifurcated, they typically believe their actions are laudable and will improve their stature in society – thus making the world a better place. This discussion will focus on villains' internal motivations and the way those motivations translate to actions deemed deplorable by society. While there are surely limitations to this approach, the aim is to identify certain trends consistent with villains who have stood the test of time.

It should be noted that in many films, the villain is not an individual literally or figuratively battling the story's hero. Rather, the villain is sometimes a detrimental personality trait of the hero, a force of nature, or a ticking clock. In *Leaving Las Vegas* (1995), the villain is ultimately the hero, Ben Sanderson, and his inability to control his alcoholism and depression. In *Twister* (1996), the villain is the tornado. In *Nick of Time* (1995), the ultimate villain is time itself.

This chapter focuses on villains who are actual characters desiring legitimacy. These are the characters we love to hate – personalities whose existence frightens and excites us at the same time. We may root for our heroes, but it is often the villain's myopic view of the world that captures our attention, creates the most entertaining dramatic conflict, and provides a sense of clarity for the importance of the hero's journey.

Examples of the various ways in which villains desire legitimacy are depicted in Table 2, which I created from villains who appear on AFI's list of *100 Years… 100 Heroes & Villains*.

Table 2: Anatomy of a Villain			
Villain	External Motivation	Internal Motivation	Hero
Hannibal Lecter *The Silence of the Lambs* **(1991)**	: To be free : To help Clarice catch Buffalo Bill	: To be understood and accepted for his "genius"	: Clarice Starling
Darth Vader *The Empire Strikes Back (1980)*	: To squash the Rebellion	: To be seen as a legitimate father and make peace with his son, Luke : To be respected as a leader	: Luke Skywalker
The Wicked Witch of the West *The Wizard of Oz* **(1939)**	: To obtain the ruby slippers from Dorothy	: To be respected and feared by the other witches and residents of Oz	: Dorothy Gale
Annie Wilkes *Misery* **(1990)**	: To keep Paul captive until he finishes his new book… and beyond	: To be taken seriously as Paul's "number one fan" and be accepted by him	: Paul Sheldon
Joan Crawford *Mommie Dearest* **(1981)**	: To maintain and grow her Hollywood career	: To be respected by the Hollywood establishment and her family	: Christina Crawford
Hans Gruber *Die Hard* **(1988)**	: To successfully steal $640 million in bearer bonds	: To be appreciated as a criminal mastermind	: John McClane

Interestingly, while the villains in Table 2 have similar internal motivations, their films represent a variety of genres – from action-adventure films like *Die Hard* to dramatic biographies like *Mommie Dearest*, to fantasies like *The Wizard of Oz* and *The Empire Strikes Back*.

While villains can appear in all shapes and sizes and in all types of films, many still have a common thread with regard to their motivations – an inherent need for respect that triggers their wicked ways.

Why Do Villains Do What They Do?

Villains and their evil deeds have never been out of vogue. As Martin Norden wrote in "The Changing Face of Evil in Film and Television" (*Journal of Popular Film and Television*, 28.2), "Evil has proved a particularly serviceable attraction for legions of film/TV practitioners... In doing so, they have turned evil into nothing short of a ubiquitous commodity for our consumption" (50).

Adds Ken Burke in "Heroes and Villains in American Film (*International Journal of Instructional Media*, 17.1):

> "... Film is especially rich in the complexities of the hero story and in the use of not only the traditional superhero-archfiend contest but also the modern evolutions of common heroes and villains, anti-heroes, and situational villains – whose value is relative to the audience member" (64).

But evil deeds are only half of the equation. The intent – or motivation – of villains is essential in understanding them as authentic three-dimensional characters with emotions as complex as their heroic counterparts.

According to Vogler (74), many villains do what they do simply because they believe they are morally superior to the hero, concluding, "a villain is the hero of his own myth, and the audience's hero is his villain." He adds:

> "Keep in mind that while some villains... exult in being bad, many don't think of themselves as evil at all. In their own minds they are right, the heroes of their own stories... The arcs of their stories are mirror images: When the hero is up, the villain is down. It depends on point of view" (169-70).

While moral superiority is an authentic belief among many villains, one cannot escape the notion that villains often want to be a part of the hero's world. Deep down, it is the innate insecurities of villains that fuel their desire for accolades so often thrust upon heroes. Whether it is Michael Corleone in *The Godfather: Part III* (1990), who seeks to legitimize his crime family's business interests, the Queen in *Snow White and the Seven Dwarfs* (1937), who is determined to be "the fairest of them all," or Annie Wilkes in *Misery* (1990), who wants to be taken seriously as Paul Sheldon's "number one fan," villains often want what they never can have – acceptance.

Outsiders Yearning for Legitimacy

While the specific motivations of the villains in Table 2 vary, there is a common personality trait we see over and again in American film – namely, villains yearning to be a legitimate part of the same societies that shun them.

For example, in *Mommie Dearest* (1981), Joan Crawford (Faye Dunaway) will do almost anything to maintain her stardom, even if at the expense of her children's happiness. Externally, she is motivated to maintain (and grow) her celebrity. To that end, she is the consummate movie star, projecting an image to the public as the perfect mother and professional. Internally, however, she struggles with living the same reality seen by the public. In her personal life, she has battles with alcohol and men, and is a perfectionist to the extreme, consistently taking out her shortcomings on her innocuous adoptive children, Christina and Christopher (Mara Hobel (as a child) and Diana Scarwid (as an adult) and Jeremy Scott Reinbolt (as a child) and Xander Berkeley (as an adult)).

But, how could this villainous movie star – seemingly an insider – actually be an outsider wanting to be taken seriously? First of all, the adoption of Christina and Christopher is Joan's attempt to show the public she can be a traditional mother. Like a true Hollywood public relations professional, Joan consistently puts forth the perception that she and her children are the personification of a perfect family – even if striving for this objective results in the mental and physical abuse of her son and daughter.

This behavior vigorously backfires on her, causing an irreparable rift between Joan and Christina (from a screenplay by Robert Getchell, Tracy Hotchner, Frank Perry, and Frank Yablans, based on the book by Christina Crawford).

>   JOAN
>   Why can't you give me the respect that
>   I'm entitled to? Why can't
>   you treat me like I would be
>   treated by any stranger on the street?
>
>   CHRISTINA
>   Because I am not one of your fans!

Even in her career, she is eventually nothing more than an outsider, desperately trying to regain the legitimacy she once enjoyed, as depicted in this scene with the head of MGM, Louis B. Mayer (Howard Da Silva):

>   LOUIS B. MAYER
>   Joan, my Joan, you're in a
>   position to do me a favor that
>   will be as big a favor for you as
>   it is for me.
>
>   JOAN
>   You don't have to ask. You only
>   have to tell me.
>
>   LOUIS B. MAYER
>   Good. I want you to leave Metro.
>
>   JOAN
>   Leave Metro? Leave Metro?
>
>   LOUIS B. MAYER
>   Your pictures one after another
>   are losing money. Theater owners
>   (MORE)
>   LOUIS B. MAYER (CONT'D)

```
                    voted you "box office poison."
                    Still, for years I've paid no
                    attention. You know me, Joan. I
                    don't give up so easily. We'll pay
                    you off on your contract. But you
                    can't afford to make three or four
                    more losers for us.

                         JOAN
                    It's the scripts, L.B. Bad
                    pictures, bad directors...

                         LOUIS B. MAYER
                    Bad with you, good with others.

                         JOAN
                    No, listen to me L.B., I have been
                    begging you... begging you for a
                    good script. Now you've always
                    given me my share of bad movies
                    because you knew I'd make them
                    work. Well I can't keep doing it,
                    L.B.!

                         LOUIS B. MAYER
                    Listen with your ears and not with
                    your pride.
```

Alex Forrest and Gordon Gekko

On the surface, many cinematic villains are nothing more than one dimensional, outlandish characters bent on achieving some repugnant goal like the destruction of all or part of humankind. As Valerie Wee writes in "Resurrecting and Updating the Teen Slasher" (*Journal of Popular Film and Television*, 34.2), "In films such as *Psycho* (1960) and *The Texas Chainsaw Massacre* (1974), through the *Halloween* (1978), *Friday the 13th* (1980), and the *A Nightmare on Elm Street* (1984) series, the traditional villains are almost consistently characterized as psychotic, virtually indestructible maniacs" (54).

While these types of villains make for attention-grabbing Halloween costumes, it is the proverbial villains next door – those individuals whose wickedness usually cannot be recognized at first glance – who are often more appealing than their overtly maniacal counterparts. The multifaceted villain, whose foibles are more genuine and identifiable, ultimately stands the test of time and proves to be unforgettable to audiences.

For instance, in writing about Al Pacino's portrayal of Tony Montana in *Scarface* (1983), Linda Salamon states in "Postmodern Villainy in *Richard III* and *Scarface*" (*Journal of Popular Film and Television*, 28.2), "Roles as envious outsider – the marginal man driven by desire – have attracted him throughout his career" (56). As a stark contrast to Wee's "indestructible maniacs" customary in the horror genre, the concept of the "envious outsider" is also prevalent in Glenn Close's portrayal of Alex Forrest in *Fatal Attraction* (1987) and Michael Douglas' portrayal of Gordon Gekko in *Wall Street* (1987).

In addition to featuring magnetic villains with similar characteristics, both *Fatal Attraction* and *Wall Street* enjoyed critical and financial success. *Fatal Attraction* earned six Academy Award nominations (with Glenn Close being nominated for "Best Actress in a Leading Role") and four Golden Globe awards (with Glenn Close being nominated for "Best Performance by an Actress in a Motion Picture – Drama"). In addition to its critical acclaim, the film earned over $156 million in domestic box office revenue (EDI FilmSource).

Wall Street earned one nomination in the Academy Awards and Golden Globes, yielding winning statues for Michael Douglas (who coincidentally is also featured in *Fatal Attraction*), as "Best Actor in a Leading Role" and "Best Performance by an Actor in a Motion Picture – Drama," respectively. While not as robust a box office performer as *Fatal Attraction*, *Wall Street* earned a respectable $43 million in domestic box office revenue (EDI FilmSource).

Beyond the critical accolades and financial success of these films lie striking similarities in the motivations of the two villains – Alex Forrest and Gordon Gekko. When we first meet Alex Forrest, she is depicted as a smart, bold, attractive, self-actualized woman with an infectious matter-of-fact personality. During her first one-on-one meeting with Dan Gallagher, Alex bluntly approaches the possibility of them having an affair (from a screenplay by James Dearden).

> ALEX
> We were attracted to each other at
> the party — that was obvious. You're
> on your own for the night — that's
> also obvious. We're two adults.

This is the beginning of a slow reveal of the character – while we initially are privy to her innate sexuality, it is only after the first sexual encounter between Alex and Dan that the audience is introduced to Alex's true self. Thirty-five minutes into the film, after Dan makes it clear he will not leave his wife for Alex, she responds by cutting her wrists in a pitiable plea for help – a plea that, consciously or not, may be more manipulative than piteous. Regardless, this action achieves her goal of forcing Dan to come to her aid, thus extending their weekend rendezvous.

Slowly and methodically throughout the film, we learn what Alex truly wants with Dan: a legitimate family. But, when she reveals she is pregnant with his child, his response is the polar opposite of what she hopes.

> DAN
> You're so sad. You know that,
> Alex? Lonely and very sad.

> ALEX
> Don't you ever pity me, you smug
> bastard.

> DAN
> I'll pity you... I'll pity you.
> I'll pity you because you're sick.

> ALEX
> Why? Because I won't allow you to
> treat me like some slut you can
> just bang a couple of times and
> throw in the garbage?

Adds Sandra Joshel in "Fatal Liaisons and Dangerous Attraction" (*Journal of Popular Culture* 26.3), "The demand that Dan uphold his responsibilities for their child becomes a demand that he remain in her life" (61). Dan's refusal to leave his family and begin anew with Alex is just another way of his refusing to acquiesce to her plea for a legitimate family.

Alex believes she deserves the same nuclear family Dan enjoys and will go to any length to obtain it. Unfortunately, that simply is not possible for this perpetual outsider. When she follows Dan to his new suburban home and watches his family in a loving tableau, she turns away and vomits. Concludes Joshel, "The narrative placement of Alex's nausea makes her vomiting more than a symptom of pregnancy: in effect, she purges the fact of the wife and the child she wants her pregnant body to replace" (63).

Ultimately, Alex's villainous behavior (e.g., killing the family pet rabbit and abducting Dan's daughter) is beyond the boundaries of societal mores, even though she thinks her actions are commendable and will help her achieve her goal of legitimacy. To once again echo Vogler (74), Alex never stops believing she is "the hero of [her] own myth."

To say *Fatal Attraction* was a social phenomenon would be an understatement. Besides the film being featured on the cover of *Time* magazine, it became an integral part of the nation's zeitgeist – illustrating the dangers of casual sex. According to Stuart Fischoff (Professor of Media Psychology, California State University, Los Angeles), "The impact of *Fatal Attraction* on society, at least in the short run, was like the impact of *Jaws* on swimming."

In other words: Attention all men – do not ever, under any circumstances… cheat.

While the above discussion focused on Alex's role as villain, it should be noted that the question of her villainy versus the film's flawed hero, Dan Gallagher, has been debated. Writes Burke, "Another [situational villain] is the Glenn Close character in *Fatal Attraction* (1987), who for some is a homicidal psychopath and for others is an avenging angel, giving Michael Douglas his just desserts for violating his family obligations" (64).

It could be argued, in fact, that the hero of the story is none other than Dan's wife, Beth. At the end of the film, it is Beth who is able to bring closure to Alex's attempts to destroy the Gallaghers. "Beth shoots Alex dead," observes Ray Pratt in *Conspiratorial Visions in American Film* (2001), "effectively cleaning up Dan's mess and preserving the family" (162).

The villain of *Wall Street*, Gordon Gekko, shares similar traits with Alex Forrest in that he too yearns for legitimacy – not as a family man, but as a rightful captain in the world of New York City high finance. Before we meet Gekko, we meet the film's hero, Bud Fox, who divulges his goal to his colleague, Marvin, by stating, "You know what my dream is? To someday be on the other end of that phone." The two men go on to talk about the legend of Gordon Gekko as the audience gets a glimpse of this villain's persona before we meet him on screen. It is Marvin who best prepares us for the introduction of Gekko by exclaiming, "He had an ethical bypass at birth."

When director Oliver Stone was asked about the villain he created in *Wall Street*, he likened Gordon Gekko to a shark. "We did enormous amounts of moving camera in this film," he says, "because we are making a movie about sharks" (Raymond Arsenault, "Wall Street (1987): The Stockbroker's Son and the Decade of Greed," *Film & History*, 28.1, 22). Continues Arsenault, "In actuality, the shark metaphor does not do justice to Gekko's complex persona, which is an eminently human mixture of ruthless venality and roguish charm" (23).

At Fox's first meeting with Gekko, however, the Wall Street legend seems anything but complex. While his external motivation is clear – money and power ("Nothing ruins my day more than losses," he warns Fox) – his internal motivation is a bit of a conundrum. But later, at Gekko's country club, his complexity becomes apparent (from a screenplay by Stanley Weiser & Oliver Stone).

BUD
This is very a nice club, Mr. Gekko.

> GEKKO
> Yeah, not bad for a City College
> boy. I bought my way in, now all
> these Ivy League schmucks are
> sucking my kneecaps. I just got on
> the Board of The Bronx Zoo. It
> cost me a mil. That's the thing
> you gotta remember about WASPs –
> they love animals; they can't
> stand people.

This exchange begs the question, "Why would Gordon Gekko pay one million dollars to have a seat on a non-profit organization?" The answer lies in his need for legitimacy – to be a part of an upper-crust society that would not normally accept membership from a "City College boy." In "Evil in the Early Cinema of Oliver Stone," (*Journal of Popular Film and Television*, 28.2), John Stone writes, "These aren't characters who push forward despite a burden on their back. They do so because of a chip on their shoulder" (81).

Later in the scene, Gekko further espouses his philosophy on what he believes makes a successful person in the world of Wall Street.

> GEKKO
> I've been in this business since
> '69. Most of these Harvard
> MBA-types – they don't add up to
> dogshit. Give me guys that are
> poor, smart, and hungry – and no
> feelings.

Clearly, there is an internal conflict present with Gekko. On the one hand, he is the venerable outsider willing to pay to be a part of "the club." On the other hand, however, he has disdain for the very people with whom he must conduct business.

In the end, his desire to be an insider wins out – and it is this obsession with legitimacy that ironically results in his illegitimate acts, leading to his definitive demise.

summary

This chapter endeavored to explain why villains do what they do in American film. Clearly, this is a topic worthy of further discussion because memorable villains are complex characters who are often difficult to generalize. That stated, the definition put forth is a starting point:

> "Externally, a villain is someone who strives to achieve a goal without regard to the welfare of the other characters or norms of society. Internally, however, the villain is an outsider yearning for legitimacy – desperately wanting to be a part of the same society that will forever shun him/her."

Surely, there are exceptions to this definition – testament to the intricacies of memorable villains – but it is nonetheless a foundation that can facilitate the creative process for students, development executives, and writers of all levels.

Villains like Alex Forrest and Gordon Gekko have captivated audiences for as long as storytelling has existed. Storytellers who have created classic films like the ones that appear on AFI's *100 Years… 100 Heroes & Villains* list understand that crafting compelling and memorable villains is one of the most important elements a filmmaker can achieve. We may have disdain for these characters who battle our heroes and live their lives on the outside of society, but we love to watch what they will do next.

And, it is precisely these outsiders yearning for legitimacy whom we love to hate… and never will forget.

(*Note*: These exercises are interchangeable with the hero exercises at the end of Chapter One.)

1. Re-watch your three favorite films, paying special attention to the villains. Take notes during your viewings and determine their motivations for villainy.

2. Watch three trailers from upcoming films. What can you ascertain about each movie's villain? Are their goals clearly stated?

3. Write down three favorite novels in which the villains are people (as opposed to places, forces of nature, and the like), and see if the villains are actually "outsider(s) yearning for legitimacy – desperately wanting to be a part of the same society that will forever shun (them)." If not, what motivates them to do their evil deeds?

Will Peter Parker (Toby Maguire) ever find true love? In the film's tragic climax, Parker walks away from Mary Jane Watson (Kirsten Dunst) – literally and figuratively.

chapter 3

Meet Ten Memorable Heroes

Spoiler Alert: These discussions about heroes include spoilers aplenty, so beware as you read on.

Peter Parker (*Spider-Man*):
The Hero With Girl Troubles

"Who am I? You sure you want to know? The story of my life is not for the faint of heart. If somebody said it was a happy little tale... if somebody told you I was just your average ordinary guy, not a care in the world... somebody lied."

And so begins *Spider-Man* (2002), the most successful comic book ever translated to the silver screen (the box office jury is still out on *Batman*). What is it about this tale and its hero – Peter Parker (Toby Maguire) – that has captured the imaginations of millions since its introduction in August 1962?

It is Parker's everyman qualities – that he is not the big man on campus, but far from it. In fact, our first image of Parker reveals a nerdy teenager awkwardly running after his school bus. He is taunted, teased, and ridiculed. We sympathize with this hero-to-be, this sad soul desperately in love with his neighbor, Mary Jane Watson (Kirsten Dunst). It takes only a few minutes for us to come to the conclusion that, yes, Parker is one of us and we will champion him throughout his journey.

And his journey begins quickly. In a testament to the economical writing of screenwriter David Koepp, a radioactive spider soon bites Peter. While most of us know the ramifications of such a bite, we are nonetheless intrigued as to how he will become "the webbed one." We are engaged as Parker tests his newfound abilities, but it is not until about forty minutes into the film when everything changes. Parker inadvertently, and indirectly, causes the murder of his beloved Uncle Ben – Parker's one true mentor.

This event becomes the primary catalyst for the rest of the *Spider-Man* films, as he is motivated by guilt. As David Koepp says, "Had [Parker] stopped the guy who later killed his uncle, then none of this would have ever happened. Spider-Man probably would have hosted his own variety show. But, because he witnessed firsthand what happens when you don't fulfill your responsibility, he now feels compelled to use his powers for justice at all times."

But, there's more going on with regard to Parker's motivation. The guilt he feels and his longing for Mary Jane become a void he may never fill – an eternal quest to become complete.

Specifically, Parker's "incompleteness" is twofold: 1) He is haunted by the belief he indirectly caused the death of his Uncle Ben; and 2) He is hopelessly in love with Mary Jane, yet knows he can only be her friend because, as he laments at the end of the film, "The ones I love will always be the ones who pay."

When Parker meets up with the crook who shot his Uncle Ben, the interaction is brief and predictable. The scene ends with the bad guy tripping over a pipe and falling through a window – a bittersweet moment for Parker that does not quell the despair he feels over his uncle's untimely demise.

As an aside, I find it fascinating how many times villains essentially "kill themselves" instead of the hero doing the killing. Think about it. The Green Goblin is the victim of his own weapon; the Beast in *Beauty and the Beast* plunges off the roof of a great castle; the predatory dinosaur in *Dinosaur* plummets off a mountain; Hans Gruber drops thirty floors from a building in *Die Hard*; Belloq meets his maker when he opens the Ark of the Covenant in *Raiders of the Lost Ark*; Jack Torrance dies of hypothermia in *The Shining*. And so on, and so on, and so on.

Traditional Hollywood films are more than happy to have their villains kill second- and third-tier bad guys along the way, but when it comes to the moment of truth, primary villains often do themselves in. It is as if the filmmakers feel the audience will think less of the hero if he actually does away with the villain utilizing his own means. A mistake, I believe, as I would rather experience Beth Gallagher putting a bullet through Alex Forrest in *Fatal Attraction* than watch Doc Ock meet his demise via his own botched invention.

Which brings us back to Peter Parker and *Spider-Man*.

About halfway into the film, the Green Goblin (Willem Dafoe) has his first battle with our hero. Afterwards, Parker's friend Harry Osborn says, "What was that thing?" and Parker replies, "I don't know. Whatever it is, somebody has to stop it."

And so, we are ushered into the second half of the film, which is all about "somebody" (Spider-Man) stopping "it" (the Green Goblin). But, wait. After the Goblin temporarily paralyzes Spider-Man with his noxious gas, he speaks to our hero as if they are one and the same. The following exchange takes place, illustrating the "shadow" existing between hero and villain (from a screenplay by David Koepp, based on the Marvel comic book by Stan Lee and Steve Ditko).

```
            GREEN GOBLIN
You're an amazing creature,
Spider-Man. You and I are not
so different.


            SPIDER-MAN
I'm not like you. You're
a murderer.


            GREEN GOBLIN
Well, to each his own. I chose my
path, you chose the way of the
hero. And they found you amusing
for a while, the people of this
city. But the one thing they love
more than a hero is to see a hero
fail, fall, die trying. In spite
of everything you've done for them,
eventually they will hate
you. Why bother?
```

```
          SPIDER-MAN
     Because it's right.


          GREEN GOBLIN
     Here's the real truth. There are
     eight million people in this city.
     And those teeming masses exist for
     the sole purpose of lifting the
     few exceptional people onto their
     shoulders. You, me. We're
     exceptional. I could squash you
     like a bug right now, but I'm
     offering you a choice. Join me.
     Imagine what we could accomplish
     together... what we could create.
     Or we could destroy! Cause the
     deaths of countless innocents in
     selfish battle again and again and
     again until we're both dead! Is
     that what you want? Think about
     it, hero.
```

This scene, coupled with Norman Osborn's forays with his alter ego, are perfect examples of the *Reflections of the Shadow* – the multiple dimensions that exist within memorable heroes and villains. This concept is best exemplified with the one sheet for *Spider-Man 3* that depicts Spider-Man in his usual costume gazing at a reflection of his villainous alter ego in a window – donning evil-looking black attire.

In *Spider-Man*, Norman Osborn, aka the Green Goblin, remains conflicted. After a Thanksgiving dinner where Osborn effectively discovers that Spider-Man is none other than Peter Parker, Osborn goes home, only to hear his villainous self say, "Spider-Man is all but invincible, but Parker – we can destroy him... the heart, Osborn, first we attack his heart." Here we see a villain who is conflicted, yet, easily succumbs to his dark side. The Green Goblin will attack those closest to Parker, then try to kill Parker himself. After all, Spider-Man is the only obstacle in the way of the Green Goblin's grandiose plans. Interestingly, the Green Goblin never specifically states his plans, which is a bit odd for a villain, but nonetheless we must assume his intentions are only of the most nefarious kind and must be thwarted.

In the beginning of the film's climactic sequence, Spider-Man is forced to choose between saving the life of his true love, Mary Jane, and a gondola filled with children. Once again, the Green Goblin explains his theory on the foolishness of heroism:

```
                    GREEN GOBLIN
          Spider-Man. This is why only
          fools are heroes — because you
          never know when some lunatic will
          come along with a sadistic choice.
          Let die the woman you love or
          suffer the little children. Make
          your choice, Spider-Man, and see
          how a hero is rewarded.
```

The Green Goblin is not just consumed with killing Spider-Man. No, he must taunt him until the very last moment – challenging this hero's deepest beliefs.

As discussed, Spider-Man is not only motivated by guilt, but he is also searching for a way to complete his persona. Something is perpetually missing in Peter Parker's life and one of the roles of Spider-Man is to fill that void. How? 1) Spider-Man attempts to minimize his guilt by becoming the greatest crime fighter the world has ever known; and 2) As long as he is protected by his costume, Spider-Man is completely comfortable courting his alter ego's lifetime love – something Parker simply cannot do without the mask.

In the end, Spider-Man must follow his heart. He saves Mary Jane first, then the children. Of course, there is no doubt in the audience's mind he will fulfill both objectives.

Mary Jane will live to see another day and Peter Parker continues his unending search for becoming complete.

When Atticus
Finch (Gregory
Peck) talks,
people listen –
as evidenced by
the captivated
courtroom of
townspeople
behind him.

Atticus Finch (*To Kill a Mockingbird*):
The Hero Next Door

When you think of movie heroes, you may immediately gravitate toward valiant World War II generals, bold and fearless sheriffs, courageous intergalactic fighters, impenetrable superheroes, or warriors from the Old Testament. Yet, the hero who garnered more votes than any other on the American Film Institute's series, *100 Years... 100 Heroes & Villains* is not depicted on the battlefront, doesn't carry a gun, has no cape, and isn't from Biblical times.

He is none other than an unassuming country lawyer named Atticus Finch (Gregory Peck).

Who is Atticus Finch and why has he been so revered since the film opened in 1962?

The movie starts slowly, so for those budding filmmakers out there, be patient. There is no murder on page one of this screenplay; no explosion in the first two minutes; no gratuitous sexual escapade. This film was made at a time when moviegoers had a bit more patience and filmmakers had the luxury of developing characters. For example, it takes about seventeen minutes before we learn Finch is being appointed to defend an accused rapist – a man who just so happens to be African American and just so happens allegedly to have raped a Caucasian woman.

Seventeen minutes.

Imagine your summer tent-pole blockbuster du jour waiting seventeen minutes to get going. Not too likely.

But, *To Kill A Mockingbird* was made in a galaxy far, far away and thus must be viewed with a bit more patience. It is worth the wait.

Thirty-seven minutes into the film, Finch tells his family what his father said to him when he was given his first rifle.

> ATTICUS
> ... Remember, it was a sin to kill
> a mockingbird. Well, I reckon
> because mockingbirds don't do
> anything but make music for us to
> (MORE)

```
              ATTICUS (CONT'D)
       enjoy. They don't eat people's
       gardens, don't nest in the
       corncrib, they don't do one
       thing but just sing their
       hearts out for us.
```

This metaphor works on a number of levels – from the arrest of an innocent man to the film's climax with the Finches' mysterious neighbor, Boo Radley.

This is our first sense of the origins of Finch's moral code – the standards by which he will hold himself and his brethren throughout the movie. Later, he explains his motivation for defending Tom Robinson to his daughter, Scout (Mary Badham) (from a screenplay by Horton Foote, based on a novel by Harper Lee).

```
                 ATTICUS
       There are some things that you're
       not old enough to understand just
       yet. There's been some high talk
       around town to the effect that I
       shouldn't do much about defending
       this man.


                 SCOUT
       If you shouldn't be defending him,
       then why are you doing it?


                 ATTICUS
       For a number of reasons. The main
       one is that if I didn't, I
       couldn't hold my head up in town.
       I couldn't even tell you or Jem
       not to do somethin' again.
```

Finch simply would not feel complete if he refused to represent Robinson. He is a man of deep principles and must do what is right not only because it is the right thing to do, but also because defending Robinson helps him feel whole – as an attorney and a father.

After Finch hears Tom Robinson is being moved to the county jail, Finch justifiably is concerned for the accused man's safety. Thus, he does what any hero would do – he sits outside the jail, reading – guarding the man he will defend the following day. This marks the infamous midpoint of the story – that moment halfway through a film when the stakes are raised. Finch is greeted by a mob of several men with weapons who have one goal in mind: to kill Tom Robinson.

But, how will Finch defeat this horde of angry residents? After all, he is only armed with a book and a three-piece suit. His stare is enough to quell the residents – and the six-foot-three regal presence of Gregory Peck doesn't hurt.

Still, Finch is ultimately a man who demonstrates his heroism through words. And, his words really begin about an hour and seven minutes into the film, when the rape trial of Tom Robinson commences. It is a packed courtroom in the sleepy town of Maycomb, Alabama, and Finch is poised to perform the most unpopular duty of his professional life – defend an African American man accused of raping a Caucasian woman.

As the trial begins, things don't look too good for Robinson. The sheriff's testimony is damning and the testimony from the victim's father, Bob Ewell, indicates he saw his daughter in the arms of Robinson. The victim, Mayella Ewell, seems to drive the final nail in the proverbial coffin as she recounts a graphic testimony of her ordeal – presumably being accosted by Robinson. Add the all-white male jury to the mix and Robinson doesn't seem to have much of a chance. But, he does have one significant advantage in the name of Atticus Finch.

Finch delivers a closing statement that would be the envy of any attorney, espousing the inherent bias in the court and exposing the town for its racism that runs deep throughout the community. Still, the jury delivers a "Guilty" verdict.

But this hero has gained the respect of the African American contingency. As Finch packs up his briefcase in the empty courtroom, the African American onlookers (who have been relegated to the balcony), stand with respect. The Reverend Sykes (Bill Walker) looks down at Finch's daughter and says, "Jean Louise, stand up. Your father's passing." It is as if Finch is the first Caucasian to stand up in a courtroom and defend an African American. And, perhaps, he was.

Throughout the film, Finch embodies the definition I put forth in Chapter One: "A hero is someone who accomplishes a clear goal for a greater good by overcoming obstacles with the help of a mentor at significant risk to the hero's livelihood." While he did not successfully defend Robinson, he did accomplish the greater goal of exposing the town to the evils of racism at significant risk to his livelihood.

Interestingly, Finch maintains his heroism without the help of a mentor. His children help him along in his pursuits, but for the most part, Finch does what he does without the assistance of a Yoda in his life.

Maudie (Rosemary Murphy), Finch's neighbor, sums up this hero best by saying, "Some men in this world are born to do our unpleasant jobs for us... your father is one of them."

Indiana Jones (*Raiders of the Lost Ark*):
The Hero With a Whip

His face is not revealed until three minutes and seventeen seconds into the film. No matter. We feel Indiana Jones' presence from the first frame of the movie – as his silhouette confidently glides across the jungles of South America. We like this guy from the very beginning. Not just because he's Harrison Ford, but also because he's a man on a mission. Specifically, he needs to get to the lost Ark of the Covenant before the Nazis. And we also want him to get there first. Badly.

Structurally, *Raiders of the Lost Ark* (1981) is pitch perfect. It begins with a twelve minute-plus action sequence that introduces our hero, his brand of heroism, and the story's primary villain, Belloq (Paul Freeman). The next ten minutes are devoted to explaining what Jones must accomplish by the end of the film. This scene brings out the affable and professorial side of Jones, as he effortlessly educates his guests from Army Intelligence (and the audience) about the history of the Ark and its importance to the world. This scene achieves two objectives: 1) It demonstrates Jones' instructional "yin" to complement his macho and adventurous "yang" we witnessed in the film's opening scene – thus

Indiana Jones (Harrison Ford) is on the verge of capturing a prized idol. Too bad it will soon be in the hands of his nemesis, Belloq.

giving him a sense of three-dimensionality; and 2) It provides the audience with much needed exposition in an entertaining way.

At the end of the scene, Jones' colleague, Marcus Brody (Denholm Elliott), succinctly summarizes the stakes of the story by exclaiming, "An army which carries the Ark before it is invincible."

Now, we don't want the Nazis to take possession of the Ark before Jones — we fully understand the ramifications — so we are on the same page as our hero. We will now dutifully and diligently root for him throughout the film. At the twenty-three minute mark, Act One is complete, Jones is on a plane, and our story has set sail.

What is Jones' motivation to leave the relative safety of academia for a precarious trek around the world? As a professor, he lectures college students about great adventures of antiquity, but longs for the same excitement in his life. Without personally embarking upon an adventure, he will forever be incomplete. It is this journey that fills the void in his life and allows him to be a part of the history he teaches, instead of just another archeology professor researching and lecturing on the accomplishments of others.

In *Raiders of the Lost Ark*, Jones has no family and a scarcity of friends to help him fill this void. This characteristic, however, should not be a surprise to students of film heroes. More often than not, there are few — if any — loved ones surrounding our memorable heroes. For instance, think about how many animated films feature heroes who are orphaned or only have one parent: *Beauty and the Beast*, *Finding Nemo*, *Aladdin*, *Toy Story*, *The Lion King*, *Pinocchio*, *The Little Mermaid*, *Bambi*, *Cinderella*, and so on.

And if anyone is there for them at the beginning, they are more often than not absent at the end. Why? Because a hero's solitude elicits more sympathy from the audience. Besides, we like our heroes to go at it alone — to slay the dragon without the help of best friends, lovers, or parents.

In the case of Jones, the quest itself is the love of his life — his cinematic spouse — the perfect antidote to his "incompleteness." He risks his life because he believes he is pursuing "a clear goal for a greater good." Yet, his actions sometimes bring him closer to the methods of the film's villains.

For example, in Jones' pivotal meeting with his nemesis, Belloq, it is clear Belloq understands the fine line between a hero and a villain. "I am a shadowy reflection of you," he tells Indiana. "It would take only a nudge to make you like me. To push you out of the light." Belloq further illustrates the similarities between the two by exclaiming, "Men will kill for [the Ark]. Men like you and me."

Jones is relatively soft spoken during the conversation, neither agreeing nor disagreeing with Belloq's views. He knows Belloq is not too far off the mark. Jones already has killed for the Ark, and he certainly will kill again. Yet, he knows there is a material difference between himself and Belloq. Belloq's motivations for obtaining the Ark are purely selfish (He later tells Jones, "[The Ark] is a radio for speaking to God. And, it's within my reach.") while Jones only wants to make sure it becomes a permanent fixture of his university's museum. Same goal – different rationale.

Toward the end of the movie, Belloq and the Nazis carry the Ark toward its final destination when Jones suddenly greets them from above, pointing a missile launcher at the Ark. When Jones threatens to destroy it, Belloq responds by speaking to Jones' passion for archeology (from a screenplay by Lawrence Kasdan, based on a story by George Lucas and Philip Kaufman).

```
                    BELLOQ
        All your life has been spent in
        pursuit of archeological relics.
        Inside the Ark are treasures
        beyond your wildest aspirations.
        You want to see it opened as well
        as I. Indiana, we are simply
        passing through history. This,
        this is history.
```

At this point, Jones simply has no choice. The contents of the Ark fill a void in him – a void that cannot be filled even by Marion Ravenwood, the love of his life. He must put down the missile launcher. He must see the contents of the Ark. That is why he embarked on this journey in the first place. In the words of David Koepp (screenwriter, *Indiana Jones and the Kingdom of the Crystal Skull*), Jones is "perhaps the most goal-directed hero in movie history." He never waivers from pursuing his goal and that's exactly what the audience loves about him.

And, his actions speak louder than his words. Watch the film closely and you'll undoubtedly notice Jones does not have a lot of dialogue. Except for the scene at the beginning of the film when he describes his mission and the importance of the Ark, he has very little to say – it is simply not his in character to explain what he's doing or how he's feeling.

His whip is his spokesperson – and Jones would have it no other way.

Rick Blaine (*Casablanca*):
The Hero Out for Himself

"I stick my neck out for nobody." Never has there been a more self-serving, cynical, and sarcastic hero in American film. The famous line of dialogue comes seventeen minutes into *Casablanca* (1942), but we know exactly who Rick Blaine is long before the utterance. He's dark, mysterious, and out for himself – and he always leaves us wanting more. Maybe it is the fast-paced and witty dialogue from Julius Epstein, Philip Epstein, and Howard Koch; maybe it is the swift direction from Michael Curtiz; or maybe it is just Bogart being Bogart. Hard to say. But, we're enthralled with this masterpiece as soon as it begins and can't wait to hear what our hero will say and do next.

In Chapter One we discussed Blaine's "incompleteness" and that saving Ilsa is necessary to make him a complete character. In this section, we will discuss that fine line between Rick Blaine the hero and Rick Blaine the villain – the "shadowy reflection" that exists when Blaine looks at himself in the mirror.

As mentioned, in Act One of the film, Rick Blaine does not in any way resemble a heroic character. He's moody, mysterious, and misanthropic. As the owner and manager of "Rick's Café Américain,"

Rick Blaine
(Humphrey Bogart)
selflessly tells Ilsa
Lund (Ingrid Berg-
man) to board the
plane, knowing
they will never see
each other again.
Fortunately, they
will always have
Paris.

Rick is just happy to be alive and has little interest in the welfare of others. There are some, however, who disagree with this assessment. When Captain Renault (Claude Rains) takes Rick aside, warning him not to sell valuable exit visas to revolutionary Victor Laszlo, the following exchange takes place (from a screenplay by Julius and Philip Epstein and Howard Koch, based on a play by Murray Burnett and Joan Alison):

> RICK
> Louie, what ever gave you the
> impression that I might be
> interested in helping Laszlo
> escape?

> CAPTAIN RENAULT
> Because, my dear Ricky, I suspect
> that under that cynical shell, you
> are at heart a sentimentalist.

Renault goes on to explain that Blaine has helped revolutionaries in the past (a clever piece of exposition to help the audience embrace Blaine as someone who may have a sympathetic side), but Blaine is quick to reply that he only did it for the money. Still, this is the first time we hear a hint of his possible benevolence. And we soon see a hint of his perceived malevolence.

When his colleague, Ugarte (Peter Lorre), is arrested by the police in the café, he pleads for help. "Rick, hide me. Do something. You must help me. Rick!" But, Blaine either cannot or will not come to Ugarte's assistance. He steps back and allows the police to capture Ugarte.

Having witnessed the unemotional side of Blaine, we are given a glimpse at his softer side. Soon after he sees his former love, Ilsa, we see a broken man – drinking alone after hours in his café, muttering: "Of all the gin joints, in all the towns, in all the world, she walks into mine." We feel compassion for this complex character, yet it is difficult to juxtapose these feelings with our disillusionment elicited by his previous behavior. The shadow is alive and well in the form of Rick Blaine.

For instance, when Laszlo asks Blaine to sell him the exit visas, Blaine maintains the neutrality that has defined his character throughout the film. "I'm not interested in politics," he tells Laszlo. "The problems of the world are not in my department. I'm a saloon keeper."

Later on, he reiterates his self-centered mantra by telling Ilsa, "I'm not fighting for anything anymore except myself. I'm the only cause I'm interested in." One gets the feeling, however, that Blaine's crusty exterior is about to crumble.

In the film's climax, this conflicted character finally makes the full transition from selfish to selfless. His cantankerous personality can no longer protect what Renault knew along – that Blaine is at heart, a sentimentalist.

Blaine concocts a plan with Renault to help him arrest Laszlo, but at the last moment double-crosses the Captain, thus allowing Laszlo and Ilsa to leave Casablanca for America. The extraordinary aspect of this character transformation is that Blaine could have used the exit visas himself – he could have left with the love of his life without any risk to himself.

However, he performs the ultimate selfless heroic act by acknowledging she will be happier leaving with Laszlo. This surprise ending – with all its emotional weight – is one of the reasons *Casablanca* has been revered since 1942.

And Blaine's final speech to Ilsa exemplifies how sometimes a villain on the outside is actually a hero on the inside.

```
        RICK
Last night we said a great many
things. You said I was to do the
thinking for both of us. Well,
I've done a lot of it since then,
and it all adds up to one thing:
You're getting on that plane with
Victor where you belong.


        ILSA
But, Richard, no, I... I...
```

                    RICK
Now, you've got to listen to me.
You have any idea what you'd have
to look forward to if you stayed
here? Nine chances out of ten,
we'd both wind up in a
concentration camp. Isn't that
true, Louie?

                    CAPTAIN RENAULT
I'm afraid Major Strasser would
insist.

                    ILSA
You're saying this only to make me
go.

                    RICK
I'm saying it because it's true.
Inside of us, we both know you
belong with Victor. You're part
of his work, the thing that keeps
him going. If that plane leaves
the ground and you're not with
him, you'll regret it. Maybe not
today. Maybe not tomorrow, but
soon and for the rest of your
life.

                    ILSA
But what about us?

                    RICK
We'll always have Paris. We
didn't have, we, we lost it until
you came to Casablanca. We got it
back last night.

>   ILSA
> When I said I would never leave
> you.
>
>   RICK
> And you never will. But I've got
> a job to do, too. Where I'm
> going, you can't follow. What
> I've got to do, you can't be any
> part of. Ilsa, I'm no good at
> being noble, but it doesn't take
> much to see that the problems of
> three little people don't amount
> to a hill of beans in this crazy
> world. Someday you'll understand
> that. Now, now... here's looking
> at you kid.

There is little doubt Blaine still loves her, yet he knows his personal journey will be a precarious one and she will only find true happiness with Victor in America. This hero makes the ultimate sacrifice – letting go of the love of his life in exchange for her happiness without him. It is not a decision many of us would make (wouldn't you be more inclined to get on that plane with Ingrid Bergman?).

But then again, as much as we may try, not many of us are Rick Blaine.

Clarice Starling
(Jodie Foster) is all
alone when she
heroically draws
her weapon on
serial killer Jame
"Buffalo Bill"
Gumb.

Clarice Starling (*The Silence of the Lambs*):
The Hero With a Past

Let me get this straight: a student at the FBI academy in Quantico, Virginia – presumably in her early twenties – is given the responsibility essentially to take the lead on one of the highest profile serial killer cases in the country? I'm supposed to believe this imperative initiative is being bestowed upon a trainee?

The short answer is, "Yes," you have to buy into the general premise or you will not buy into the rest of the movie. It is commonly referred to as "suspension of disbelief" and in the case of *The Silence of the Lambs* (1991), it is our job as compliant members of the audience to suspend our disbelief for the duration of the film.

Clarice Starling (Jodie Foster) is unwittingly thrust into a situation for which she did not volunteer and is not prepared for what is to come. A perfect storm for any heroic premise and one that immediately grabs our attention and elicits our sympathy.

Like many movie heroes, Starling doesn't seem to have any familial support – there are no signs of parents, siblings, or significant others. In true Hollywood form, this hero has no one to call when things get rough. No shoulder to cry on. She is on her own and the stakes could not be higher.

Starling lives in the shadow of her deceased father, a police officer who never got the chance to share her accomplishments. And, it is apparent Starling is traumatized by his death. Throughout the film she is depicted as a little girl – literally, in flashbacks of her childhood, and figuratively, as the unfortunate recipient of Hannibal Lecter's (Anthony Hopkins) interrogations. It is clear in all of these depictions that her void – her "incompleteness" – is the absence of her father... a void Lecter eerily fulfills as her paternal proxy.

As the story begins Starling is given an assignment by one of her FBI supervisors, Jack Crawford, to observe Lecter and see if he can shed any light on an at-large serial killer named Buffalo Bill. In her initial meeting with Lecter, Starling shows she can act years beyond her age. After all, one would not think she would be able to hold her own with someone like Lecter. However, even after Lecter condescendingly chastises Starling, she has the gumption to put him in his place (from a screenplay by Ted Tally, based on a novel by Thomas Harris).

> HANNIBAL LECTER
> You know what you look like to me, with your good bag and your cheap shoes? You look like a rube. A well scrubbed, hustling rube with a little taste. Good nutrition's given you some length of bone, but you're not more than one generation from poor white trash, are you, Agent Starling? And that accent you've tried so desperately to shed: pure West Virginia. What is your father, dear? Is he a coal miner? Does he stink of the lamp? You know how quickly the boys found you... all those tedious sticky fumblings in the back seats of cars... while you could only dream of getting out... getting anywhere... getting all the way to the FBI.

> CLARICE
> You see a lot, Doctor. But are you strong enough to point that high-powered perception at yourself? What about it? Why don't you — why don't you look at yourself and write down what you see? Or maybe you're afraid to.

Good for you, Starling. Not everyone can hold her own with Dr. Hannibal the Cannibal. Still, even though he is captive behind impenetrable Plexiglass, we remain a little concerned for her safety. Our brains tell us it is impossible for him to get to her. Our guts, however, tell us a different story. Just like Starling, we are scared of what he will say – terrified of what he might do. There is no doubt as to who "owns" the scene. It is Lecter – it is always Lecter (in Chapter Four, we will delve deeper into this memorable villain).

As the story progresses, Starling becomes more consumed with finding the identity of serial killer Buffalo Bill as well as apprehending him. Again, you have to wonder why the FBI doesn't assign a team of seasoned agents on this important case instead of handing the reins over to a sole newbie. But this is a Hollywood movie and in Hollywood movies, teams don't save the day.

Individuals save the day.

Starling continues to make progress on the Buffalo Bill case and, throughout, we learn more about her childhood, via Lecter's "quid pro quo" cross-examinations. She is haunted by the death of her father and this void is filled to a certain extent by her pursuit of law enforcement. So, maybe – just maybe – Starling can complete her persona by bringing the evil Buffalo Bill to justice. Of course, she realizes the potential boost to her career, but she also understands that saving Catherine (Buffalo Bill's latest victim) will have a dramatic and overwhelmingly positive effect on her as a person.

Later on in the film, Lecter entices Starling to reveal more about her childhood.

> HANNIBAL
> You still wake up sometimes, don't
> you? You wake up in the dark and
> hear the screaming of the lambs.

> CLARICE
> Yes.

> HANNIBAL
> And you think if you save poor
> Catherine, you could make them
> stop, don't you? You think if
> Catherine lives, you won't wake
> up in the dark ever again to that
> awful screaming of the lambs.

>   CLARICE
>   I don't know. I don't know.
>
>   HANNIBAL
>   Thank you, Clarice. Thank you.

Lecter is, of course, toying with her. This interrogation with Starling is his version of intimacy. Since he cannot physically be with her, getting inside her mind is the next best thing – which satisfies him, at least temporarily. And this "intimate" relationship also benefits Starling in that Lecter is her mentor throughout the film. Like so many memorable heroes, Clarice is guided by her own version of a "tutelary figure," even though this particular figure is a convicted murderer.

One would think Crawford would fill the role of mentor, but the teacher-student association is far less dramatic. We don't want to see Starling talk through the logistics of the case with her boss – we want to experience the creepy conflict emanating from her interactions with Lecter.

And let us not forget: Our hero has a job to do and like all memorable heroes, Starling moves into proactive mode. She must find Buffalo Bill and she must do so before he kills Catherine. So, she goes off and investigates like the seasoned special agent she is not, yet we have long forgotten the Bureau has given her so much responsibility – we are on the same page as Starling and are loyally along for the ride.

At the film's climax director Jonathan Demme performs an incredible cinematic sleight of hand, as he makes the audience believe an entire team of police officers and FBI personnel are about to storm into Buffalo Bill's home and save the day.

But, remember the rule on saving the day? In the world of movies, it is never a team effort.

Unbeknownst to Starling she is about to enter the real home of Buffalo Bill – hundreds of miles away from her colleagues. No backup. No experience. No problem.

Starling goes it alone in a harrowing seven-minute denouement. In true heroic form, she doesn't call the local authorities for help. She delves right into the belly of this beast by following him into the dungeon where he tortures his victims. In it, she sees Catherine and promises her the cavalry has arrived and she is going to be okay. Heroes love to console regular people, even if they're not so sure of the outcome themselves.

In the final confrontational moment Starling is forced to meander through a labyrinth of dim hallways, creaky doors, and creepy vestibules filled with exotic moths. In the end, she must take a shot in the dark – literally – at her nemesis.

It is always comforting to know that heroes never miss their targets – even if they can't see them.

Rocky Balboa
(Sylvester Stallone)
is "Gonna Fly
Now" as he
celebrates at the
top of the steps of
The Philadelphia
Museum of Art.

Talk about being a part of the American zeitgeist. Is there anyone who hasn't exercised to Bill Conti's majestic theme from *Rocky* (1976) and exuberantly raised his hands in victory? I, for one, am guilty as charged.

In Chapter One we discussed how Rocky Balboa fits the definition of a hero. In this section, we will take our analysis a step further and follow his journey "from zero to hero."

As our story begins, Rocky Balboa is fighting in a less-than-desirable ring at the pleasure of a less-than-desirable audience. He wins and is given $40.55 for his efforts. When he asks when he can fight again, the response is, "Two weeks." By the look on Balboa's face, we immediately get the sense he may not have many other sources of income. An understatement.

This is not someone with extensive health benefits or a six-figure, diversified 401(k). As we will learn, this is someone who has nothing – no money, no significant other, no family, and no steady income. Many of the most memorable heroes in cinema are those who have been stripped of everything, and they are precisely the characters we cheer for until the final frame of the film.

Next, we are introduced to Balboa's world on the streets of Philadelphia. In the first thirteen minutes, here's what we learn: 1) Balboa's apartment is not exactly one you would find in an Ethan Allen catalogue; 2) He likes animals (always an easy tactic to get the audience to sympathize with the hero); 3) He likes Adrian, who works at the local pet store; and 4) Although he is the "muscle" for a loan shark, he's not interested in beating up any of the debtors – even if they're late with a payment or a little "light."

All in all, we like this guy. And that is exactly how the filmmakers want us to feel.

At the thirty minute mark, Apollo Creed – the current boxing world champion and ultimate showman – comes up with a novel idea: He will fight an unknown local Philadelphian on January 1, 1976, to commemorate the nation's 200th birthday. Any guess as to which unknown Philadelphian is going to get a shot at the title? You got it. So, not only do we like our hero, but he is also about to be pitted against a man who no one thinks he will defeat – an underdog tale from the very beginning.

On his first date with Adrian, Balboa is kind, charming, and chivalrous. He treats her with respect and is able to help her come out from her shy persona. At this point in the story, we know Balboa will have two goals that will drive him forward: 1) To win Adrian's heart (he is aware of this goal); and 2) To go the distance with Apollo Creed (since he has not been told he will be fighting Creed, he is not yet aware of this goal). Throughout the rest of the film, Balboa's journey will be guided by these two dramatic objectives.

At one hour and fourteen minutes into the movie, we see how far Balboa has to go in order to become even the slimmest threat to Creed. After his predawn jog takes him through the streets of Philadelphia, Balboa barely makes it up the famous steps of the Philadelphia Museum of Art.

We know that will change. In fact, that's the way we want our heroes to be depicted. We want them to fail. We need them to have obstacles. Everything must be difficult. It makes their journey – and our viewing experience – that much more satisfying.

The importance of Adrian in Balboa's journey and his 'completeness' cannot be overstated. In a scene with Paulie (Burt Young) – Adrian's brother – Balboa is asked about his relationship with her (from a screenplay by Sylvester Stallone).

> PAULIE
> You like her?

> ROCKY
> Sure, I like her.

> PAULIE
> What's the attraction?

> ROCKY
> I dunno... she fills gaps.

> PAULIE
> What's "gaps"?

> ROCKY
> I dunno, she's got gaps, I got
> gaps, together we fill gaps.

In his own way, Balboa realizes they complement each other – filling in each other's emotional missing parts and thus enabling each other to become complete. From an audience's perspective, his successful wooing of Adrian is one goal on the road to being fulfilled, one more to go.

Ah, but that other goal is a tough one. Like all unforgettable heroes, Balboa shows doubts about getting into the ring with Creed. Major ones. You see, heroes are not stupid.

When they are called to pursue a goal, it is rare said goal can be attained without significant risk to their livelihood. And, what sensible person wants to risk his livelihood voluntarily? Thus, initially, heroes are often reluctant.

In a pivotal scene with Adrian (Talia Shire), Balboa explains his initial reluctance and definition of "beating" Creed.

> ROCKY
> I can't beat him.

> ADRIAN
> Apollo?

> ROCKY
> Yeah. I been out there walkin'
> around, thinkin'. I mean, who am
> I kiddin'? I ain't even in the
> guy's league.

> ADRIAN
> What are we gonna do?

> ROCKY
> I don't know.

```
              ADRIAN
You worked so hard.


              ROCKY
Yeah, that don't matter. Cause I
was nobody before.


              ADRIAN
Don't say that.


              ROCKY
Ah come on, Adrian, it's true. I
was nobody. But that don't matter
either, you know? Cause I was
thinkin', it really don't matter
if I lose this fight. It really
don't matter if this guy opens my
head, either. Cause all I wanna
do is go the distance. Nobody's
ever gone the distance with Creed,
and if I can go that distance,
you see, and that bell rings and
I'm still standin', I'm gonna know
for the first time in my life,
see, that I weren't just another
bum from the neighborhood.
```

While this goal may seem out of place for your typical film hero, Balboa's self-reflection is inspiring and refreshing. Surprisingly, winning the fight is not his goal – he simply wants to go the distance with Creed. Easier said than done. He understands his capabilities and is, in a sense, managing the expectations of Adrian and the audience for a scenario where he is not the victor, but still victorious.

The fight between Balboa and Creed is classic – moving briskly to encapsulate a fifteen-round match. Like most finales of this kind, the hero is up, then he is down, then he is up again, and so on. In the end, Balboa accomplishes his goal by going the distance with Creed. As the announcer briefs the audience on the judges' decision, Balboa is only fixated on seeing Adrian, who is making her way to the ring.

True to his character, he doesn't even care about the outcome of the fight – and neither do we. Purposely, the results are muffled (Creed wins in a split decision), because the filmmakers clearly want us to focus on Balboa reuniting with Adrian.

And, reunite they do. In the film's final moments, Adrian makes it onto the ring and professes her love for Balboa. He, of course, returns the gesture. All along, Bill Conti's sweeping theme music blares to a crescendo as we blissfully witness Balboa and Adrian embrace.

Typically, a hero does not achieve two goals in a film. But, Balboa is not a typical film hero. We are equally happy he goes the distance with Creed and falls in love with Adrian. That these goals are achieved in the closing seconds of the film makes it that much more satisfying.

If you got a chill down your spine when Balboa and Adrian finally embrace, don't worry. You're only human and you're not alone.

Even though we might have been able to predict the ending, it is Balboa's journey and the uniqueness of his character that set this film apart and makes us want to watch it over and over.

Who knew Ellen Ripley (Sigourney Weaver) had maternal instincts? Her relationship with Rebecca "Newt" Jorden (Carrie Henn) brings dimensionality to Ripley and becomes the spine of the story.

Ellen Ripley (*Aliens*):
The Hero With a Score to Settle

For those of you who have seen *Alien* (1979), you undoubtedly will never forget the trials and tribulations of poor Kane (aptly played by John Hurt). You know the scene I am referencing. Here's a guy – simply doing his job – and he ends up screaming on a table while the most vile creature you have ever seen bursts from his abdomen. Never again would I complain about an upset stomach.

With the success of *Alien* I can't blame 20th Century-Fox for concocting *Aliens* (1986) – yet another way for Ripley (Sigourney Weaver) to engage with this "perfect organism." Since she is the sole survivor of her ship, the *Nostromo* (presumably named after the Joseph Conrad tome), it makes perfect Hollywood sense for her to somehow reunite with the malevolent beast that took the lives of her entire crew.

As mentioned in Chapter One the hero of *Aliens*, Ellen Ripley, is yet another example of a character yearning to be complete. Specifically, she must destroy The Alien and has a strong desire to act on her maternal instincts.

We begin our story with Ripley being awakened from hyper sleep and brought to a space station just outside the Earth's atmosphere. The company that owned the *Nostromo* does not believe her account of the events that occurred and, to her frustration, orders the case closed. Like any competent hero, however, she warns the "suits" about the likelihood of thousands of more Alien eggs on the planet her team originally investigated (LV-426) – ready to hatch and burst out of a lot more abdomens.

As luck would have it the company – represented by Paul Reiser as Carter Burke – loses contact with the colony on LV-426 and asks Ripley to accompany a team of interstellar marines to explore the situation. Ripley, of course, declines – no real hero simply goes into the unknown on a whim. But, she can't seem to get rid of the demons haunting her. Understandably, The Alien and all it represents took quite a toll on Ripley and she's not itching to dance with it again.

But there's a problem. She must go back to LV-426 because if she doesn't, there's no movie. We all know that, but are still curious as to how the character will come to this realization. Seventeen minutes into the film, it comes in the form of one final sweat-infused nightmare. In order to cleanse herself of the demons, she must confront them one more time (actually, based on the financial success of the film, she will have other opportunities to confront her demons on a profit-seeking planet called "sequel").

After Burke assures her their mission is to destroy the Alien eggs (as opposed to bringing them back for research), Ripley agrees to go. Clearly, there's still a void in her – an "incompleteness" – she is hoping will be filled by embarking on this journey.

At twenty-four minutes into the movie Ripley addresses the crew and basically summarizes the first film. These obligatory scenes (there is another one at about ten minutes into the movie) are necessary evils to ensure the fifty people who did not see *Alien* are brought up to speed – mandatory exposition of sorts.

The crew – who are supposed to be an elite group of marines – seem to be a better fit in *Animal House*, as their insubordination frustrates their superiors, Ripley, and most likely the audience. It is ironic the military would assemble a group akin to that in *The Bad News Bears* for such a critical assignment, but maybe their behavior gives us more sympathy for Ripley and, in turn, transforms her into a more heroic character.

Perhaps screenwriter and director James Cameron decided that a group of sarcastic misfits was best poised to tackle this mission or he simply was looking for a free spirit to balance against Ripley's ultra-serious, tough-as-nails personality. Whatever the reason, these are the cards our hero has been dealt and we must support her in the against-all-odds battles to come.

Forty-five minutes into the film we meet Newt (Carrie Henn) – a cute little girl who has somehow survived the countless deadly aliens inhabiting LV-426. For Ripley, this may be the beginning of a beautiful friendship, as we slowly are introduced to her capable maternal instincts. Maybe the forever-single Ripley can feel complete as a mother to the orphaned Newt. We'll see.

Quick tangent: For those writers and film enthusiasts out there, I just wanted to spend a moment discussing the midpoint of a screenplay. This is that difficult beat – the one writers fear – that essentially breaks Act Two in half. There are many theories as to what should happen at a film's midpoint (e.g., the stakes are raised for the hero), but one that seems to work quite often is this: At the midpoint of a film, the hero transitions from being reactive to proactive. *Aliens* is a perfect example supporting this theory.

For the first half of the movie, Ripley is a reactive hero. She explains what happened to her on the *Nostromo*; she agrees to accompany the marines on LV-426 as a consultant; and she sits back and watches as the crew investigates the planet. But, at one hour and four minutes into the film (*Aliens* runs about two hours and fourteen minutes), things change. Ripley goes from the passive, reactive character helping out those on the front line to the heroic, proactive character we experience for the rest of the film. The transformation literally happens in an instant and has a profound effect on the character for the balance of the movie.

As the marines investigate a colony where they think there may be human activity, Ripley and Lieutenant Gorman sit safely on the ship, hoping for the best. But when things get messy and marines start dying at the hands (and mouths) of aliens, Ripley's heroic switch is suddenly turned on as she takes command of the ship, usurping the power of the weak and indecisive Gorman. It is a harrowing rescue sequence, executed by one woman. From this point on, it is Ripley's show. She knows it and the rest of the crew is about to know it.

Her newfound proactive heroism couldn't have come at a better time. Moments later, the entire crew (what's left of them) finds themselves stranded without a ship to take them home. The stakes go up, the obstacles multiply, and we're officially at the edge of our seats.

But first, we experience Ripley's maternal instincts in action. While she puts Newt to bed, we witness the development of this special mother-daughter relationship (from a screenplay by James Cameron, based on a story by James Cameron, David Giler, and Walter Hill).

```
            NEWT
My mommy always said there were no
monsters — no real ones. But, there
are.


          RIPLEY
Yes, there are, aren't there?


            NEWT
Why do they tell little kids that?


          RIPLEY
Most of the time it's true.
```

Later in the scene, Ripley comforts Newt like only a mother can comfort her child.

```
          RIPLEY
Newt, I'm going to be right in the
next room. And, you see that
camera right up there? I can see
you right through that camera —
all the time to see if you're
safe. I'm not going to leave you,
Newt. I mean that. That's a
promise.
```

It is not easy being a mom and the leader of a military unit, trying to survive while thwarting a bunch of nearly indestructible aliens, but Ripley is up to the challenge.

As we transition into the nonstop, nail-biting Act Three, Ripley finds herself on a ship that will offer her and the remaining crew members safe haven. They have plenty of time to fly off before the place explodes. Mission accomplished. She can finally go home, right?

Not so fast. In the previous scene, Ripley lost Newt and it appears the little girl may no longer be alive. But, we're savvy film aficionados and know deep down in our hearts that children don't usually perish in Hollywood films. And, true heroes never leave children behind.

So, even though Ripley has a free pass to go home, she chooses to go back into the belly of the beast and look for Newt. Alone. She has no choice. It is in this hero's DNA.

When Ripley finds Newt, she finds her covered with Alien goo. The scene is enough to induce vomiting in the average person, but film heroes don't seem to have any problem removing alien bodily fluid with their bare hands. It is as if they have been doing it all of their lives.

In the film's climax Ripley and Newt are suddenly in a hatching ground of aliens and there is one mad female at the helm. So, it will be Ripley the mother vs. Alien the mother and the odds don't look too good for our hero.

That is, until we see Ripley in the giant yellow loader (she demonstrates her proficiency with the apparatus in an earlier scene, so there's no surprise when we see it again). I don't remember the audience reaction when she looked the mother Alien in the eyes and said, "Get away from her, you bitch," but I am going to guess the moment was met with great fanfare. After a traumatic battle, Mother Ripley sends Mother Alien into the vastness and emptiness of space – right where she belongs.

And Ellen Ripley can now be at peace – having achieved her goals of destroying the aliens and becoming a "mother" to Newt. For now, she is complete – until, of course, *Alien³* rears its head six years later.

Oskar Schindler (Liam Neeson) can do no more, as he addresses his workers and announces the end of the war.

Oskar Schindler (*Schindler's List*):
The Hero With a Conscience

My guess is director Steven Spielberg had a cinematic predicament: How could he capture the horror of the Holocaust while depicting the humanity that only sporadically co-existed? Oskar Schindler, a real life figure, was the perfect hero to drive *Schindler's List* (1993) – an epic film about the depravity of the Final Solution.

He doesn't utter a word until six minutes into the film. But, there is no question as to who owns every scene he occupies. Liam Neeson, who was nominated for an Academy Award for his portrayal of Schindler, is an imposing presence every time we see him. By the end of the first scene, we recognize that Schindler is a master show-man – a man who understands that wine, women, and song can win the hearts of many men, even SS officers.

When Schindler meets the accountant, Itzhak Stern, for the first time, he makes him an offer: Schindler will obtain SS approval for Army contracts and Stern will help raise money to buy Schindler a company to make items needed for the war (from a screenplay by Steven Zaillian based on a book by Thomas Keneally).

> STERN
> Let me understand. They put up all
> the money. I do all the work.
> What, if you don't mind my asking,
> would you do?

> SCHINDLER
> I'd make sure it's known the
> company's in business. I'd see
> that it had a certain panache.
> That's what I'm good at. Not the
> work, not the work — the
> presentation.

At this point in the film we are not looking at Schindler as a hero. He is a member of the Nazi party and a businessman who clearly wants to take advantage of the Jews' newfound quandary as slave laborers. Is it possible we will feel differently about Schindler at the end of the movie – that his "shadowy reflection" will manifest itself in the form of a just, selfless character? The answer is an unmitigated "Yes."

But like all heroes, Schindler is on a journey that will test him to his core. While at dinner with his wife (you can add "adulterer" to his list of "shadow-like" traits), he talks about his goal in life:

> SCHINDLER
> They won't soon forget the name
> "Oskar Schindler" around here.
> "Oskar Schindler," they'll say,
> "everybody remembers him. He did
> something extraordinary. He did
> what no one else did. He came with
> nothing, a suitcase, and built a
> bankrupt company into a major
> manufactory. And left with a
> steamer trunk, two steamer trunks,
> of money. All the riches of the
> world."

He's right "they won't soon forget the name 'Oskar Schindler'" and he will do "something extraordinary," but he will not be immortalized because of his business acumen. Of course, he does not know this yet. Ultimately, Schindler's journey is one of self-discovery, which will immortalize him for something far greater than managing a profitable business.

That is not to diminish Schindler's mastery of marketing and self-promotion. Scene after scene, he uses his charm to convince SS officers that doing business with Oskar Schindler is the best way to do business. And it works. For the rest of the film he strengthens his influence with the SS to get what he wants when he wants it.

For instance, at forty-five minutes into the film Schindler discovers his accountant, Stern, has mistakenly been placed on a train, presumably en route to a concentration camp. Schindler is understandably upset – after all, Stern is essential to Schindler's financial livelihood – and he goes to great lengths to get him off the train. When he is questioned by two junior SS officers, Schindler confidently warns them they will "both be in southern Russia by the end of the month" if they don't help him locate Stern. These are the words of a man who feels quite comfortable displaying his influence with SS senior management.

At this point in Schindler's character arc it is clear he is still motivated by money, power, and the success of his business. That's why he saves Stern. His motivations, however, will soon change.

A catalyst for Schindler's change comes in the form of Amon Goeth (Ralph Fiennes), who is introduced fifty minutes into the movie. If there is a villain's villain, it is Goeth. He is the one – even amongst his Nazi brethren – who is the most void of humanity.

Unfortunately for Schindler, he will soon learn that Goeth's cooperation is vital for Schindler's business to succeed.

But first, we must witness Goeth's viciousness – his complete and unadulterated lack of regard for Jewish life. After approaching a building under construction in the forced labor camp, a Jewish woman named Reiter (Elina Löwensohn) pleads with him to rebuild the structure because of safety issues.

                    REITER
        I'm a graduate of Civil
        Engineering from the University
        of Milan.

                    GOETH
        Ah, an educated Jew... like Karl
        Marx himself. Unterscharfuehrer!

                    HUJAR
        Jawohl?

                    GOETH
        Shoot her.

```
                REITER
       Herr Kommandant! I'm only trying
       to do my job!

                GOETH
          Ja, I'm doing mine.
```

Of course, Goeth does not shoot Reiter himself – he has one of his henchmen do the deed. Still, he orders the execution in a warped effort to show the Nazis and the Jews who is in charge. After a bullet is put through Reiter's head, Goeth turns to one of his subordinates and says, "Take it down. Re-pour it. Rebuild it. Like she said." It is an instant of utter hypocrisy and cowardliness – and there will be plenty more similar moments to come.

During the liquidation of the ghetto Schindler finds himself on horseback, overlooking the area and horrified at what is transpiring – the senseless murder, the screams from helpless children, the cacophony of rapid-fire automatic weapons.

Surely, Schindler knows how the Jews were being treated, but this is the moment when he truly understands the gravity of their hopeless situation. Afterwards, he goes back to his empty production facility, only to gaze at thousands of pots with no workers inside.

It is impossible to hypothesize how much of Schindler is saddened by the loss of workers versus the loss of innocent life. Is he a hero who selflessly saves the lives of those who cannot help themselves or simply a "shadowy reflection" of a hero – taking advantage of cheap (or free) labor to become the champion of a business he so badly desires? At this point, we don't know. But, one thing is for certain: He is changing.

An hour and thirty-seven minutes into the film (just about the midpoint of this epic), Schindler undergoes a metamorphosis. Much like Ellen Ripley in *Aliens*, who is largely reactive for the first part of her story, Schindler also suddenly transitions into a proactive hero. It is a meeting with Stern that propels the change.

Schindler tries to rationalize Goeth's barbaric behavior – concluding he might not be so bad under different circumstances – but even the persuasive Schindler cannot convince himself. He realizes that although he cannot stop the Holocaust, he can do his part by employing as many Jews as possible – hence the germination of "The List."

From now on, Schindler will save as many Jews as possible, risking his livelihood and his company. But then again, heroes never think of themselves first.

After a party, Schindler meets with Goeth with the hope of breathing some humanity into him.

> SCHINDLER
> Power is when we have every justification to kill, and we don't.

> GOETH
> You think that's power?

> SCHINDLER
> That's what the Emperor said. A man steals something, he's brought in before the Emperor, he throws himself down on the ground. He begs for his life, he knows he's going to die. And the Emperor... pardons him. This worthless man, he lets him go.

> GOETH
> I think you are drunk.

> SCHINDLER
> That's power, Amon. That is power.

Schindler's less-than-obvious appeal does temporarily convince Goeth to think of himself as merciful, but this is one villain who does not change an iota. Still, Schindler's compassion is showing and continues to grow. When he meets up with several SS officers at a train waiting in blazing heat to go to a death camp, it is Schindler who hoses off the trains, providing a moment of relief to the thousands of

Jews piled into the cars. "This is very cruel, Oskar," says Goeth. "You're giving them hope. You shouldn't do that. That's cruel." But, Schindler knows otherwise.

Later, Schindler and Stern share an emotional moment – a "good-bye" of sorts. When Stern asks him what he will do now that all of his employees are being sent away, Schindler responds by saying, "I'm going home. I've done what I came here for. I've got more money than any man can spend in a lifetime."

This seems like the old capitalist Schindler talking, as opposed to the new and improved humanist. He may be telling Stern that all he wants to accomplish are financial gains, but both men know Schindler has found a higher purpose. Will he really call it a day and go home with a clear conscience? Not a chance. This "incomplete" hero can only feel "complete" by preventing as many Jews as possible from being shipped to the death camps.

So, after an obligatory epiphany scene, Schindler cuts a deal with Goeth and renews his famous list – Jews who will work for him instead of making the perilous and ultimately deadly trek to the death camps. He pays for each of them and does not care that his fortune is dwindling. He is on a new mission, one that will give him much greater satisfaction than any material goods.

After bribing more SS officers (again, at great risk to his livelihood) and maintaining a factory that purposely does not produce any usable munitions, Schindler is told he is broke. In true heroic fashion, rather than surreptitiously running away to save his own life, he stays to save the lives of others.

When it is announced the war is over and Germany has surrendered, Schindler gathers his workers to bid farewell.

> SCHINDLER
> ... Many of you have come up to me
> and thanked me. Thank yourselves.
> Thank your fearless Stern, and
> others among you who worried about
> you and faced death at every
> moment. I am a member of the Nazi
> Party. I'm a munitions

```
manufacturer. I'm a profiteer of
slave labor. I am... a criminal.
At midnight, you'll be free and
I'll be hunted. I shall remain
with you until five minutes after
midnight, after which time — and
I hope you'll forgive me — I have
to flee.
```

In the end Oskar Schindler is a man who knows he rightly chose humanity over greed. Yet, like many heroes, he never is satisfied. "I could have got more out," he says in his final moments with his workers. "I didn't do enough." We finally see an emotional side of Schindler that eluded us throughout the film. Fittingly, his transformation is complete.

It is his workers who give him the final gift by providing Schindler and his wife with clothing worn by Jews in the ghetto. Yes, he will be hunted, but we all hope Oskar Schindler will live to fight another day.

Norma Rae
Webster (Sally
Field) is through
dealing with
management,
as she strongly
recommends her
coworkers join
the union.

Norma Rae Webster (*Norma Rae*):
The Hero With a Cause

We like her. We like her. We get it. Sally Field walked away with Academy Awards for her performances in *Norma Rae* (1979) and *Places in the Heart* (1984). While her acceptance speech for the latter victory has been misquoted, parodied, reviled, and revered, one cannot lose sight of the extraordinary heroic performance she delivered in *Norma Rae* as a Southern union organizer.

We first meet Norma Rae in a textile mill amidst the dissonance of machinery accompanying an average day at the job. It is loud. It is overwhelming. The employees are overworked and underpaid. And, it is the only job in town.

It doesn't take long for us to see that Norma Rae is an "incomplete hero" searching for something to make her whole. Eleven minutes into the film we see her getting dressed with a strange man in a motel. It is probably not a business dinner and most definitely is an affair she's having with a married man that has been going on for quite some time. So, the "shadow" is alive and well in Norma Rae – we've now seen the adulterous side of her (even though she does express remorse about the tryst); the heroic side is still to come.

Enter Reuben Warshowsky (played by Ron Leibman, who is clearly channeling Woody Allen in a relentlessly neurotic performance), a union organizer from New York City. He's from the Textile Workers Union of America and as far as a lot of folks are concerned, he's there to cause a heap of trouble. Not that Norma Rae minds his company. There is an odd chemistry between these two characters who could not be further apart in terms of geography, upbringing, religion, and education. Yet, Warshowsky is there to help workers of the textile mill unite and Norma Rae may be the only one to get it done.

Let us not forget our working definition of a hero from Chapter One: "A hero is someone who accomplishes a clear goal for a greater good by overcoming obstacles with the help of a mentor at significant risk to the hero's livelihood." As we will see, this definition works perfectly with Norma Rae, with Warshowsky serving as her mentor.

As Warshowsky meets with the plant's hostile management, he progresses very little toward making an impact on the workers. It is clear they want to keep their jobs and are afraid a union may jeopardize their employment. But, Norma Rae is enthralled with Warshowsky's mission. Perhaps this is the cause she is looking for. Perhaps it will make her complete.

At fifty-five minutes into the film, the infamous midpoint rises like the phoenix. Up until now, our hero has been largely reactive – watching, observing, and contemplating – but now it is time for action. She can't own the hero label unless she has a goal that must be achieved at the risk of her own livelihood. When she meets Warshowsky in his ad hoc union headquarters, she says one simple line – "I'll go along with you" – and presto, she is a member of the union and Norma Rae's journey as hero has begun.

She asks her reverend if he will allow a union gathering at his church and when he refuses her request, she quits. To the distaste of her neighbors, she holds the meeting in her home with African Americans present. Both of these acts, while forwarding her cause, do little to endear her to the community. But, like all memorable heroes, Norma Rae doesn't care what others think of her. She knows what's right and is not about to let an obstacle or two get in her way of achieving her goal.

Later, we see another aspect of this "incomplete" hero. In a scene with Warshowsky, Norma Rae asks him about his girlfriend, Dorothy (from a screenplay by Harriet Frank Jr. and Irving Ravetch).

```
                  NORMA RAE
         How come she's so smart?


                  WARSHOWSKY
         Dorothy? Books.
```

We feel Norma Rae's maudlin reaction without her saying a word. To be sure, she's insecure about her lack of education and wants to make herself more appealing to the educated Warshowsky. So, what's a hero to do? She, of course, tries to rectify the situation. She picks up a nearby Dylan Thomas book and asks, "Is he hard to read?" After flipping through a few pages, she concludes by saying, "I'll try him."

On the union front, things go bad quickly when Warshowsky learns the management of the textile mill has cut the workers' pay in half while increasing their hours. Not good. And it is about to get worse. Back at the plant, Norma Rae's father, Vernon, complains of numbness in his arm – only to be met by a member of management telling him he can take a break "in fifteen minutes." Moments later, Vernon dies (another example of a hero losing a loved one in the midst of her journey). While she doesn't need further incentive to continue her trek, this unfortunate event certainly bolsters her cause.

Adding to her obstacles is an unethical management team. Feeding off the inherent racism among the workforce, Norma Rae's bosses underhandedly post a notice claiming black employees will somehow gain more power if a union is established. So, she defiantly copies the memo for Warshowsky, who will use it to take legal action. With an entire management team hovering over her, she continues copying the document – once again risking her livelihood for a greater good.

Management then asks her – make that, orders her – to leave the plant. But, they obviously do not know with whom they are dealing. This is someone who will achieve her goal at any cost. In a memorable mutinous moment, Norma moves to the center of the plant and tells management exactly what it will take to remove her.

```
             NORMA RAE
    Forget it! I'm stayin' put. Right
    where I am. It's gonna take you
    and the police department and the
    fire department and the National
    Guard to get me outta here! I'll
    wait for the sheriff to come and
    take me home and I ain't gonna
    budge until he gets here.
```

What happens next is one of those great movie moments – like Rocky running up the steps of the Philadelphia Museum of Art, Atticus Finch delivering a powerful closing argument, or Indiana Jones tearing through a cave with a menacing boulder at his back. Norma Rae writes the word "Union" on a piece of cardboard, defiantly stands on a table, and passionately displays it to every worker in the plant – the ultimate act of blissful insubordination.

One by one, the workers turn off their machines in support of Norma Rae and her cause. Maybe they needed to see how important this is to her before they could realize how important it should be to them. It is one of those moments that reminds you of the power of film and the impact a memorable character can make when she does the right thing in the right place at the right time.

But, for true cinematic heroes, everything is hard – that's why we love to root for them as they struggle past obstacle after obstacle. You can't defy your bosses and cause the factory to shut down without ramifications. She is arrested and goes to jail. Call this event the end of Act Two of the story. For those of you who are consumers of books on screenplay structure, you are probably familiar with this "all is lost" moment. It typically occurs about five to twenty minutes before the end of the film and is the instant when the hero is furthest from her goal. It may only last for a moment, but the best Act Two conclusions elicit the question from the audience, "How in the world is she going to achieve her goal now?"

Fortunately, this is a Hollywood movie and we know in our hearts things usually work out in the end.

For Norma Rae, it comes down to a vote. In a tense scene with the workers inside the plant and Norma Rae and Warshowsky anxiously waiting outside, the vote is in favor of creating a union.

In the final scene, Norma Rae and Warshowsky say good-bye. While we get the sense she is more "complete" during this scene than at the beginning of the story (especially regarding her confidence), it is a bittersweet ending to a complex relationship that could have evolved in another place at another time. We get the sense they both wanted it to progress in such a way, but alas, the obstacles to love are sometimes too great for even the most memorable of heroes to overcome.

When General
Maximus (Russell
Crowe) tells Com-
modus (Joaquin
Phoenix) "I only
have one more life
to take. Then it
is done," he isn't
kidding. With a
finishing blow,
Maximus is finally
at peace.

General Maximus Decimus Meridus (*Gladiator*):
The Hero Who Wants to Go Home

Gladiator (2000) begins not with the face of its hero, but with its hero's hand gently caressing a wheat field, as we hear the faint sounds of a family in the background. Joy. Serenity. Love. However, we soon realize this is the vision of what Maximus (Russell Crowe) wants, as we see him donning full military gear in a dark and unforgiving Germania – a stark contrast to the yellow brilliance of the opening image.

Maximus' goal is clear before we see his somber expression or hear a word of dialogue: he wants to go home. And that is precisely what will complete him as a character. "Three weeks from now, I will be harvesting my crops," he soon proclaims to his soldiers. He does not talk about going to Rome or valiantly leading another war. Rather, like any unforgettable hero, he is fixated on a goal: to go home.

And as in most memorable stories, our hero will have to overcome insurmountable obstacles throughout the balance of the film to become complete and achieve his goal.

Approximately fifteen minutes into the film, the emperor Marcus Aurelius (Richard Harris) approaches Maximus after his victory and asks, "How can I reward Rome's greatest general?" Again, Maximus does not ask for money, a promotion, or to be acknowledged throughout the empire. He simply restates his goal: "Let me go home."

At thirty-six minutes into the film, all bets are off. Maximus will need to put his desire to go home on hold. For that is the very moment Commodus (Joaquin Phoenix) extinguishes the life from his father, Marcus Aurelius, and becomes the de facto ruler of Rome. Maximus no longer has the luxury of contemplating Marcus Aurelius' offer. No, the moment Commodus commits patricide, Maximus cannot go home. The stakes have changed. Commodus is in charge and, in order to achieve his goal, Maximus will embark on a journey never imagined.

The moment Maximus discovers his wife and son have been murdered by Commodus' cronies, his definition of "home" changes. For the rest of the film, when Maximus speaks of reuniting with his family, he will do so in the afterlife. Ironically, this character will only be complete in death, when such a reunion finally will take place.

Later in Act Two, Maximus has a crucial meeting with Proximo (Oliver Reed), who owns and manages the gladiators. Maximus approaches Proximo with great intensity and says, "You asked what I want. I too want to stand in front of the Emperor, as you did." At this point, Maximus is a man with nothing to lose. He knows he will never be complete until he is once again with his family. Yet, he is not the type to take his own life; nor is he the type who will not defend himself in the Coliseum. It is not in his DNA.

Thus, the second half of the film is now set in place. Maximus has a singular objective before he transitions to the afterlife and reunites with his family. He will kill Commodus – giving Rome back to the people and fulfilling the dying wish of his surrogate father, Marcus Aurelius.

This goal and the way Maximus ultimately achieves it illustrates the "shadow" that sometimes exists between a hero and a villain. The means by which Maximus achieves his goal are sometimes the same means by which Commodus achieves his goal. Like Commodus, Maximus will kill to accomplish his objective. Yet, we give him a pass – we cheer him on, knowing his tactics are justifiable and are the acts of a just man. The same cannot be said for Maximus' rival.

When the two meet again in the Coliseum, Maximus reiterates his goal for the audience and states it for the first time directly to Commodus by saying, "My name is Maximus Decimus Meridius, commander of the Armies of the North, General of the Felix Legions, loyal servant to the true emperor, Marcus Aurelius. Father to a murdered son, husband to a murdered wife. And I will have my vengeance, in this life or the next."

At this point, Maximus knows he could perish with a simple "thumbs down" from Commodus – that is why he is just as content exacting his vengeance "in this life or the next." His bottom line remains constant: He wants to go home. But, his preference is to complete this one mission before he does so. It is our hatred for Commodus that allows us to root for Maximus – no matter how Maximus' "shadow" manifests itself when he exacts his revenge.

One hour and forty-nine minutes into the film, a decisive moment takes place. After Maximus defeats Rome's greatest gladiator, Tigris of Gaul, Commodus again comes down into the Coliseum and the following exchange takes place (from a screenplay by David

Franzoni, John Logan, and William Nicholson based on a story by
David Franzoni):

```
          COMMODUS
Are we so different, you and I?
You take life when you have to,
as I do.


          MAXIMUS
I only have one more life to take.
Then it is done.
```

In this scene, Commodus – like Belloq in *Raiders of the Lost Ark*
or the Green Goblin in *Spider-Man* – is a villain who truly believes his
methods and morals are not unlike those of his heroic counterpart.
Ultimately, he embraces the "shadow" to rationalize his loathsome
behavior.

Like all great heroes, Maximus knows exactly what he wants and
has no problem restating his goal to every other character in the story. It
keeps us focused, engaged, and following him every step of the way.

In the film's climactic ending – the *mano-a-mano* duel between
Maximus and Commodus in the Coliseum – we are further reminded
of the similarities between hero and villain as Commodus is dressed in
traditional white, heroic garb while Maximus is dressed in traditional
black, or villainous garb. This is no accident, as director Ridley Scott
is undoubtedly sending a mixed message to the audience.

But, there is no ambiguity as to whom we want to win. Commodus puts up a respectable battle, but let's face it, he is no match
for the great General Maximus. Commodus dies, but even Maximus
cannot withstand the wounds that have been inflicted upon him. In the
end, Maximus instructs Quintus to free his men and reinstate Senator
Gracchus. Thus, Marcus Aurelius' vision of Rome finally will be realized.

Maximus falls to the ground in front of a silent Coliseum audience. When Commodus' sister Lucilla (Connie Nielsen), who has
always loved Maximus, comes to his side, she earnestly looks down at
a dying Maximus and says, "Go to them."

She knows what Maximus knows – he will be reunited with his
wife and son. It is time for him to go home. And go home he does.

summary

As we have seen, heroes come in a multitude of shapes and sizes. Sometimes they are blessed with superhuman powers (Spider-Man); sometimes they are blessed with the gift of persuasion (Atticus Finch); and sometimes they are just like you and me, but find themselves in extraordinary circumstances that bring out levels of heroism they never thought possible (Clarice Starling).

The most unforgettable heroes are those who are multidimensional and looking for ways to complete their personas. More often than not, classic film heroes are also frequently at odds with the "reflections of their shadows." These are the heroes we root for because they represent who we want to be. Few of us are ready, willing, or able to risk our livelihood for a greater good, but we like to think it is possible.

And maybe that's why heroes like the ones discussed in this book are so enduring – because they make us feel better about ourselves and help us identify the hero lying dormant in all of us.

(*Note:* These exercises are interchangeable with the villain exercises at the end of Chapter Four.)

1. Watch three of the films featured in this chapter and write down the primary traits of each hero. Do you see commonalities? If so, what conclusions can you make of their common characteristics and motivations?

2. If you are writing a screenplay, write down ten words that best describe your hero and compare these traits to heroes we have discussed. Can you think of ways to make your heroes more memorable?

3. Take a look at the American Film Institute's *100 Years... 100 Heroes & Villains* list and watch as many of the films featured in the "Hero" category as possible (*www.afi.com/tvevents/100years/handv.aspx*). You will find this to be an invaluable exercise in discovering ways to make your own heroes unforgettable.

4. Do you know anyone in your life who is heroic? Write down their traits and examples of their heroic behavior. Then, try to ascertain their motivations and see if these real life heroes can help you with your fictitious heroes.

Hannibal Lecter (Anthony Hopkins) dutifully stands at attention as he awaits the first meeting with his soon-to-be student, Clarice Starling.

chapter 4

Meet Ten Memorable Villains

Spoiler Alert: These discussions about villains include spoilers aplenty, so beware as you read on.

Dr. Hannibal Lecter (*The Silence of the Lambs*):
The Villain With a Bite

Let's begin by stating what we know about Dr. Hannibal Lecter (Anthony Hopkins) from what *The Silence of the Lambs* (1991) tells us. By this, I mean we will not delve into the source text, nor will we with any of the heroes and villains discussed. Exploring heroes and villains in novels, while a worthy pursuit, is perhaps also worthy of another book. So, we will use what we see and hear on the screen.

As we have discussed, the hero of the film – Clarice Starling (Jodie Foster) – has a void in the form of the absence of her father – a void Lecter gladly takes advantage of and fills.

We first meet the doctor about twelve minutes into the film.

Prior to the famous meeting between Lecter and Starling, we get a glimpse of who Lecter is from other characters in the movie. This tactic is often effective in building suspense before we meet a main character – we hear what others have to say about him so by the time we are acquainted, we feel as if we already know him.

Starling's supervisor, Jack Crawford (Scott Glenn), plants the seeds after giving her the assignment of interviewing Lecter (from a screenplay by Ted Tally, based on a novel by Thomas Harris).

>   CRAWFORD
>   Be very careful with Hannibal
>   Lecter. Dr. Chilton at the Asylum
>   will go over all of the physical
>   procedures used with him. Do not
>   deviate from them for any reason
>   whatsoever. And, you are to tell
>   him nothing personal, Starling.
>   Believe me, you don't want Lecter
>   inside your head. Just do your job,
>   but never forget what he is.

In the next scene, our preview of Lecter continues, raising our level of anticipation of what is to come. At the asylum, Dr. Chilton (Anthony Heald) continues to intensify our expectation for the villain Starling and the audience are about to meet.

>   DR. CHILTON
>   Oh, he's a monster. Pure
>   psychopath. So rare to capture
>   one alive. From a research point
>   of view, Lecter is our most prized
>   asset.

Chilton then takes Starling through a number of hallways and maximum security doors while continuing to pique our interest.

>   DR. CHILTON
>   Do not touch the glass. Do not
>   approach the glass. You pass him
>   nothing but soft paper — no
>   pencils or pens. No staples or
>   paperclips in his paper. Use the
>   sliding food carrier, no
>   exceptions. If he attempts to
>   pass you anything, do not accept
>   it. Do you understand me?

At this point, we are ready to meet Lecter — and that's exactly what the filmmakers want to achieve by telling us all about him before his grand entrance. We are just like Starling – giddy and nervous with anticipation. But, we're not done yet. Chilton has one more anecdote to relay to Starling and the audience – one final tidbit to put us on the edge of our seats before Lecter even appears on screen.

```
              DR. CHILTON
      I am going to show you why we
      insist on such precautions. On
      the evening of July 8th, 1981, he
      complained of chest pains and was
      taken to the dispensary. His
      mouthpiece and restraints were
      removed for an EKG. When the
      nurse leaned over him, he did this
      to her.
              (pulls out photo)
      The doctors managed to reset her
      jaw more or less. Saved one of
      her eyes. His pulse never got
      above 85, even when he ate her
      tongue.
```

These scenes are perfect examples of heightening audience ex- pectation before meeting a villain. Imagine if the filmmakers simply CUT TO a close up of Starling and Lecter without the prelude from Crawford and Chilton. It would be much less effective and we would feel far less sympathy for our hero. The film barely has begun and we are already cheering for Starling at full throttle. Why? Because we know she will be up against a more-than-worthy adversary.

We love heroes who look like they're about to fail at any mo- ment. The more we hear about Lecter, the more we want Starling to succeed. It is David vs. Goliath and we're hoping our David has more than a slingshot at her disposal.

The Silence of the Lambs is unique in that Hannibal Lecter is not the true villain of the story. That designation, of course, belongs to the serial killer Buffalo Bill. Lecter is more of an obstacle and catalyst to Starling discovering the identity of Buffalo Bill and learning more about herself. We know Lecter is mad, but we only see his violent behavior on one occasion (the sequence in question – one of the film's best – begins at about one hour and fourteen minutes into the story).

When we finally meet Lecter, he doesn't disappoint. Even though he is completely confined to his cell, he is clearly in charge. He quickly sums up Starling and hypothesizes about her childhood. Whether he is partly right or wrong, we never know – but we do know that somehow Lecter always has the upper hand, even if he is confined. Never has a villain felt so menacing and dangerous without being able to lay a single hand on the hero.

As the story progresses, it is clear Lecter's internal goal is to be accepted for his genius – he draws detailed European vistas, plays classical music, and is not shy demonstrating his persuasive and erudite questioning techniques. But, what of his external goals?

They are twofold: 1) Escape from the jaws of law enforcement and become a free man; and 2) Help Starling solve the Buffalo Bill case. But, wait a second. Surely we understand his first goal – no one wants to be confined to a small cell for eternity, right? But, why the second goal? He doesn't need to help Starling. He could string her along with misinformation and still ultimately escape.

Lecter helps Starling because there is a benevolent side of his "shadow" – however modest – that wishes her well. He wants her to succeed and even be happy.

Thus, the "shadowy reflection" that is Hannibal Lecter.

Lecter is literally the villain as an outsider, as, in most of the film, he is incarcerated – the ultimate outsider who cannot be reunited with the same society that has shunned him. And while he may interrogate Starling and inject fear into all those who share his space, he ultimately wants one thing in life: to be free.

> LECTER
> I have been in this room for eight
> years now, Clarice. I know they
> will never ever let me out while I
> am alive. What I want is a view.
> I want a window where I can see a tree
> — or even water. I want to
> be in a Federal institution far
> away from Dr. Chilton.

While Lecter's version of freedom is undoubtedly different than what you and I consider freedom, the subtext is that he wants to be free and the foreshadowing suggests he will, in fact, achieve his goal.

Yes, he is a cold-blooded murderer who probably never will change his ways and accept the mores of society. But, there is another side of Lecter – the side that counsels Starling throughout the film and helps her grow as a hero. Their exchanges are reminiscent of the verbal banter of *The Paper Chase*, with Professor Kingsfield continuously grilling law student James Hart. Lecter is the professor; Starling is his student. An unorthodox relationship, but one that effectively keeps our attention and drives the story forward.

Lecter likes Starling and even though we know he is a convicted serial killer, we like him because he is fond of our hero and helps her achieve her goal. Through their scenes together, Starling grows as a person and a professional, giving her the confidence and knowledge to catch Buffalo Bill.

This duality of Lecter is unexpected, but present in the most memorable villains. The monosyllabic, unidimensional characters who laugh maniacally at every turn come and go – we usually forget about them minutes after leaving the theater.

But the complex, multidimensional villains like Hannibal Lecter – whose personas and motivations make us ponder – are the ones we love to watch over and over again.

Darth Vader (David
Prowse, with voice
by James Earl
Jones) taunts his
former mentor,
Obi-Wan Kenobi
(Alec Guinness)
as the two former
friends battle to
the death.

Darth Vader (*Star Wars*):

The Villain in Black

Is it possible I could say something about Darth Vader and *Star Wars* (1977) that has not already been said? After all, this six-chapter saga has probably been written about more than anything in the history of pop culture. Yet, there's always a sliver of light that could be shed on the juggernaut that is George Lucas' intergalactic epic. While I will reference Vader's character arc that propelled him through Episodes IV, V, and VI, most of this discussion will be reduced to the original film, now known as *Star Wars: Episode IV – A New Hope*.

In the Prelude I chronicled the first time I saw the film (on opening day) and the profound effect it had on me. I am not alone. Talk to any movie lover who was at least ten years old in 1977 and he or she will have a similar story – the wonder of witnessing a movie that looked like no other before it (we can argue about *2001: A Space Odyssey* at another time).

While we all wanted to be Luke Skywalker (Mark Hamill), it was Darth Vader (David Prowse, with a voice by James Earl Jones) who kept us glued to the screen. There was no blinking allowed when Vader was on screen – we simply couldn't afford to miss a single frame.

When Vader first appears, we are struck by his presence. Not only does he don a black costume with a cape and angular mask concealing his identity, he is a towering figure (David Prowse, who plays Vader, is a former bodybuilder and reportedly about six foot six). And, how many villains have their very own menacing theme music? We always know when Vader is about to appear because composer John Williams respectfully tells us in advance.

Bottom line: We fully understand this is the bad guy of the story and if we want him defeated, we don't want it to happen until the bitter end.

In our next encounter with Vader, we witness his power as well as his malfeasance. With one hand, he lifts a rebel representative off the ground, squeezes the life out of his neck, and discards him. Now, we get it: He not only looks like the toughest guy in the room, he *is* the toughest guy in the room. We're six minutes into the movie and already have a good idea of what the good guys are up against.

Vader wants to squash the Rebels; the Rebels want to destroy the Death Star and gain independence from Vader and the "evil Galactic Empire." Sounds simple enough. Simple, but far from easy.

At seventeen minutes into the film, we meet Luke Skywalker – a long time to wait for our hero's introduction, but then again, the audience and Skywalker have something in common – namely, we don't know he's a hero... yet. As an aside, take notice that Skywalker – like so many live action and animated heroes – has no parents (at least none he is aware of). Skywalker is being raised by his aunt and uncle. Perhaps George Lucas had Peter Parker in mind, who was raised by his Aunt May and Uncle Ben (Spider-Man first appeared in the *Amazing Fantasy* comic book in 1962).

At thirty-four minutes into the film, Skywalker sits with his soon-to-be mentor, Obi-Wan Kenobi (Alec Guinness) and we learn a bit more about Vader (from a screenplay by George Lucas).

LUKE
How did my father die?

OBI-WAN
A young Jedi named Darth Vader,
who was a pupil of mine until he
turned to evil, helped the
Empire hunt down and destroy the
Jedi knights. He betrayed and
murdered your father. Now the
Jedi are all but extinct. Vader
was seduced by the dark side of
The Force.

For the moment, try to forget you know Vader is really Skywalker's father. The point is that Vader was once good, then "seduced" into evil. Interestingly, Kenobi's choice of words detracts a bit of the blame from Vader. He did not choose to go to the Dark Side of The Force. He was "seduced." Semantics, perhaps, but also a hint that maybe there is a "shadowy reflection" present in this villain – a fragment of his personality that is not willingly evil.

In the next few scenes Kenobi and Skywalker meet up with Han Solo and our story is set into motion. It is them versus Vader and his gang of intergalactic thugs.

Speaking of thugs, it is interesting to note Vader is not the ultimate authority in the Galactic Empire. Governor Tarkin is clearly his superior, as is the Emperor. That relegates Vader to a general, chief of staff, or secretary of defense of sorts. Again, this is not to minimize his inexcusable behavior; rather, it helps us understand his role in the Empire and authority to make decisions.

For instance, when the Empire wants to get information from Princess Leia about the whereabouts of the rebel base, it is Tarkin who incinerates her home planet of Alderon, not Vader. Of course, Vader doesn't object to obliterating a planet and killing millions of innocent people, but it is not his idea nor is it executed on his command. When it comes to interfacing with his old friend Kenobi, however, Vader does not ask for permission.

"I must face him alone." That is what Vader tells Tarkin when he realizes Kenobi is inside the Death Star. Without the knowledge of the other episodes under our belt, we take this statement at face value – like a good Western flick, it comes down to a battle between the sheriff and the stranger who just rode into town. It is Will Kane battling Frank Miller in *High Noon*, except Kenobi and Vader are armed with light sabers instead of six-shooters.

And a battle it is. In a scene epitomizing good against evil, Vader and Kenobi finally meet face to face. In a fight akin to an Olympic fencing competition, Kenobi issues the following warning to Vader:

```
            KENOBI
You can't win, Darth. If you
strike me down, I shall become
more powerful than you can
possibly imagine.
```

Darth Vader is not someone who has a history of taking advice from others, so he forges ahead until Skywalker and Co. approach. Kenobi smiles ever so slightly, then allows Vader to slice right through him, reducing Kenobi to the equivalent of a big, empty, burlap sack.

Is it possible Vader knew Kenobi was right and ends his life because a part of him recognized Kenobi's death would ultimately benefit his son, Skywalker? Was this actually a "shadowy" moment displaying Vader's "light side" – a selfless act he knew would ultimately lead to his demise?

It is hard to say for sure, but if you take the premise that Vader must know Kenobi will be more powerful in death, you can then conclude that the act of ending Kenobi's life ironically illustrates the softer side of Vader.

Where Kenobi goes, we do not know. But, we do know Skywalker's mentor is gone and it is at the hand of Darth Vader. Like in so many memorable stories, the hero's mentor dies, leaving the hero with yet another obstacle in achieving his goal – in this case, he is alone and can no longer benefit from the wisdom of his teacher.

Skywalker appropriately mourns the loss of his friend, but "the needs of the many outweigh the needs of the few... or the one" (at least that's what I learned from *Star Trek: The Wrath of Khan*), so he must now focus his newfound Jedi knowledge to help the Rebellion destroy the Death Star... and Vader.

But, Vader has tracked the good guys back to their base. His obsession with squashing the Rebellion may be more of a reality than we thought possible.

In the film's climax Skywalker accompanies a group of Rebels bent on maneuvering their ships into a narrow corridor and blowing the Death Star to bits. Do you think any of those anonymous rebels we just met are going to do the job – or even help Skywalker? Of course not. One by one, they are picked off by messengers of the Empire. Skywalker is our hero and he is going to save the day (and the galaxy) all by himself.

And save the day he does. With Vader on his tail and seconds before the entire Rebellion is about to be eradicated, Skywalker uses the Force to fire that one in a million shot to destroy the Death Star. It explodes and all is well.

Except for one minuscule complication: Vader gets away unscathed. He's just too malicious a villain not to be featured in the sequel.

In *Star Wars*, Vader is a true presence and clearly a villain to be remembered. As discussed in the Prelude, his "shadowy reflection" becomes most prevalent in *Return of the Jedi*. In that film, he reveals himself to Skywalker as his father and essentially repents for his sins. This is the Vader we were waiting to see – the human side of this villain who elicited unconditional fear in the Rebels for three films. I remember feeling a bit sad when the revelation occurred and could only think, "Why didn't he tell Skywalker earlier?"

What I didn't realize is that memorable villains don't always work on the audience's timetable. They do what they need to do when they need to do it – and in rare cases like Darth Vader… actually leave The Dark Side behind.

The Wicked Witch of the West (Margaret Hamilton) happily hurls a fireball, indicating how badly she wants Dorothy's ruby slippers.

The Wicked Witch of the West (*The Wizard of Oz*):
The Villain With a Broom

"I'll get you, my pretty."

It is one of the most quoted lines in American film. And it belongs to none other than the Wicked Witch of the West (Margaret Hamilton) in *The Wizard of Oz* (1939). Just as we did not probe the literary origins of our villainous Dr. Lecter, we will not explore the source text of this timeless villain, L. Frank Baum's classic novel. Rather, we will see what we can glean from the movie itself.

So, who is the character? What does she want? And, why does she want it?

We first meet Elmira Gulch – the Wicked Witch's alter ego – about eight minutes into the film. Everything about her appearance (motored by her broomlike bicycle and its rich staccato accompaniment) suggests Gulch is a character worthy of attention – someone whose wickedness will soon be apparent to all.

It bears repeating that like so many heroes we have discussed, Dorothy Gale (Judy Garland) has no parents – she is being raised by her aunt and uncle – and is thus yet another example of a film's attempt to elicit more sympathy for its hero and encourage the audience to root for her throughout her journey.

In the next scene, we get another glimpse of Gulch and what's to come. When she tells Dorothy she has an order from the sheriff to take her dog, Toto, Dorothy responds by calling her a "wicked old witch." After the tornado arrives, Dorothy is knocked out and hallucinates, providing us with our third moment that foreshadows the entrance of the Wicked Witch. In it, Dorothy sees a vision of Gulch peddling away on her bike, which immediately transforms into a tableau of Gulch as a Witch, snickering while gliding away on a broomstick.

Once in the Land of Oz – twenty-nine minutes into the film – the Wicked Witch of the West finally appears in full Technicolor.

Her external goal, as she clearly explains, is to obtain the ruby slippers worn by Dorothy, the film's hero. We don't know the benefit of acquiring said slippers, but can only hypothesize that they will endow the Wicked Witch with unimaginable powers. She does say when she obtains the slippers, she'll have the greatest powers in Oz, but what does that mean? As a plot point, it does not disengage us emotionally from the film, but it would be nice to better understand her intentions. Still, this external goal clearly falls within our definition of a villain since the Wicked Witch strives to achieve an objective "without regard to the welfare of the other characters or norms of society."

Since the Wicked Witch is seen as an outcast, it is also safe to say the ruby slippers equal some form of legitimacy in her mind. We cannot, however, minimize the motivation of power, which keeps many villains ticking and continues to inspire them to concoct evil plots to thwart our heroes.

Clearly, she is not after the slippers to make a fashion statement.

The Wicked Witch's internal goal is to be taken seriously as a powerful force in the Land of Oz since she receives little respect from her benevolent counterpart, Glinda, the Good Witch of the North (Billie Burke), who is adored by all (from a screenplay by Noel Langley, Florence Ryerson, and Edgar Allan Woolf – adapted by Noel Langley, based on a novel by L. Frank Baum).

```
        WICKED WITCH OF THE WEST
    You stay out of this, Glinda, or
    I'll fix you as well!

        GLINDA
    Oh, rubbish! You have no power
    here. Be gone, before somebody
    drops a house on you, too.
```

While, externally, the Wicked Witch is motivated by vengeance (Dorothy's house fell on her sister, killing her) and the desire to obtain the ruby slippers, internally it is apparent she still has a desire to be respected and adored like Glinda – a respect and adoration she will surely never achieve. She is, and always will be, an outsider yearning for legitimacy.

And she has a score to settle with our hero. Dorothy wants to see the Wizard of Oz, who will apparently help her go home. But, the Wicked Witch is not about to let her get away with those slippers. Thus, the core dramatic conflict of our story.

The next time we see the Wicked Witch is thirty-nine minutes into the film. Dorothy and her new straw-filled friend, the Scarecrow, enter an area populated by misanthropic apple trees (presumably some of the Wicked Witch's many minions) as the Wicked Witch menacingly waits in the wings.

I'm not sure why Dorothy and the Scarecrow are suddenly hungry for apples — after all, the tangent puts their journey on pause — but they go up to the apple trees nonetheless and start picking. It is a mistake, as the trees have serious personality disorders. This encounter causes little harm to Dorothy and the Scarecrow, yet it is a sample of what the Wicked Witch has planned for them.

Minutes later, she raises the stakes by appearing atop a roof and threatening Dorothy, the Scarecrow, and their new metallic friend, the Tin Man.

```
            WICKED WITCH OF THE WEST
       Helping the little lady along
       are you, my fine gentlemen? Well
       stay away from her, or I'll stuff
       a mattress with you! And you, I'll
       use you for a beehive. Here
       Scarecrow, want to play ball?
```

And with that, she hurls a fireball at the scarecrow. This is the Wicked Witch's first overtly violent act toward Dorothy and her colleagues — and she's far from done. She wants those ruby slippers and will do anything to get them.

The Wicked Witch tries another tactic a few moments later when she laces a poppy field with poison intended to put the dynamic foursome to sleep (the Lion has also joined the former triumvirate). Thankfully, Glinda comes to their rescue and releases some snowlike antidote that awakens our hero and her friends.

When the four arrive at the Emerald City, they are given Extreme Makeovers to prepare for their meeting with the Wizard himself (Frank Morgan). Meanwhile, the Wicked Witch has not given up, writing the warning "Surrender Dorothy" in the air with the smoke from her broomstick — a not-so-subtle message that things are about to get a lot worse for the girl from Kansas.

Their meeting with the Wizard is a letdown for the gang. Most likely, they were hoping for a benevolent, grandfatherly type who would graciously grant them their wishes. Instead, the Wizard would seem more at home as a *Star Trek* villain, with his bulging frontal lobe and pulsating veins. To make matters worse, he's not exactly the warmest guy in the room. One by one, he berates the quartet into submission – ending with the following command:

```
          THE WIZARD OF OZ
      The beneficent Oz has every
      intention of granting your
      requests. But first, you must
      prove yourselves worthy by
      performing a very small task.
      Bring me the broomstick of the
      Witch of the West.
```

Not exactly the reception they were expecting. Just when they thought their dreams were about to come true, the Wizard has suddenly inserted a wrench in their plans and has become the catalyst to pit Dorothy against the Wicked Witch in an Act Three battle till the bitter end. They know they'll never obtain the broomstick from her while she's still alive. So, onward they go – and kill her they must.

Back at the Wicked Witch's worldwide headquarters, she deploys her army of flying monkeys (a group of creepy creatures who have unquestionably caused countless nightmares for generations of unsuspecting children) to grab Dorothy. And grab her they do – while leaving the other three behind.

When Dorothy is delivered to the Wicked Witch, things get ugly. The Wicked Witch threatens to drown Toto, then concludes she will never be able to take possession of the ruby slippers while Dorothy is still alive. Not good for Dorothy or Toto. Meanwhile, the Scarecrow, Tin Man, and Cowardly Lion are determined to save our hero.

At this point, one has to wonder why the Wicked Witch doesn't simply do away with Dorothy in some quick and definitively wicked fashion. As an alternative, she turns over an hourglass and exclaims that Dorothy will be kicking the bucket when all of the sand falls through.

How this is going to happen and why she chose such an ambiguous way to bump off Dorothy, we'll never know.

We do know, however, that villains — even three-dimensional memorable ones — typically do not try to kill their heroes in an expeditious manner. They usually create some complex way for the hero to die, then leave the room, giving her just enough time to break free or be rescued. When will villains ever learn? (See Chapter Nine for Villain "Don'ts").

In the film's climax, the Wicked Witch lights the Scarecrow on fire, which motivates Dorothy to unload a bucket of water on him. The water accidentally drenches the Wicked Witch and, unbeknownst to anyone, she starts to evaporate while bellowing her infamous, "I'm melting!" line.

Who would have known water would have such an effect on her? And if water is so deadly to this pugnacious villain, why would she have a filled bucket nearby?

Who cares? The Wicked Witch is dead — as are her unjust goals and dreams of power and legitimacy. And Dorothy wakes up in Kansas, finally appreciating that "there's no place like home."

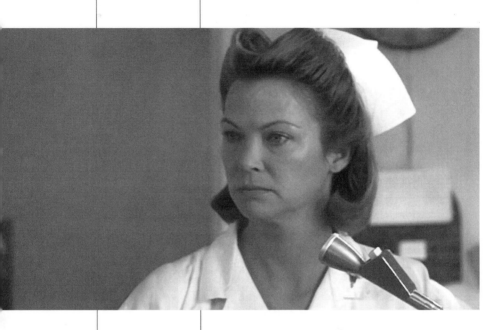

There is no doubt
who is in charge
on the floor. It is
Nurse Ratched
(Louise Fletcher),
accompanied by
her most evil gaze.

Nurse Ratched (*One Flew Over the Cuckoo's Nest*):
The Villain in White

"I've loved being hated by you." These were the words of Louise Fletcher, upon accepting her Academy Award for Best Actress in a Leading Role for her portrayal of Nurse Ratched in *One Flew Over the Cuckoo's Nest* (1975). It is true. Nurse Ratched has effectively become one of the most despised characters in American cinema. And we can't get enough of her.

We first meet her in the film's opening scene. She enters the mental institution in which she works draped in black and is immediately greeted by a trio of respectful orderlies – not unlike Darth Vader entering the Death Star for the first time. While their attire may be similar, some would say Vader is a Boy Scout next to the villainous ways of our beloved nurse.

We immediately get a strong sense of the strict regimen Ratched has created as, one by one, the patients take their daily medication while soothing music plays to create a serene backdrop. This is her world. The rules are known to all. They must not be broken.

And if that was it, *One Flew Over the Cuckoo's Nest* would be as exciting as a C-Span weekend marathon. But, things are about to change for Ratched and the sense of equilibrium she has worked so long to establish.

Randall P. McMurphy has come to town.

McMurphy, memorably played by Jack Nicholson, is not like any of Ratched's sedate, passive patients. He is a fast-talking, funny, and loquacious fake who has gotten himself transferred to a mental institution instead of serving time in a penitentiary. He is an injection of insubordination – and therein lies the struggle between the two for the entire film.

During Ratched's group therapy session, she delves into the psyche of the patients, almost as if she received her training from Dr. Hannibal Lecter. When the patients start yelling at one another, Ratched stoically sits back, enjoying the theater. She is the Svengali of her world and revels in manipulating the subjects in her fiefdom.

If her goal is to maintain power and influence on the ward, it is certainly achieved "without the welfare of the other characters or norms of society."

In McMurphy and Ratched's first one-on-one encounter, she makes it crystal clear as to who is in charge and the ramifications of breaking her rules. When he initially refuses to take his medication, Ratched's ice cold response foretells the conflict the two will experience throughout the movie (from a screenplay by Lawrence Hauben and Bo Goldman, based on a novel by Ken Kesey).

```
              NURSE RATCHED
     If Mr. McMurphy doesn't want to
     take his medication orally, I'm
     sure we can arrange that he can
     have it some other way. But I
     don't think that he would like it.
```

To be sure, there is a duality to Ratched's personality – a reflection of her "shadow." On the one hand, she is the coldhearted queen of a very dysfunctional kingdom, quick to use her power to intimidate her patients and maintain their low morale. On the other hand, however, she is, at her core, a caregiver and one cannot ignore her seeming interest in the welfare of the men on the ward. While she is guilty of manipulating them, she is also their sole maternal figure, responsible for their physical and mental well-being.

But, would you want a mother like Nurse Ratched?

Another aspect of her "shadow" comes to fruition during a meeting of the mental health professionals who run the institution. The psychiatrists agree that while McMurphy is a dangerous and unpredictable individual, it is their unanimous belief he is not crazy. They therefore agree to send him back to the penitentiary. But our movie can't end here – there are simply too many juicy confrontations to come.

Nurse Ratched speaks up amongst the otherwise all-male room of psychiatrists and makes the case to keep McMurphy in the mental institution.

> NURSE RATCHED
> Well, gentlemen, in my opinion if
> we send him back to Pendleton or
> we send him up to "Disturbed,"
> it's just one more way of passing
> on our problems to somebody else.
> And you know we don't like to do
> that. So, I'd like to keep him on
> the ward. I think we can help
> him.

What's intriguing about this moment is McMurphy has already proven himself to be a major thorn in Ratched's side. He is a nuisance, incites others, and is argumentative. You would think Ratched would be thrilled at the opportunity to be rid of him. But her "shadowy reflection" is in full force. You could argue she is a sadist and only wants McMurphy around to abuse him, but I think there is a component of her – even if it is a small component – that genuinely wants to help him. Like Rick Blaine in *Casablanca*, perhaps I am a bit of a sentimentalist.

The cynic in me, however, wonders if Ratched truly wants the other men on the ward to get better. After all, if they become well enough to re-enter society, she will forever lose her power and influence over them to the outside world. Something to ponder.

In Act Three, our story takes a major turn that sheds some light on our adored nurse. After McMurphy orchestrates a party on the floor of the ward – complete with alcohol and women from the outside – the place is left in shambles and everyone is a drunken mess.

Except for Billy Bibbit (Brad Dourif).

He is the twentysomething voluntary patient with a stutter and unusually low self-esteem. An innocent, friendly lad, Bibbit also has been on the receiving end of Ratched's verbal abuse. For instance, Ratched is friends with Bibbit's mother (Ratched has friends?) and is comfortable invoking her name when trying to pry information out of him. She knows Bibbit's mother is his weakness and is more than happy driving a stake into his emotional Achilles' heel.

When Ratched arrives for work the next morning, she is horrified to see what has transpired during the night – her once pristine ward now looks like the aftermath of a fraternity party gone bad. After discovering Bibbit had sex with one of the women brought in from the outside, she instinctively approaches him – the most vulnerable member of the group – and goes straight for his jugular.

> NURSE RATCHED
> You know Billy, what worries me is
> how your mother is going to take
> this.

> BILLY
> You don't have to tell her, Ms.
> Ratched.

> NURSE RATCHED
> I don't have to tell her? Your
> mother and I are old friends. You
> know that.

Bibbit's reaction is immediate and visceral – he goes ballistic and is taken away by the orderlies. Moments later, we hear a nurse scream as we discover Bibbit has taken his own life. To McMurphy, there is a direct correlation between Ratched's verbal castigation of Bibbit and his subsequent suicide. McMurphy attacks Ratched, strangling her to near death, until an orderly saves her.

In the next scene, it seems like business as usual in the ward. Except McMurphy is nowhere to be found. There are rumors he has escaped, but we don't know the truth. We do, however, feel the absence of his magnanimous, larger-than-life presence.

And we'll never experience it again.

In the film's final haunting scene, Chief Bromden – a McMurphy confidante – discovers McMurphy bedridden in a vegetative state. Bromden notices two scars on McMurphy's forehead and quickly concludes that McMurphy will never be the same again (he apparently is the victim of a lobotomy). So Bromden puts McMurphy out of his misery and escapes from the ward.

Perhaps that is what Nurse Ratched wanted all along.

We will never know her true motivations when she was sitting in that meeting and deciding the fate of McMurphy. Did she really want to help him or did she want him to stay to break his spirit?

As in the famous 1930s radio show, "Only her 'shadow' knows."

After a physical clash with Dan Gallagher, Alex Forrest (Glenn Close) delivers one of the most spine-chilling stares in film.

Alex Forrest (*Fatal Attraction*):
The Villain and the Bunny

In Chapter Two, we discussed Alex Forrest (Glenn Close) as an "outsider yearning for legitimacy." In this section, we will further delve into the Alex Forrest character and contemplate her "reflections of the shadow."

At six minutes into *Fatal Attraction* (1987), she delivers the look. It is after Dan Gallagher's colleague, Jimmy (Stuart Pankin), says, "Hi there" to Forrest at a business party. Her nonverbal response is one for the ages, as she coldly dissects him with her stare, then walks off with complete confidence. She is dressed in black and her wild, blonde, curly hair further accentuates her angular facial features. She has presence and she has zest – that much we know.

In the next scene, Forrest and Gallagher (Michael Douglas) bump into one another at the bar. To be sure, there's some sort of connection between the two. She's friendly, affable, and has a pleasurable disposition and he possesses a likeable 'everyman' charm.

When she watches him go to his wife, however, we see something else in her face – an "incompleteness" – a longing for someone who is not yet in her life.

In their next encounter, Forrest and Gallagher find each other in a business meeting. Again, she could not be more appealing. She's dressed in an angelic white suit and in a touching (and telling) moment, lets Gallagher know he has some cream cheese on his nose, which he promptly wipes off.

On the one hand, it is a simple, kind gesture that can be taken at face value. On the other hand, there's something comfortable about the moment – foreshadowing the intimacy between the two.

Thirteen minutes into the film, Gallagher and Forrest have an impromptu drink and the stage is set for the rest of the film – but not without some initial verbal foreplay that would make Tracy and Hepburn green with envy (from a screenplay by James Dearden).

                    GALLAGHER
          It's funny being a lawyer. You
          know, it's like being a doctor.
          Everybody's telling you their
          innermost secrets.

                    FORREST
          You must have to be discreet.

                    GALLAGHER
          Oh, God yeah.

                    FORREST
          Are you?

                    GALLAGHER
          Am I what?

                    FORREST
          Discreet?

                    GALLAGHER
          Yes, I'm discreet.

                    FORREST
          Good. Me too.

Forrest is charming with an infectious giggle. Other than show-ing interest in a married man, up to this point she has only revealed the light side of her "shadow." She is smart, attractive, clearly educated, and has a respectable career. Sounds like the marrying type, right? Not so fast. The dark side of her "shadow" looms in the not-too-distant future — and we'll soon discover just how "discreet" she is.

The inevitable occurs — Forrest and Gallagher have sex, complete with lots of water — and she coaxes him to spend the following day with her. This is not an unusual request, per se, but we get the sense she may view their rendezvous as more of a relationship while Gallagher views it as no more than a one (or two) night stand. Still, there's nothing to give us pause with regard to the darkness of her character.

After a day of frolicking throughout Central Park, they go back to her apartment. She makes dinner, they drink wine, and they talk about *Madame Butterfly* (foreshadowing elements of how this relationship is going to end). In short, they seem like a happy, loving couple. The problem, of course, is that they are not a couple. Far from it. While it has been argued Gallagher is every bit as much a villain as Forrest, her reaction to the dissolution of their relationship proves otherwise.

At thirty-three minutes into the film, the other side of her "shadow" comes to fruition. After another session of intimacy, Gallagher suddenly jumps out of bed and says he has to leave. Reality has suddenly thrown Gallagher a right hook and he now wants nothing more than to get back to his legitimate life and leave his illegitimate life behind. And, if it were as easy as that, our story would be over. But, in a way, it has just begun. While Gallagher is emotionally detached over their weekend together, Forrest doesn't want it to end – rather, she wants it to intensify. They have an argument, ending with Gallagher stoically storming toward the door.

But when she asks for a farewell good-bye, Forrest reveals she has slit her wrists. If it is her way of keeping Gallagher with her for an extra day, it works. Gallagher, however, is quickly becoming aware he is dealing with someone who is capable of unpredictable and unsettling behavior.

About ten minutes later in the film, Forrest unexpectedly shows up at Gallagher's law office, apologizing for her prior behavior and hoping he will accompany her to a production of *Madame Butterfly*. It should be noted she is no longer dressed in angelic white. Rather, she is wearing a form-fitting black leather jacket – another hint there is more darkness to come.

At this point in the story, Gallagher is thinking, "Can't she take a hint? I have no intention of seeing her again and jeopardizing my marriage." But, Forrest doesn't see it that way. She eternally is hopeful and not about to give up on him. The scene has a tense, disturbing undertone concluding with Forrest awkwardly saying, "So… ummm… I'll see you around sometime."

She will most definitely see him again – but it will now and forever be on her terms.

At the story's perfectly-placed midpoint (remember, that's when the stakes are typically raised for the hero), Forrest meets Gallagher outside and delivers a one-two punch: 1) She tells him she loves him; and 2) She tells him she's pregnant and he is the father. What's an adulterer to do? His instincts are, in his mind, justifiable in that he offers to pay for an abortion. But, Forrest has another plan: She will keep the baby and doesn't care if Gallagher is a part of the process or not. The scene ends with a warning of sorts from Forrest: "You play fair with me and I'll play fair with you."

Clearly, she has a loose definition of the word "fair."

She shows up at their apartment, posing as a prospective buyer; she threatens to tell his wife; she destroys his car; she records an eerie tape of incoherent ramblings; and most of all, she makes it clear to Gallagher she will "not be ignored." The dark side of Forrest's "shadow" is successfully taking over any light side that previously existed.

At an hour and twenty-seven minutes into the film, Forrest brings her brand of emotional terrorism to a new level when Gallagher's wife, Beth (Anne Archer), discovers their pet bunny has been boiled to death in their kitchen.

At this point, Forrest has reached a point of no return. Whatever goodness existed in her "shadow" has all but disappeared. She has lost her sense of reality and Act Three of *Fatal Attraction* suddenly begs the question, "How far will she go?"

After Gallagher admits his affair to Beth, there is an unforgettable and poignant scene. It is Beth — arguably the movie's victim and hero — who puts Forrest in her place in a classic movie moment that according to screenwriter James Dearden, elicited the greatest applause in theaters.

> BETH
> This is Beth Gallagher. If you
> ever come near my family again,
> I'll kill you. You understand?

It is the moment we have been waiting for in that Forrest has, at least for now, lost a bit of control. Up until this scene, she held all the cards. She could always tell Gallagher's wife about the affair and her pregnancy. No longer. At this point, the run-of-the-mill villain may give up and call it a day. But, not Alex Forrest – she's a villain with nothing to lose. And those are exactly the characters we fear the most.

Forrest demonstrates her villainous muster by kidnapping Gallagher's daughter, Ellen, and taking her on a bizarre trip to an amusement park. While looking for her daughter, Beth finds herself on the receiving end of a car accident. With Ellen missing and Beth in the hospital, things couldn't get much more dire for Gallagher.

Ah, but this is a great thriller and great thrillers must end with a great bang.

Ellen is returned unharmed (with Forrest using the incident as a maternal test drive), Beth is released from the hospital, and Gallagher explodes into Forrest's apartment – almost killing her. Incredibly, not a word of dialogue takes place during this fight laced with verisimilitude. At the end of the scene, Gallagher's conscience gets the best of him (he can't kill her), yet Forrest longingly gazes at him as he leaves. Even after this near-death experience, a part of her still loves him.

There is a reconciliation of sorts between the Gallaghers and all seems well – until the chilling finale to this tale. Forrest is one villain who simply will not give up. She surprises Beth in the bathroom of their home, brandishes a lengthy stiletto, and finds herself fighting Gallagher himself. He drowns her to death and we reach the end of Alex Forrest. Or, do we? Any astute film aficionado knows villains rarely die the first time around. And, Forrest is no exception.

She rises out of the water with the knife, but before she can stick it in Gallagher, she is shot dead (this time, really dead) by Beth. Who could have predicted Gallagher's sweet and caring wife would rub out the movie's monstrous villain?

It is a satisfying ending – because while we may have been initially ambivalent about Forrest's demise, the moment her "shadow" became fully dark, we knew she reached the point of no return and had to be defeated. And who better to do the deed than the film's only true victim?

Gordon Gekko
(Michael Douglas)
is part statesman,
part corporate
raider, and all
egomaniac while
lecturing to his
audience on the
benefits of greed.

Gordon Gekko (*Wall Street*):
The Villain With Greed

In Chapter Two, we discussed Gordon Gekko (Michael Douglas) as an "outsider yearning for legitimacy." In this section – like our discussion on Alex Forrest – we will delve into Gordon Gekko's character and reflect upon his "reflections of the shadow."

After a prelude with the film's hero (and I use the term "hero" lightly), Bud Fox (Charlie Sheen) spends the day waiting outside Gekko's office with the hope of gaining entrance to the Wall Street legend's den.

Once inside, Fox pitches Gekko a few investment ideas, none of which is of any interest to Gekko – until Fox surprises him with some inside information. "Bud Fox," says Gekko, "I look at a hundred deals a day. I choose one." Well, we all know the one he will be choosing today – it is the inside information Fox knew he shouldn't have handed Gekko on a silver platter.

So, the Faustian deal is made and the movie has set sail. The young Fox is about to make the elder Gekko money and, in turn, Gekko will bring Fox into his world of deal making, deception, and more money than the Wall Street novice could ever imagine. Fox will leave his ethics at the door and enjoy the fringe benefits (of which there are many) of living large in New York City in the 1980s.

Is it possible there is more to Gekko than a quest to buy low and sell high? Could there actually be a light side to the man who quips, "Greed is good"? Is he simply a coldhearted bastard of a broker who cares for no one except himself? Clearly, there must be a reflection to this three-dimensional "shadow," right?

Of course. Gekko's "shadow" is illuminated in their next conversation. He calls a purchase order into Fox – he is going to give the kid a chance. Gekko is, of course, motivated to make a profit from the transaction, but one gets the sense he is happy to reward the young Fox with a sizeable piece of business.

In a meeting the next day at New York's famous 21 Club, Gekko hands Fox a check for a million dollars to open an account. Altruistic? Probably not, but Gekko realizes Fox can make him money while Gekko helps his career. And Gekko sets the rules quite succinctly for the up-and-comer (from a screenplay by Stanley Weiser and Oliver Stone).

```
              GEKKO
    I don't like losses, sport.
    Nothing ruins my day more than
    losses. Now, you do good, you get
    perks. Lots and lots of perks.
```

So far, so good. But, this is a movie, and circumstances only stay so good for so long.

Gekko hires a prostitute for Fox, brings him to his swank country club, and offers up some thoughtful advice on winning on Wall Street, compliments of Sun Tzu ("Every battle is won before it's ever fought."). This is the professorial, lighter side of Gekko's "shadow" – wanting to deploy wisdom to his apprentice. Perhaps there was never such a teacher in Gekko's early career; perhaps Gekko sees a reflection of himself in the young Fox. Whatever his motivation, Fox is not receiving an education available in traditional business schools. Whether it is an education wholly beneficial to his career and sense of morality, however, remains to be seen.

Gekko tests Fox's commitment to his way of business by uttering, "You stop sending me information and you start getting me some." The next scene – thirty-three minutes into the film – is pivotal in the Gekko-Fox relationship. In a clear test of Fox's diminishing ethics, Gekko asks him to follow Gekko's financial nemesis, Sir Larry Wildman, in order to obtain inside information on his next deal. This is the moment Fox decides whether he can live a morally ambiguous (or by some accounts, morally bankrupt) life on Wall Street. "If you're not inside, you are outside," Gekko smugly tells Fox, who finally responds, "All right, Mr. Gekko. You got me."

And with that, the deal with the devil has been solidified.

With the help of Gekko, Fox's career and his net worth catapult. While Gekko's motivation remains wealth building, there is a part of him that enjoys the camaraderie with Fox – the reflection of himself as a newcomer to the ways of The Street – and takes joy in seeing him succeed. "I'm gonna make you rich, Bud Fox," Gekko tells him with complete confidence (further demonstrating the positive side of his "shadow"). Gekko will make good on his promise, but at what cost to Fox?

At an hour into the film, the midpoint is crystal clear. As we have previously discussed, more often than not, the stakes are raised for our hero at the midpoint. Rarely, however, is this moment as obvious as it is in *Wall Street*. In the scene in question, Fox sits with Gekko and his lawyer, discussing how their business relationship will proceed. Fox is given power of attorney on all Gekko trades and provided with information relating to offshore accounts. It is clear that from now on, Fox is being given more money, more responsibility, and more risk.

Amazingly, Gekko ends the scene by telling Fox (and the audience), "The stakes are going up. No mistakes."

This is a moment when we see the darker side of Gekko's "shadow." He is essentially absolving himself of any knowledge of any financial transaction, even though we all know Gekko is pulling the strings. Even though he has grown fond of Fox, his apprentice is still disposable.

An excerpt of Gekko's famous "Greed is good" speech is worth reprinting for the following reasons: 1) He perfectly plays both sides of the "shadow." On the one hand, he espouses the importance of greed in our society (typically a pejorative term, but Gekko somehow makes it sound like a positive character trait). On the other hand, he talks about giving power back to the people – in this case, the employees and shareholders of Teldar Paper; and 2) This is Gekko's moment to shine in public – to show the world (in this case, hundreds of Teldar Paper shareholders), he is a patriot, a visionary, and ultimately "an outsider yearning for legitimacy."

```
                  GEKKO
        ... America has become a second-rate
        power. Its trade deficit and its
        fiscal deficit are at nightmare
        proportions. Now, in the days of
        the free market when our country
        was a top industrial power, there
        was accountability to the
        stockholder. The Carnegies, the
        Mellons, the men that built this
        great industrial empire, made sure
                  (MORE)
```

                    GEKKO (CONT'D)
of it because it was their money
at stake. Today, management has
no stake in the company! All
together, these men sitting up
here own less than three percent
of the company... You own the
company. That's right, you, the
stockholder. And you are all
being royally screwed over by
these, these bureaucrats, with
their steak lunches, their hunting
and fishing trips, their corporate
jets and golden parachutes.

                    CROMWELL
This is an outrage! You're out of
line, Gekko!

                    GEKKO
... One thing I do know is that our
paper company lost 110 million
dollars last year, and I'll bet
that half of that was spent in all
the paperwork going back and forth
between all these vice presidents.
The new law of evolution in
corporate America seems to be
survival of the unfittest... I am
not a destroyer of companies. I
am a liberator of them! The point
is, ladies and gentleman, that
greed, for lack of a better word,
is good. Greed is right, greed
works. Greed clarifies, cuts
through, and captures the essence
of the evolutionary spirit.
Greed, in all of its forms; greed
                    (MORE)

```
          GEKKO (CONT'D)
for life, for money, for love,
knowledge has marked the upward
surge of mankind. And greed, you
mark my words, will not only save
Teldar Paper, but that other
malfunctioning corporation called
the USA. Thank you very much.
```

In this speech, Gekko brilliantly plays both sides of the "shadow" – part statesman, part corporate raider. But, we know the truth – not emotion nor conscience nor humanity will ever influence the way he conducts business. And unfortunately, Fox has chosen to travel the same road. When Gekko betrays Fox by planning to break up his father's airline, Gekko can only respond by saying, "It's all about bucks, kid. The rest is conversation."

If we had any doubt as to Gekko's motivations, those doubts can now be laid to rest. The dark side of his "shadow" is all we will see for the rest of the film and it will be up to Fox to save himself.

And like all capable heroes, Fox has a plan. He thwarts Gekko's purchase and breakup of an airline and sets him up to be arrested for insider trading – but not before he gets himself arrested for the same charge. At the very moment Fox is met at his office with police handcuffs, his boss, Lou Mannheim (Hal Holbrook), takes him aside – restating the "shadowy reflections" theme.

```
          LOU
Man looks in the abyss, there's
nothing staring back at him. At
that moment, man finds his
character. And that is what keeps
him out of the abyss.
```

Fox ultimately finds the abyss far too tempting and Gekko – while at times affable, charming, and insightful – never bothered to stare into the abyss in the first place... for he was there all along.

The Joker (Heath Ledger) happily burns a mound of his own cash, explaining, "It's not about money. It's about sending a message."

The Joker (*The Dark Knight*):
The Villain With a Smile

I wanted to hate *The Dark Knight* (2008) and was already skeptical of Heath Ledger's performance before viewing a single frame of film. I read dozens of articles about a posthumous Academy Award for Ledger's portrayal of the Joker and assumed it was all Hollywood hot air.

So, I sat down in my local IMAX theater, overflowing with skepticism.

Boy, was I wrong.

For starters, I was mesmerized by the six-minute opening sequence. Billy Wilder would have been proud, as director Christopher Nolan clearly bought into his edict: "Grab 'em by the throat and never let 'em go."

And against my initial will, I was effectively grabbed by the throat for the next two and a half hours, enjoying the best cinematic experience I have had in years.

But, enough fawning. This section will focus on the scrumptious evil that is the Joker.

The revelation that one of the crooks in the opening bank robbery is none other than the Joker is superb in its timing and shock value. "I believe whatever doesn't kill you, simply makes you stranger" are the first words we hear from this villain encased with clown makeup gone bad.

To say the Joker is strange is an understatement of millennial proportions. He is an outlandish, misanthropic rogue filled to the brim with malfeasance – and the moment he concludes a scene, we can't wait to see what he'll do next.

In this memorable opening – as the Joker's colleagues in crime kill each other one by one (leaving the remaining members of his gang to die at his own hand), it is clear the Joker perfectly fits our definition of a villain as "someone who strives to achieve a goal without regard to the welfare of the other characters or norms of society."

Before we are once again graced with the Joker's presence, there is a pivotal scene at a swank restaurant between Bruce Wayne, his girlfriend of the moment (Natasha), District Attorney Harvey Dent, and Wayne's old flame, Rachel Dawes. The scene has gravitas because it not only communicates the theme of the film, but also clearly spells out the "reflections of the shadow" that so often exist within memorable characters and the movies they inhabit. When talking about the dire straits of the city and its unyielding wave of crime, Dent exclaims, "You either die a hero or you live long enough to see yourself become the villain." This is a powerful statement for Wayne, aka Batman, to digest, and it is a mantra he struggles with throughout the film.

And what about our dapper reprobate dressed in purple?

In a memorable scene, the Joker crashes a meeting of Gotham's most notorious criminals. Remarkably, even in the midst of a dozen or so treacherous felons, it is the Joker who owns every frame of the scene. He offers to kill Batman for half of their collective net worth, rationalizing the usurious offering by saying, "If you're good at something, never do it for free." He leaves the group dumbfounded, yet impressed with his boldness. And we are left with the question, "Who is this guy?"

Is it possible this cartoon-influenced villain actually has a backstory that could give us a window into his wickedness? Maybe. In a subsequent scene, the Joker and a couple of his underlings sabotage Gambol, a gangster who placed a price on the Joker's head. With a strategically-placed knife inside Gambol's mouth, the Joker explains a little about who he is (from a screenplay by Jonathan Nolan and Christopher Nolan, based on a story by Christopher Nolan and David S. Gayer).

                    THE JOKER
        Wanna know how I got these scars?
        My father was a drinker. And a
        fiend. And one night he goes off
        crazier than usual. Mommy gets
        the kitchen knife to defend
        herself. He doesn't like that.
        Not. One. Bit. So, me watching,
        he takes the knife to her,
                    (MORE)

> THE JOKER (CONT'D)
> laughing while he does it. He
> turns to me and he says, "Why so
> serious?" He comes at me with the
> knife, "Why so serious?" He
> sticks the blade in my mouth.
> "Let's put a smile on that face!"
> And, why so serious?

Apparently, the Joker was not raised in a *Leave it to Beaver* household. While this speech does not elicit a plethora of sympathy from the audience, it partially explains who he is, the seeds of his psychopathic behavior, and the potential existence of a light side of his "shadow."

In his next appearance, the Joker commandeers a benefit for District Attorney Dent, hoping to do away with the dapper D.A. Instead, he discovers Dawes, and once again finds it imperative to explain his ghastly appearance by reminiscing about his past.

> THE JOKER
> Come here. Hey! Look at me. So I
> had a wife, beautiful, like you,
> who tells me I worry too much.
> Who tells me I ought to smile
> more. Who gambles and gets in
> deep with the sharks. One day,
> they carve her face. And we have
> no money for surgeries. She can't
> take it. I just want to see her
> smile again, hmmm? I just want
> her to know that I don't care
> about the scars. So, I stick a
> razor in my mouth and do this...
> > (mimics slicing his mouth
> > open with his tongue)
> ... to myself. And you know what?
> She can't stand the sight of me.
> She leaves. Now I see the funny
> side. Now I'm always smiling.

Wait a second. The Joker was married to a woman he loved so much he practically devoured a razor? Did they have friends? Go to the movies together? Did he have a career that did not involve criminal activity?

Is it possible the filmmakers are teasing us – blatantly revealing another side of his "shadow" – and attempting to provide the audience with a humane side to this iniquitous villain? And, what about the origins of his scars? Are the Joker's deformities the result of an abusive father or a bout of self-mutilation?

I'm not sure it matters.

The point is that he was not necessarily born the villain depicted in *The Dark Knight*. He was made. Perhaps the Joker is nothing more than an "outsider yearning for legitimacy" – someone who only wishes he could face a judgmental world without makeup. Someone who is a product of a cruel upbringing and an ungrateful spouse.

We will never know, but we do feel a modicum of sympathy for a character who is clearly the product of an environment that may have adversely affected the best of us. Furthermore, it is interesting to watch this villain explain himself to his victims – a bizarre form of catharsis, helping him rationalize who he is and what he does.

On the other hand, is it plausible the Joker's motivation is non-existent? Would someone really wreak as much havoc as he does without a clear goal? Wayne's loyal friend, Alfred Pennyworth, sums up the possibility.

> ALFRED
> ... Some men aren't looking for
> anything logical, like money.
> They can't be bought, bullied,
> reasoned, or negotiated with.
> Some men just want to watch the
> world burn.

As disheartening as it may sound to those students of Holly-wood cinema, I think Pennyworth is onto something. We expect the Joker to be after money, power, or revenge – something grandiose and immoral we can embrace. All villains need a tangible goal, right?

Right, but there are exceptions. Even with blockbuster films that make hundreds of millions of dollars across the globe. The truth is the Joker's true goal is to create chaos – "to watch the world burn." Pure and simple. While this amorphous objective may defy traditional Hollywood constructs, the character is nonetheless intriguing enough to keep our eyes glued to the screen. Ideally, we want to know what this villain is after, but we also want to give him a pass, hoping each time we see him, we'll get a little more insight into what makes him tick. Hoping.

When Batman corners mob boss Salvatore Maroni and asks the whereabouts of the Joker, his reply adds to the mystery of this memorable villain.

> MARONI
> No one's gonna tell you anything.
> They're wise to your act. You got
> rules. The Joker, he's got no
> rules. No one's gonna cross him
> for you. You want this guy, you
> got one way. And you already know
> what that is. Just take off that
> mask and let him come find you.
> Or do you want to let a couple
> more people get killed while you
> make up your mind?

Maroni illustrates an important theme of this film, in that heroes typically play by a set of rules – a moral code – while villains like the Joker are unencumbered by established social mores. Not a fair fight, and that's exactly why we root for our heroic underdogs to be victorious.

Later, when Dawes challenges Wayne about the idea of giving up his role as Batman, he counters by saying, "I have enough blood on my hands. And I see now what I would have to become to stop men like him." Clearly, the moral code Wayne adheres to can only be stretched so far – his "shadow" has limits.

The first face-to-face meeting between Batman and the Joker does not disappoint, with our hero taking joy in using our villain as a punching bag. Even though the Joker is no match for the physical prowess of Batman and he is sans his deadly toys, it is the Joker who owns every moment of the scene. Why? Because he is able to keep his cool while infuriating Batman — all while receiving the beating of his life.

"The only sensible way to live in this world is without rules," he exclaims while Batman precariously props him up by his neck. Once again, we are reminded this villain is not after the typical goals we see from the typical cinematic scoundrels. All he wants is a world without borders where he can inflict arbitrary damage wherever and whenever he wishes — an anarchist to the core.

When the Joker meets up with one of the mob bosses, The Chechen, he again finds the need to espouse his views of the world, educating the mobster on his philosophy of villainy by nonchalantly stating, "It's not about money. It's about sending a message."

And one can argue that few villains in modern film have been better at "sending a message" than the Joker. For instance, in the film's climactic sequence, he concocts a classic "prisoner's dilemma" scenario (a non-zero-sum game where the participants may either cooperate or betray one another). In the Joker's sadistic version, he has placed explosives on two ferries — one carrying a large cluster of Gotham citizens and the other carrying an assemblage of prisoners.

Both parties are told the following: Each boat has a detonator that, if pressed, will blow up the other boat. If neither detonator is pressed, the Joker will blow up both boats at midnight. The message the Joker is sending is simple: No matter how much planning and protection the authorities provide, he can still construct a scenario where hundreds of people will die. And he does it not for money, power, nor revenge — but simply because he can.

It is a harrowing sequence as the minutes tick toward midnight. There is considerable debate and discourse on each boat — and the Joker watches with giddy anticipation from a nearby high-rise. But as the clock strikes midnight, the basic goodness of humanity wins out, and both ferries decide not to detonate one another. By the time the Joker tries to take matters into his own hands by igniting both boats, it is too late — predictably, it is Batman to the rescue.

In the Joker's final scene, we see him hanging by one of Batman's apparatuses, taunting the caped crusader and joyfully predicting, "I think you and I are destined to do this forever." I can only assume the filmmakers shared the same sentiment.

Which brings us back to Ledger. What a shame this talented thespian could only grace us with his villainous presence on one precious occasion. One can only imagine the sheer entertainment a sequel to *The Dark Knight* would have delivered with an encore of the Joker and his revolving band of misfits.

Instead, we are forever robbed of this intoxicating psychopath and left with the genius of Ledger's singular performance – and the comfort knowing we can enjoy this hypnotic, complex, and unforgettable villain over and over again.

If he wasn't a cold-blooded killer obsessed with stealing millions, one just might confuse Hans Gruber (Alan Rickman) for a Fortune 500 CEO.

Hans Gruber (*Die Hard*):
The Villain With a Plan

In *Die Hard* (1988), Hans Gruber (Alan Rickman) is intent on stealing $640 million in negotiable bearer bonds from the Nakatomi Corporation. In doing so, it is evident he needs to demonstrate to his captors he is not a common criminal; rather, he is – in his mind – a highly educated constituent of the cultural elite. He needs to show he has two very distinct sides of his "shadow."

For instance, when he enters the office of Mr. Takagi, the CEO of the company he is holding hostage, he surveys the giant room, taking the opportunity to show Takagi he is not a common criminal (from a screenplay by Jeb Stuart and Steven E. de Souza, based on the book by Roderick Thorp).

> GRUBER
> And when Alexander saw the
> breadth of his domain, he wept –
> for there were no more worlds
> to conquer. The benefits of a
> classical education.

These are the words of a conflicted villain – one who has one foot as an outsider in the underbelly of society and another foot as a member of the intelligentsia.

But, who is Gruber? What can we glean from what is presented to us in the film? We first hear this villain's baritone coolness twenty-five minutes into the story. He and his crew have taken control of the Nakatomi Corporation via a well-orchestrated sequence – culminating with Gruber's ominous intrusion into the company's Christmas party on the thirtieth floor. He is well-groomed, well-financed, well-suited, and clutching a small leather book, which he opens, as if he is about to deliver a sermon to a gaggle of loyal followers.

"Ladies and gentlemen," he says while flanked by a posse brandishing a litany of automatic weapons that would be the envy of most law enforcement agencies. "Due to the Nakatomi Corporation's legacy of greed around the globe, they are about to be taught a lesson in the real use of power. You will be witnesses."

Gruber presents himself as a Godlike figure who has ascended this great skyscraper to address his "parishioners," immediately putting forth the notion that the Nakatomi Corporation is the true evil character of this story and Gruber and Co. are the "outsiders" who will provide some sense of justice to a world controlled by corrupt global conglomerates.

But, we know what's really going on here. We know Gruber cares not for righting a "legacy of greed." He cares not for punishing a corporation for its cancerous capitalism. No, he is guilty of the same material desires as the company he has sabotaged. And, by his projected persona of perfection, one can only deduct that, ultimately, he craves the same niceties in life that are enjoyed by the corporate elite he shuns.

Soon after he takes control of the Nakatomi Plaza, he escorts CEO Takagi away from the group with the hope of obtaining a password to the company's vault. While in the elevator, Gruber wryly glances at Takagi's suit and says, "Nice suit. John Phillips – London. I have two myself." Clearly, this is a villain who wishes to place himself on the same level as the CEO of one of the world's largest corporations – a not-so-subtle attempt at legitimacy.

Gruber is the ultimate outsider gazing through a window at the wealthy and influential, longing to be one of them and convinced that achieving his malicious goal will be a shortcut to power and privilege.

One of the first acts we witness with Gruber displays his apparent sociopathic ambivalence for human life. When Takagi refuses to give him the code to open the vault (containing $640 million in negotiable bearer bonds), Gruber stoically fires a bullet through his head. Like most memorable villains, Gruber has a clear goal and will stop at nothing to achieve it.

So, we know Gruber has a dark side, but is there also a light side to his "shadow"?

In a later scene, we find him sitting at the end of a buffet, eating finger foods while addressing the hostages. There is a civility about him when he is in a group setting. To be sure, he is in charge, but one gets the feeling he is not motivated to murder a group of innocent people. He would find the act uncivilized. Even when his lieutenants' tempers flare and chaos encompasses him — like when the police and FBI enter the scene — it is never Gruber who loses his cool.

A moment displaying the light side of Gruber's "shadow" is telling, as he once again sets himself apart from the run-of-the-mill villain in the run-of-the-mill action film. In this scene, Holly Gennaro (unbeknownst to Gruber as McClane's wife), approaches him with a question.

                    HOLLY
        I have a request.

                    GRUBER
        What idiot put you in charge?

                    HOLLY
        You did, when you murdered my
        boss. Now, everybody's looking to
        me. Personally, I'd pass on the
        job. I don't enjoy being this
        close to you.

                    GRUBER
        Go on.

                    HOLLY
        We have a pregnant woman out
        there. Relax, she's not due for a
        couple of weeks. But, sitting on
        that rock isn't doing her back any
        good. So, I would like permission
        to move her to one of the offices
        where there is a sofa.

                    GRUBER
        No, but I'll have a sofa brought
        out to you. Good enough?

```
               HOLLY
Good enough. And, unless you like
it messy, I'd start bringing us
in groups to the bathroom.

               GRUBER
Yes. You're right. It will be
done. Was there something else?

               HOLLY
No. Thank you.
```

If you can somehow get past the unrealistic hubris of Gennaro (Would anyone ever say, "I don't enjoy being this close to you," to the leader of a gang that has her company at gunpoint?), does this genial scene sound like a conversation between a hostage and a murderous, malicious malcontent? I think not. And, that's exactly the point. Gruber doesn't always speak and act like a traditional villain and thus, perfectly plays both sides of his "shadow."

In arguably the film's best scene, Gruber pokes around an unfinished floor in the building and literally bumps into McClane (Bruce Willis) – the first time they meet in the movie. Instinctively – and without missing a single beat – Gruber loses his accent and transforms into a terrified "hostage" with a perfect American Midwest dialect. The metamorphosis is astonishing. He coyly glances at the company directory and chooses the name "Bill Clay" as his name, but ultimately, McClane senses he is a fake.

The purpose of the scene is not only to bring the hero and villain together for the first time in the film (it takes an hour and thirty minutes for the union to take place), but to demonstrate the seemingly endless layers to Gruber – he's smart, creative, charming, and does accents too. He has all you want in a villain.

Toward the end of the film, Gruber succeeds in accessing the vault. It is this moment that accentuates his symbolic transformation from "outsider" to "insider" status. The scene is heightened by the melodic Beethoven's Ninth Symphony – Ode to Joy, (a score used brilliantly throughout the film) a heroic low camera angle, pungent lighting, and a whisper of wind blowing through Gruber's perfectly groomed hair. The beat ends with him confidently telling his associate, "By the time they figure out what went wrong, we'll be on a beach earning twenty percent."

In the movie's climax, we see a villain who is no longer expressing both sides of the "shadow." As in so many films of its kind, the ending leaves little room for ambiguity – Gruber has both feet in the Dark Side and is not stepping out. His final diversion is to escort all of the hostages onto the roof, where he will promptly detonate the entire area and kill many innocent people (and make the authorities think he too is among the dead). He doesn't care about "the welfare of the other characters or norms of society."

He has his bearer bonds and will now be on his way, thank you very much.

In their second and final on-screen confrontation, Gruber conveniently uses Gennaro (Bonnie Bedelia) as a hostage while McClane hopelessly drops his only gun. But, this is a Hollywood movie, right? And heroes in Hollywood movies always have an extra gun tucked away, right?

Of course they do.

McClane shoots him, but in typical big-budget fashion, Gruber doesn't die from a single bullet wound. He must perish in style – plummeting thirty floors to his final demise.

Gruber's quest for materialism and legitimacy is not unlike that of many villains in film and as is most often the case, it is an objective that never will be achieved. But, Gruber also presents himself in a very refined, likeable manner – "shadow-like" traits that set him apart from the typical one-dimensional maniac and make him a villain we will remember for years to come.

Jake Gittes (Jack
Nicholson) is
clearly getting on
Noah Cross' (John
Huston) nerves as
Gittes slowly
unfolds the dark-
ness in Cross' life.

Noah Cross (*Chinatown*):
The Villain We Seldom See

A villain who is on screen for only a precious few minutes? Doesn't sound very threatening. But, alas, threats can come in many forms. The first time we see Noah Cross' (John Huston) image is fifty-one minutes into *Chinatown* (1974). It is private investigator Jake Gittes (Jack Nicholson) who catches a glimpse of Cross in an old photograph. Cross appears to be an older, genteel, benevolent man leaning on a walking stick. But, as we will learn, there is nothing genteel or benevolent about Mr. Cross.

Gittes makes the mental connection that Cross is indeed the father of Evelyn Cross Mulwray (Faye Dunaway) – the woman with whom Gittes becomes entangled regarding her husband's mysterious death – but a mental connection is all that is made.

Later in the scene, Gittes discovers Cross was partners with Evelyn Mulwray's husband, Hollis Mulwray, in the Water Department. The two owned the entire water supply for the city of Los Angeles. If you can get past this implausible plot point (is it possible two men owned all of the water for a major American city?), we can focus on this new bit of information that will shed some light on Cross. Namely, we now know this villain is a wealthy, influential man who was partners with another man who is now deceased. That's enough to make Gittes want a meeting with Cross – and a meeting he soon shall have.

We are further intrigued by Cross in a subsequent scene with Gittes and Mulwray, where Gittes asks her, "Noah Cross is your father, isn't he?" While responding, she nervously reaches for a cigarette. Clearly, Gittes has touched a nerve – both in Mulwray and the audience. The very mention of Noah Cross causes Mulwray to completely change, covering her in an aura of apprehension. Something fishy is going on here, but it will be awhile before we are blessed with the truth.

It is worth noting that throughout the film, the audience and Gittes are one and the same – the story unfolds before our eyes at the exact moment it unfolds before Gittes' eyes. An equal-opportunity playing field. And, as we have seen in many other films, one effective

tactic used to amplify the expectation of meeting a character is to feature other characters talking about him. By the time we meet Cross,
we know quite a bit about the man and are more than ready for the
introduction.

In Gittes' scene with Cross, we get a glimpse into a tale that is
much more than meets the eye — a saga where Cross plays an unlikely,
yet pivotal role. While Cross is about as unnerving as they come, he
is able to put on the façade of an absentminded professor. You get
the sense he is always one step ahead of the other characters and in
total control of every scene in which he appears (from a screenplay
by Robert Towne).

>   CROSS
>   You're dealing with a disturbed
>   woman who just lost her husband.
>   I don't want her taken advantage
>   of. Sit down.
>
>   GITTES
>   What for?
>
>   CROSS
>   You may think you know what you're
>   dealing with but believe me, you
>   don't. Why is that funny?
>
>   GITTES
>   It's what the District Attorney
>   used to tell me in Chinatown.

Later in the scene, Gittes tries to turn the tables as he inquires
about Cross' recent involvement with Hollis Mulwray.

>   GITTES
>   Do you remember the last time you
>   saw Mulwray?

```
                 CROSS
     At my age, you tend to forget.


                 GITTES
     It was five days ago outside the
     Pig & Whistle and you had one hell
     of an argument. I got the
     pictures in my office, if that
     will help you remember. What was
     the argument about?


                 CROSS
     My daughter.


                 GITTES
     What about her?


                 CROSS
     Just find the girl, Mr. Gittes.
```

The girl in question is Mulwray's mistress, who mysteriously disappeared around the time Mulwray was found dead. Why Cross is so interested in finding her is up to our hero to find out and, so far, we don't have any more information than he does.

We don't know much about Cross, but we do know this: He is one villain not necessarily yearning for legitimacy and acceptance from society, but someone who is already a captain of his community and a business leader. In short, he desperately desires to maintain and grow the legitimacy he already possesses.

Is it possible the light side of Cross' "shadow" could be more prominent than his dark side? As we will see, not very likely.

At one hour and fifty minutes into the story, Gittes (and the audience) finally learn that Cross raped his daughter, Evelyn Mulwray, and her offspring, Katherine is her sister and her daughter. She is the one thought to be Hollis' mistress when she is really his stepdaughter of sorts. Sounds confusing? It is, and that's why *Chinatown* is a bit difficult to completely swallow on a first viewing. There are enough complex plot points to keep you fully engaged during viewings number two, three, and so on.

The revelation of incest (that Cross had sex with his daughter, Evelyn Mulwray, and fathered Katherine), is not only a critical beat in the story, but it also makes us aware of the extent of Cross' evil – even though we haven't seen him on screen in over fifty minutes. He has broken the taboo of taboos – extinguishing any light that may have been present in his "shadow" – yet, we look forward to seeing him again. Fortunately, we don't have to wait too long.

Ten minutes later, Gittes and Cross meet again in a tension-filled scene. Gittes confronts Cross, accusing him of murdering his former business partner, Hollis Mulwray, and Cross can only reply by rationalizing human behavior.

> CROSS
> ... Most people never have to face
> the fact that at the right time
> and the right place, they're
> capable of anything.

Even though Cross' actions are despicable, it is clear that everything in his career is for the sake of holding onto his legitimacy. When Gittes asks the wealthy Cross if his scheme is all about money, Cross replies that it is all about the future. These are the words of a character who yearns to be taken seriously and is ultimately concerned with his legacy.

But, Cross' true "shadow" continues to be revealed in the film's climax. When all of the major characters converge in Chinatown, he grabs Mulwray with the hope of reuniting with Katherine.

> CROSS
> Evelyn, how many years have I got?
> She's mine too.

> MULWRAY
> She's never going to know that.

Then, Mulwray brandishes a gun – pointing it at her father. Gittes begs her to put the gun down and leave this matter to the police, but Mulwray can only respond by bellowing, "He owns the police!"

Once again, it is another character informing the audience about Cross instead of us witnessing Cross' actions. While this is a rather unorthodox approach to communicating villainy (we would prefer to see a firsthand account of the villain acting villainous), the line of dialogue nonetheless adds to Cross' malevolent persona.

Also adding to Cross' sheer creepiness are the final moments of the film, when Evelyn is shot by the police. Katherine, who is unharmed, is taken away by Cross with his hand gently placed over her mouth – silencing her forever.

Annie Wilkes
(Kathy Bates) is
pretty peeved that
Paul Sheldon has
not been playing
by her rules and
she's about to
teach him a
lesson he will
never forget.

Annie Wilkes (*Misery*):

The Villain as Number One Fan

"I'm your number one fan. There's nothing to worry about. You're gonna be just fine. I'll take good care of you."

And if that were true, we would have no movie.

This is the benign introduction of Annie Wilkes (Kathy Bates), at about seven minutes into *Misery* (1990). These are words of comfort and relief to Wilkes' literary hero, Paul Sheldon (James Caan), who has just found himself upside down in his car after an accident in the hills of Colorado. But unfortunately for Sheldon, Wilkes' seemingly benevolent appearance turns out to be as compassionate as the sledgehammer she wields later in the story.

Not that Sheldon would predict such behavior during the first days of his incarceration. During that time, Wilkes is nothing less than a compassionate caregiver bent on nursing him back to health. She provides an IV drip, pain medication, and secures Sheldon's broken legs in homemade braces.

The duality of Wilkes' "shadow" is perfectly present, in that she has literally saved the life of her hero. If Wilkes doesn't show up on that snow-covered hill, there is no more Sheldon – and no more story. Like several of the memorable villains we have discussed, Wilkes does have dimensionality to her. She is not a myopic, monolithic character with a singular evil guise. There is a caring element at work. But like most of our villains, one side of the "shadow" will eventually prevail over the other – and it is not the light side of Wilkes that will triumph.

Life takes a turn for the worse about eighteen minutes into the film. Wilkes' munificent demeanor turns ugly after reading the beginning of Sheldon's new novel. While she tells him she doesn't approve of the book's profanity, a metamorphosis suddenly comes upon her, culminating in a screaming tirade and a bowl of spilled soup. Before she leaves, a sense of calm comes across her. "I love you, Paul," she says. "Your mind. Your creativity. That's all I meant."

But, we know that's definitely not all she meant. And we know something is rotten in the state of Colorado.

This is the first moment of the film when we realize Wilkes is far from what she seems. We have just experienced a glimpse that she may be psychotic – the audience knows it – and so does Sheldon.

But, what about this villain's desire for legitimacy? Clearly, she aspires to more than simply torturing her favorite author. Ultimately, she sees Sheldon as her husband – part of her legitimate nuclear family – except this husband happens to be psychologically and physically captive.

When Wilkes instructs her captor he will now write another book while locked up in her house, we get a glimpse of her delusions of grandeur and need to be a part of the society that shuns her (from a screenplay by William Goldman, based on the book by Stephen King).

> ANNIE
> It'll be a book in my honor – for sav-
> ing your life and nursing you
> back to health. Oh, Paul. You're
> going to make me the envy of the whole
> world.

She is falling in love with Sheldon and believes his feelings are mutual. But, of course, they are not. Sheldon must use what he has left – specifically, his mental acumen – to convince Wilkes they are destined to be together.

At twenty-eight minutes into the film, things take a quick and definitive turn for the worse for our hero, Sheldon. Upon reading his latest novel – featuring his recurring character, Misery – Wilkes enters Sheldon's room in the middle of the night, clearly peeved (an understatement of monumental proportions).

> ANNIE
> You. You dirty bird! How could
> you? She can't be dead. Misery
> Chastain cannot be dead!

> PAUL
> Annie, in 1871, women often died in
> childbirth. But, her spirit is the
> important thing and Misery's spirit
> is still alive.

                    ANNIE
I don't want her spirit! I want
her! And, you murdered her!

                    PAUL
No. I didn't.

                    ANNIE
Who did?

                    PAUL
No one. She, she died. She just
slipped away.

                    ANNIE
Slipped away? Slipped away? She
just didn't slip away! You did
it! You did it! You did it! You
did it! You did it! You murdered
my Misery!

                    PAUL
Annie! Annie!

                    ANNIE
I thought you were good, Paul.
But you're not good. You're just
another lying old dirty birdy –
and I don't think I better be
around you for a while. And don't
even think about anybody coming
for you. Not the doctors. Not
your agent. Not your family.
Because I never called them.
Nobody knows you're here. And you
better hope nothing happens to me.
Because if I die, you die.

So much for the light side of her "shadow." This scene is critical in our story because if we ever doubted the type of movie this is, we now know what we are watching. Sheldon is incapacitated with no access to communication and Wilkes has every intention of keeping him hostage until his dying day. Sheldon wants to escape; Wilkes wants him to stay – two characters with diametrically opposing desires. It is a perfect example of dramatic conflict, a highly effective lesson for any writer, and a marvelous moment that fully immerses the audience into the film.

Still, Wilkes remains Sheldon's caregiver for most of the movie. It is a peculiar dichotomy when a villain has a hero captive, yet also acts as his nurse – and that is just one of the elements that makes Wilkes such an unforgettable villain.

But, her most memorable scene is yet to come. Many screenwriting books will discuss the end of Act Two as the point when the hero is furthest away from his goal. It is usually about five to twenty minutes from the end of the film and is present in almost any memorable Hollywood movie. At the conclusion of Act Two (sometimes referred to as the second turning point), it is as if the filmmaker says to the audience, "There's no way your hero is going to get out of this one."

That very moment happens to Sheldon at one hour and twenty-two minutes into the film. After Wilkes discovers Sheldon has been out of his room, she decides she can no longer take any chances. He is her figurative husband and she is not looking for a divorce – not now, not ever.

So, she does what any other psychotic person would do (apologies to the medical community for diagnosing her without any formal training in psychology) – she reenacts a barbaric form of punishment called "hobbling," where a thick piece of wood is placed in between the victim's feet and a sledgehammer is used to shatter the lower extremities. If you haven't seen *Misery* yet, this is one scene you need to witness – for no description in print could ever do it justice. The result is that, physically, Paul is brought back to the early days of the crash – a dire situation for a hero who desperately wants to escape.

And a clear message to the audience that Wilkes' "shadow" is now officially void of light.

Wilkes also has an "end of Act Two moment" after killing the sheriff who comes to her house to investigate Sheldon's disappearance. With the lifeless sheriff at her feet, she peacefully gazes at Sheldon, brandishing a gun and syringe in hand.

```
                    ANNIE
        ... You and I were meant to be
        together forever. Now our time in
        this world must end. But, don't
        worry, Paul. I've prepared for
        what must be done. I put two
        bullets in my gun. One for you,
        and one for me. Oh darling, it
        will be so beautiful.
```

Here is one villain who actually wants to die with the story's hero — an unorthodox construct, to say the least, but the moment keeps us on the edge of our seats and prepares us for the climactic battle to come.

And it comes in the form of Sheldon smashing his manual typewriter onto Wilkes' head, sending her collapsing onto the floor. A teeth-clenching romp across the room follows, until Sheldon trips Wilkes, who ironically plummets face first onto his typewriter — knocking her out cold.

Ah, but let us not forget the lesson we learned from Alex Forrest in *Fatal Attraction* — namely, sometimes a villain does not die the first time she is dealt a "lethal" blow. Sometimes she gives the audience a moment to let down its collective guard and take a breath — only to give her one more shot at doing away with the hero.

So, just as Sheldon slithers into the next room — apparently leaving a deceased Wilkes in a pool of her own blood — she astonishes all of us when she falls onto him and the fight resumes. It is a nail-biter as the two purposely move toward a cast iron pig — the last weapon left at their disposal.

There will be no third chance for Wilkes. Sheldon gets to the substantial swine first, then successfully bashes it into Wilkes' face. Finally, it is game over – Sheldon has at long last done away with this most villainous of villains and will live to write again.

The most memorable villains are the ones who have dimensions to their personality far beyond their overt villainy. If Annie Wilkes wasn't a competent nurse, poor Paul Sheldon would never have lasted past the opening scene in *Misery*; if Hans Gruber wasn't a brilliant criminal strategist, the chess game he had with John McClane would have been dull and tedious; and if the Joker wasn't encompassed by an excess of internal and external scars, his presence would have been far less compelling.

Just as heroes have reflections of their "shadows," the most unforgettable villains also have positive traits to help us better understand their motivations. For example, while it is true Hannibal Lecter is a psychopathic, cannibalistic, and homicidal murderer, a part of us actually likes a part of him. We know he'll never harm Clarice Starling, and that's one of the reasons we find him so charming. "I have no plans to call on you, Clarice," he says to her upon his freedom. "The world's more interesting with you in it." And we feel the same way about our deceitful doctor and all of the unforgettable villains he represents.

(*Note*: These exercises are interchangeable with the hero exercises at the end of Chapter Three.)

1. Watch three of the films featured in this chapter and write down the primary traits of each villain. Do you see commonalities? If so, what conclusions can you make of their common characteristics and motivations?

2. If you are writing a screenplay, write down ten words that best describe your villain and compare these traits to villains we have discussed. Can you think of ways to make your villains more memorable?

3. Take a look at the American Film Institute's *100 Years… 100 Heroes & Villains* list and watch as many of the films featured in the "Villain" category as possible (*www.afi.com/tvevents/100years/handv.aspx*). You will find this to be an invaluable exercise in discovering ways to make your own villains unforgettable.

4. Do you know anyone in your life who is villainous? Write down their traits and examples of their villainous behavior. Then, try to ascertain their motivations and see if these real life villains can help you with your fictitious villains.

part 2

Creating Memorable
Heroes and Villains

chapter 5

Conversations With the Screenwriters

I had the unique opportunity to speak with four master storytellers who created some of the most enduring heroes and villains in film. Their collective cinematic canons have entertained countless movie-goers across the globe.

Steven E. de Souza (*Die Hard*):

Photo by Shane Sato

Steven E. de Souza understands what it takes to create a hero or villain who stands the test of time. With films like *Die Hard*, *48 Hrs.*, and *Lara Croft Tomb Raider: The Cradle of Life* to his credit, de Souza has created some of the most memorable characters in American film over the last twenty years.

I had the pleasure of speaking with de Souza about his experience with *Die Hard* and his approach to writing.

Jeffrey Hirschberg: Tell me how you were brought into this project.

Steven E. de Souza: *Die Hard* was based on a book entitled *Nothing Lasts Forever* by Roderick Thorp. Frank Sinatra had originated the character (who at the time was known as Joe Leland), in a movie called *The Detective* and was thus offered the lead role in *Die Hard*. When Sinatra passed, the studio changed the name of the lead character to John

McClane so it would not be considered a sequel to *The Detective*. Joel Silver and Larry Gordon had a script by Jeb Stuart that was developed a couple of years earlier that they were shopping around town. It had hit some speed bumps because the producers were having trouble casting the lead character (James Caan, Richard Gere, Sylvester Stallone, Arnold Schwarzenegger, and Burt Reynolds were among those to whom offers were made). They gave the script to me to rewrite and I wasn't given a lot of time. This was, in my opinion, a good thing. My best experiences have been working on movies that have a release date from the onset. The reason being that there is little time for studio executives to tinker with the script. Everyone is on a tight timetable and thus, the process tends to work much more smoothly. In the case of *Die Hard*, I was told production was going to begin "right away," so the pressure was on – and that's exactly how I like to work.

Hirschberg: What was the specific reaction to the McClane character, who is the hero of the film?

de Souza: The problem was that if you compared the John McClane character to other heroes in the mid-eighties, he seemed very reactive in comparison – a real wimp, if you will. He is very reactive and cautious for a good part of the movie, and these are traits I believe are prevalent in most memorable heroes. The best compliment I received on this film was, "I thought the hero was going to die."

Hirschberg: In many films, the hero is not the protagonist. Rather, it is the villain. Can you comment on Hans Gruber's duel role of protagonist and villain?

de Souza: You're right. In film, the protagonist is the character who gets the ball rolling. In *Jaws*, the protagonist is the shark. In *Die Hard*, it's Hans Gruber. In most cases, the hero cannot do anything until something else happens – and it's almost always the protagonist who inspires the hero to act. After that, it's a chess game – the protagonist (who is often the villain) makes a move, then the antagonist (who is often the hero), makes a counter-move. To be clear, nine times out of ten, the protagonist is the villain in genre movies.

Hirschberg: What changes did you make to the story that were not in the book or the original Jeb Stuart script?

de Souza: The book spends most of its time in the head of the hero – a first-person perspective. If you actually broke down the events in the book, there wasn't enough happening to fill a two-hour movie. The challenge was to transform this first-person narrative style to a third-person omniscient point-of-view. One of the major elements I added was the notion that Gruber's terrorism plot was a smoke screen and he had a hidden agenda. I needed to give Gruber and his team something to do during the story so I came up with the idea that they had to break into a high-tech vault holding $640 million in bearer bonds. I knew the villain needed a plan that would have gone off swimmingly if the John McClane character hadn't shown up. Gruber's plan, therefore, enabled the audience to keep track of the "chess game" between the hero and the villain.

Hirschberg: What changes did you make to the Hans Gruber character?

de Souza: The best villains I have experienced in plays, movies, or novels do not think they are villains. Typically, they don't wake up every morning and say, "What can I do that's evil today?" For Gruber, I approached him as a CEO of a small company that had a detailed plan to accomplish a goal. He hired a reliable staff and treated them well. This made him more real – more relatable. Because Bruce Willis was so busy shooting *Moonlighting* during the day and *Die Hard* at night, there was a practical consideration to give him a little down time. The result was that the studio asked me to spend more time with the villain. So, I started by creating the origin of the Gruber plan, which would be critical to the movie. Ironically, the backstory I made up was utterly preposterous – that the bank vault in the Nakatomi building was connected to the company's headquarters in Japan via an underwater cable. Basically, I had to invent something for Gruber and his team to do that would take the length of the movie – disengaging the bank vault. It's also important to mention that in casting Alan Rickman as Hans Gruber, we went against the casting norms of the 1980s. During that time, villains were usually a big physical presence. Rickman, however, was slight in his build. The key to creating a memorable villain is not to make him physically daunting. Rather, he should be smart and have tremendous resources.

Hirschberg: Were you faced with any story issues?

de Souza: Structurally, I felt the need to simplify the story. So, in Act One, the hero is reluctant to get involved and is trying to get help. In Act Two, the hero is trying to stay out of the line of fire between the authorities and Gruber's team. In Act Three, he realizes he has to step up to the plate and thwart the villain's plan. The next problem we faced with the story was, "How will the villains escape?" It was not until very late in the production when we came up with the idea they would create an explosion on the roof and escape in an emergency vehicle when the authorities arrived.

Hirschberg: *Die Hard* is unique because it is one of the few films in which I found myself rooting for the hero to achieve his goal (saving his wife and the rest of the hostages) and for the villain to achieve his goal (stealing the $640 million in bearer bonds and escaping). Was this your intention and if so, how did you achieve it?

de Souza: This was my intention. One of the things that made Hitchcock's films so memorable was his ability to make the audience sympathize with the villain – in other words, you were unconsciously being steered to root for the bad guy at a particular moment. In the case of Die Hard, the villain is purposely cryptic in his plan. Thus, the audience subconsciously wants Gruber to make progress because that's the only way they'll find out what he's up to. Curiosity makes us root for him.

Hirschberg: Why do you think the Hans Gruber character is so memorable?

de Souza: First of all, he's extremely entertaining with some of the best lines in the picture. Secondly, he's clearly smart and audiences always respect an intelligent villain. Finally, he comes across as being very real. So many movie villains are simply depicted as being crazy and that makes for a familiar, boring viewing experience. Gruber is different. Gruber has layers.

Hirschberg: How did Alan Rickman complement the Gruber character?

de Souza: Rickman really elevated the entire movie by playing the role so real and so smart.

Hirschberg: How do you approach dialogue and finding your characters' voices?

de Souza: That's the one thing missing in most screenplays. Every character should have a unique voice. The biggest defect in most motion pictures is that everyone sounds the same. A long time ago, a colleague once parlayed the following words of wisdom to me: "You should be able to tell which character is speaking in a screenplay even if the name is covered up. If you can't, you've done something wrong." The key is to develop your ear for dialogue and figure out the style for each of your characters.

Hirschberg: For writers who are interested in creating memorable heroes and villains, what films would you recommend?

de Souza: Sir Guy of Gisbourne from *The Adventures of Robin Hood* is an incredibly nuanced villain if you really pay attention to the character; Jaffar in *The Thief of Baghdad* is a terrific, multilayered villain; and Alexander Sebastian from *Notorious* is a great example of a villain every writer should be familiar with.

Hirschberg: It has been said that heroes often change throughout a film while villains stay the same. What are your thoughts of hero and villain character arcs?

de Souza: It's a practical consideration. There is only so much time for all of the elements of a movie to be communicated, so filmmakers often give more of a character arc to the hero as opposed to the villain. In the case of Hans Gruber, his character pretty much stayed consistent throughout the movie, except when his planning went awry and he was forced to improvise at the end.

Hirschberg: Can you talk a little about the difference between "character" and "characteristics?"

de Souza: When I speak at writers' conferences and retreats, I like to use the following example to illustrate this topic: "I am going to describe somebody and you tell me what kind of person this is: He wants to be in an artistic, creative field but feels that in the world he lives in, this must be put aside for practical matters. So, he decides to do something for society and his country. He is very health-conscious – a vegetarian – doesn't smoke, loves animals, and is a natural leader." After going through this description, I'll ask the group whom I'm speaking of and they'll rattle off a list of heroes. The truth, however, is that I am speaking about Adolph Hitler. These are all true characteristics but they do not necessarily inform us as to the complete character.

Hirschberg: What advice do you have for writers looking to sell a script in the spec market?

de Souza: 1) One of the most important aspects of a feature spec script is that it should be short. It sounds crazy, but you have a better chance of getting your material read if it's between, say, 110 and 115 pages. I can't think of a picture I have ever worked on when a studio executive hasn't said, "Can you shave a few pages?" 2) You have to know what type of movie you are writing within the first five pages. 3) Keep your stories contemporary. 4) Always remember your first audience is a reader who works at a production company or a studio. They often read dozens of scripts per week, so you have to get their attention quickly or your script may end up being tossed out.

David Franzoni (*Gladiator*):

David Franzoni, who wrote the screenplay for *Gladiator*, won an Academy Award for producing the film with Branko Lustig and Douglas Wick. His other screenwriting credits include classics such as *Amistad* and *King Arthur*.

Photo by Nancye Franzoni

I had an enlightening conversation with David about writing the screenplay for *Gladiator*, creating the legendary General Maximus character, and his experiences working in Hollywood.

Jeffrey Hirschberg: What was the origin of the *Gladiator* screenplay?

David Franzoni: In 1973, I was traveling the world on a motorcycle and everywhere in Europe I went, I saw the remnants of arenas. It occurred to me that the arena events must have been a big business. When I reached Baghdad, I picked up a book entitled *Those About to Die*, by Daniel P. Mannix. The book was a dramatic commentary of the Games at the Coliseum. While the book did not give me a storyline to work with, it did give me a modern way of looking at the Games that was very fresh and contemporary. Twenty years later, while I was writing *Amistad* for Steven Spielberg, I revisited the book and began writing *Gladiator*.

Hirschberg: How did DreamWorks get involved?

Franzoni: When I got back from Rome, I called Doug Wick (who eventually produced *Gladiator* with me) and pitched the story. He responded immediately. We then took it to DreamWorks and they said, "Yes."

Hirschberg: Did you consult with any scholars in the field while researching the screenplay?

Franzoni: I did, and here's what I discovered. Basically, there are three types of scholars: 1) those who are the defenders of what has already been written on the subject and are inflexible to alternate interpretations; 2) those who have actually gone out there and studied the work, who are typically more effective than the defenders; and 3) those who are constantly investigating to find the truth. I found the latter group to be the most helpful, especially Kathleen Coleman (my advisor, who is now at Harvard).

Hirschberg: There is a lot of conflicting information regarding the existence of a real character named Maximus. Was Maximus a true historical figure?

Franzoni: According to historical records, Commodus was murdered by a gladiator in one of the gladiatorial schools. My goal was to invent the life of the gladiator who killed him. And I needed someone who almost had a genetic code of honor – someone who was implacably straightforward and honest. When I read the Augustan Histories, I found it fascinating how Commodus would often go into the arena as a gladiator and was victorious via "fixed" fights. When I read a gladiator killed him, I knew I had my hero. So, there was no real historical foundation for Maximus. The name "Maximus" came out of a committee meeting I had with Ridley Scott, Walter Parkes, John Logan, and Steven Spielberg.

Hirschberg: At the end of Act One, Marcus Aurelius says to Maximus, "I want you to be the protector of Rome after I die." Why did Maximus turn down such an honor?

Franzoni: Because he wants to go home to his family. He doesn't want to run Rome. He feels he has done his duty for Rome and has had enough. He longs to raise his son and be with his wife.

Hirschberg: A few minutes later in the film – after Commodus murders Marcus Aurelius – Commodus offers his hand to Maximus and says, "Take my hand. I'll only offer it once." Why does Maximus refuse, knowing he has essentially signed his own death wish?

Franzoni: Maximus will always default to doing the right thing. His reaction to Commodus extending his hand is visceral. He can't touch him. Maximus is the kind of person who makes decisions almost instantaneously by doing what he deems "the right thing." That's one of the most important traits of Maximus and what helped make him an extremely strong hero. He is hopelessly heroic.

Hirschberg: What is Maximus' motivation? Is it revenge for Commodus killing his wife and child?

Franzoni: For me, the bottom line for Maximus is that he wants to go back home. Once he becomes a gladiator, his initial goal is simply to stay alive. Once he realizes he can survive as a gladiator, his next step is to kill Commodus. He's moving from moment to moment. But at the end of the day, saving Rome is impossible and revenge is empty, so this hero never strays from his overarching goal: to get home. Once his family is dead, "home" becomes defined as meeting them in the afterlife. Maximus promises his family he is coming home and he never breaks a promise. Period.

Hirschberg: How much of the action sequences in *Gladiator* were conceived by you and how much of them were conceived by the film's director, Ridley Scott?

Franzoni: Before Ridley came on board I spoke to Steven about much of the script, including the action sequences. We agreed that every gladiatorial action sequence had to advance the plot – we couldn't just have a bunch of people killing each other. So, all of the battle scenes were carefully written to achieve that objective. The idea was to create an accelerating series of fights so by the time you got to the sequences in the Coliseum, you were ready for the climax.

Hirschberg: About an hour and twenty minutes into the film, Maximus' instincts as a general take over as he bands together the other gladiators to win a battle heavily biased against them. What was your rationale for including this scene?

Franzoni: In all of the battles, the gladiators are supposed to lose. They are always the underdogs. The idea was for each battle sequence to build – with each battle being greater in scope. So, when Maximus is in the Coliseum and sees that he and his fellow fighters are about to be attacked by a massive chariot squadron, he immediately knows it is time to be a general, not just another gladiator.

Hirschberg: Why do you think Maximus is such a memorable hero?

Franzoni: First of all, Maximus' goal is pure. It is not to get rich; it is not revenge; it is not any of the usual goals one would see in a typical Hollywood movie. He wants to get home. And because his goal is so noble, we have a hero who is implacably good. Even when he is killing people, he is good. It's what makes him unique.

Hirschberg: How do you approach dialogue and finding your characters' voices?

Franzoni: The problem with so many films is that everyone talks like the writer, so all of the characters sound the same. It's critical to give every character an identifiable personality through their voice. For me, as I develop characters, they begin to take on their own personalities. I like to look for shortcuts in language that help define my characters. I sit around and talk to myself a lot.

Hirschberg: How do you avoid clichés in your screenplays?

Franzoni: I am tired of movies about movies people have seen. I want to see a movie about a life someone has lived. I went around the world on my motorcycle, lived in a grass hut in Baghdad, and stayed in a ruined castle in Greece. These are just some of my life experiences that influenced the *Gladiator* script and every other screenplay I have ever written. If you travel as much as I have, you are exposed to many cultures and dialects. Eventually, you develop an ear for dialogue. On the other hand, as a writer, you need to know when you are writing clichés. I advise young writers to take people they know and use them as models for their characters. This will help get them grounded in realistic dialogue.

Hirschberg: Do you think characters need to change?

Franzoni: After a certain age, people – and therefore characters – no longer change. They may, however, have surprising goodness or evil latent within them. These attributes can be part of their arcs. The challenge is to convince the audience it's there.

Hirschberg: What films should writers see that best illustrate memorable heroes and villains?

Franzoni: The movies Ridley Scott and I talked about were *All Quiet on the Western Front* – because of its gritty, realistic depiction of war; *La Dolce Vita* – because it's about corrupt Romans; and *The Conformist* – because of its webs of deceit, rising fascism, and evil overwhelming goodness. Those were our primary references for *Gladiator*. As far as heroes are concerned, Marcello Mastroianni's character in *La Dolce Vita* is one of the most important heroes in modern film. Another important hero is Anthony Quinn's character in *La Strada*.

Hirschberg: Any final thoughts on your writing process?

Franzoni: I never outline – I just write. The reason I do so is because the personality of the story must emerge from the personalities of the characters. In the case of *Gladiator*, the story lives inside Maximus. The movie is him.

Photo by Melissa A. Thomas

David Koepp (*Spider-Man*):

David Koepp is responsible for some of the most successful movies of the last fifteen years. With films including *Jurassic Park, Mission: Impossible, Panic Room, Indiana Jones and the Kingdom of the Crystal Skull,* and of course, *Spider-Man,* Koepp's screenplays have entertained millions of people throughout the world with his memorable characters, witty dialogue, and intricate plots.

I spoke with David about *Spider-Man* and its timeless hero, Peter Parker.

Jeffrey Hirschberg: How were you hired to write the script for *Spider-Man*?

David Koepp: After the copyright situation was resolved, I found out the studio was looking for a writer – and it was the type of project a lot of writers were pursuing. I also found out this was not the type of assignment the studio was just going to hand me – I would have to earn it. So, as a big fan of *Spider-Man* comics and the original TV show, I delved through a bunch of old material with the initial goal of finding the perfect villain for the script – knowing that a hero is so often defined by his villain. I started pulling out panels I thought were iconic, representing what I thought the film should look like. I made up a bunch of poster boards I looked at for inspiration.

Hirschberg: Did you focus on *The Amazing Spider-Man #1* or the character's introduction in *Amazing Fantasy #15*?

Koepp: I read hundreds of issues to immerse myself in the character and his world. Since I knew the studio had an eye toward making several *Spider-Man* films, my first challenge was deciding how long the origin story should run. I concluded it should continue as long as possible because it is, in my opinion, the best origin story of any superhero character I have ever seen. It's the most psychologically complex and, therefore, critical to get it right to set up the first movie and those that would eventually come afterwards.

Hirschberg: How did you choose the Green Goblin as your villain?

Koepp: I looked for the villain who best summed up Peter Parker's complex story and the Green Goblin was the obvious choice. The whole Norman Osborn-Harry Osborn-Mary Jane Watson-Peter Parker relationship was so rife for soap opera. It was rich with conflict and so natural. Ultimately, I felt this storyline was so dramatically strong it belonged in the first movie, alongside the origin story.

Hirschberg: Once you had your take on the film solidified, to whom did you pitch it?

Koepp: I pitched to John Calley, Amy Pascal, and Matt Tolmach from Sony, and Avi Arad, who runs Marvel. The poster boards I made were effective visual props – it never hurts to have office products with you when you pitch a movie idea. A few days after the pitch meeting, I was told I got the job. After several drafts, they brought in the producer, Laura Ziskin, and the director, Sam Raimi.

Hirschberg: How is the Peter Parker character different in the movie versus the comic book?

Koepp: I'd certainly like to think we fleshed him out a bit in transforming the character from drawings to a living, breathing person. We definitely minimized the wisecracking that was so prevalent in the comics. Whenever I tried to infuse that element into the script, the story jumped out of reality.

Hirschberg: Many films today cater to an impatient audience, providing action as soon as the credits roll, if not before. In *Spider-Man*, Peter Parker doesn't climb the wall until about twenty-five minutes into the film. Was this a tough sell to the studio?

Koepp: Not really. During the pitch, I told the studio there were a couple of things they needed to do that might be hard to swallow: 1) The origin story has to take at least forty-five minutes because this story will be more interesting than his battle with the villain; and 2) Peter should not get the girl at the end because ultimately, this story needs to be a tragedy. Everyone was enthusiastic about these two points, which kept us all on the same page.

Hirschberg: Did you need to alter the Peter Parker character when Tobey Maguire signed on for the part?

Koepp: Not at all. He is uniquely suited for the part, which is one of the reasons the movies have had such success. He was great at adapting to this person he was supposed to play.

Hirschberg: What was Peter Parker's motivation for his heroism?

Koepp: Guilt. Had he stopped the guy who later killed his uncle, then none of this would have ever happened. Spider-Man probably would have hosted his own variety show. But, because he witnesses firsthand what happens when you don't fulfill your responsibility, he feels compelled to use his powers for justice at all times. Guilt is a great motivator and, in Peter's case, he is trying to ease a guilty conscience. I also think heroes are heroes because they must be heroes – the challenge is finding the reason. Typically, they have an inner voice that will not be quiet unless they act heroically. I am currently working on *Angels & Demons* (the follow-up to *The DaVinci Code*) and when I was first brought on board, there was a lot of discussion about the Robert Langdon character (played by Tom Hanks) and his motivation for going on this journey. My answer was simple: He does it because it's a mystery and at his core, he's a detective. He has no choice. He must find the answer.

Hirschberg: How do you avoid clichés with your characters?

Koepp: First, I try to make each character as specific as possible. Second, I try to make each character do the unexpected. The key is to find those idiosyncratic traits that make characters interesting.

Hirschberg: Do you prescribe to the notion that characters need to undergo some sort of change throughout the film?

Koepp: Not really. In the case of *Spider-Man*, Peter Parker doesn't change – mostly because it's a serial adventure. Indiana Jones doesn't really change at the end of each movie. He may learn a lesson or two, but at the beginning of the next movie, he's right back where he started. The classic model of character change in American cinema is Michael Corleone in *The Godfather*. He went from, "That's my family – that's not me" to "I am my family." That sort of change doesn't come along too often. In most cases, I'm not sure change necessarily serves drama. That said, this is one of three comments writers constantly receive from studios: "The hero has to go through more of a transformation," "We need more sympathy for him," and "There needs to be more tension in Act Three."

Hirschberg: What is it like working through the studio process?

Koepp: The studio process can be helpful or it can be hurtful. You should think of a studio as a bunch of editors and sometimes, these editors actually make your work better.

Hirschberg: What is your philosophy on rewriting?

Koepp: It is my experience that most scripts hit their stride around the third draft. After that point, the script can become different or it can become worse, but it probably won't get better. After a few drafts, writers start to 'overthink' and 'overexplain' the story.

Hirschberg: Regarding *Indiana Jones and the Kingdom of the Crystal Skull*, how were you able to craft a story acceptable to Steven Spielberg, George Lucas, and Harrison Ford when so many other writers failed?

Koepp: A lot of it was probably good timing. I preserved several elements they had previously agreed upon over the years. The challenge was to refashion a story around these characters that worked to everyone's satisfaction. They liked the script, but more importantly, I was brought in at a time when they were ready to agree on a story and move forward.

Hirschberg: Cate Blanchett did a terrific job with the villain of the film, Irina Spalko. Do you approach writing heroes and villains differently?

Koepp: Not really. Heroes and villains are very similar, they just have different goals. The villain's goal, for instance, is usually without any shred of moral consideration.

Hirschberg: What advice do you have for writers who aspire to create their own memorable heroes and villains?

Koepp: It's all in the details, rather than the broad strokes. In the script I am currently writing, there is a scene with the villain and another character who thinks he's about to be killed. At the end of the scene, however, the villain simply offers the other character a cup of tea. We don't expect a villain to be a tea lover, but this scene ultimately works because the other character and the audience are surprised at the end. It's the small things that will often lead you to the big things.

Hirschberg: What movies would you recommend every writer watch that feature a memorable hero?

Koepp: *Raiders of the Lost Ark*, of course, because Indiana Jones is less than perfect, but perhaps the most goal-directed hero in movie history. And, the fact he's a teacher means he can really spell out his goal for the audience at the top of the movie – a virtue not to be overlooked in storytelling. Also, any of the Basil Rathbone - Nigel Bruce *Sherlock Holmes* movies, which were models for heroic storytelling – particularly the first half dozen or so, which became really proficient at setting up the recurring hero's new challenge. I'd also throw in *Bridge on the River Kwai* for something a bit more complex – watching the hero come to his heroic actions slowly, and perhaps from the wrong direction.

Hirschberg: What movies would you recommend every writer watch that feature a memorable villain?

Koepp: *The Godfather*, but in that case – "antihero" is the more appropriate term. But, the character – and his turn to darkness – are so good and so flawless that we have come to think of it as the "Michael Corleone model of character change." I'd recommend *The Silence of the Lambs* as well, because Hannibal Lecter goes from a position of total powerlessness to total power – the exact opposite we're used to seeing in a villain in a Hollywood story. Finally, Richard Donner's original *Superman*, to see how a weaker villain – Lex Luthor – can manipulate events and psychology to master a far more powerful hero. Again, this is the opposite of the usual Hollywood model, which likes to present the hero as being outmatched in order to make his triumph all the more impressive.

Hirschberg: What advice do you have for writers looking to sell a script in the spec market?

Koepp: My advice is not to think about the spec market when you are writing. You can't lead the parade from behind and if you are chasing trends and patterns that are already out there, you will be hopelessly behind them when the time comes to sell your script. It's corny, but just write what you would like to see and hope for the best. When you're sitting in a movie theater with your popcorn and Raisinets and a few hours free from work and family, what do you hope comes up on screen?

Hirschberg: Why do you think Peter Parker is such a memorable character?

Koepp: Simple identification. We like him because we know him – because he is us. But, he is more than us – which gives us hope we might be more than we think we are too.

Photo by Annabel Brooks

James Dearden (*Fatal Attraction*):

In the fall of 1987, there was a film that occupied the cultural zeitgeist of the country – a movie that found itself the topic of water cooler conversations from coast to coast and on the cover of the November 16th issue of *Time* magazine. The cover, which featured Michael Douglas and Glenn Close in an awkward embrace, was accompanied by the headline "The Thriller Is Back." The thriller in question was the invention of screenwriter James Dearden.

I spoke with James about the film and, specifically, its memorable villain, Alex Forrest.

Jeffrey Hirschberg: *Fatal Attraction* was based on a short film, *Diversion*, which you wrote and directed. How did the short influence the feature film?

James Dearden: *Diversion* is basically the first third of *Fatal Attraction*. In the short film, Alex is a sad, neurotic, single woman. When I turned it into a feature, I realized I had to continue taking the character to the next level and in the process, she became more and more insane... unbalanced... unhinged. So, she was not originally conceived as a villain but became one as I developed the script with the studio.

Hirschberg: How were you hired to write the full-length screenplay?

Dearden: I met Stanley Jaffe in London and later sent him a copy of *Diversion*. Stanley and his producing partner, Sherry Lansing, then asked me if I wanted to turn *Diversion* into a full-length feature film, set in New York City. It took about four years to get the script into production.

Hirschberg: Would you consider the Dan Gallagher character to be heroic?

Dearden: It depends. We all thought Michael Douglas would be the perfect choice to play Dan Gallagher because he has that strong, "everyman" quality. He's very relatable to the audience. Very likeable. This was important because in the film, he's an adulterer, and we needed someone the audience would still accept. This partly explains what happened to the character of Alex. In order for Dan to appear likeable, she had to go further and further to an extreme. The more extreme she becomes, the more reasonable he becomes.

Hirschberg: Did you write a backstory for the Alex and Dan characters?

Dearden: In a sense, the main characters in *Fatal Attraction* are all archetypes. Specifically, there is a husband, wife, and mistress. So, I never wanted to give too much specificity to the characters and Dan's motivation for having the affair. He is simply a bit of a philanderer.

Hirschberg: Why did so many studios pass on this project, even after Michael Douglas was attached?

Dearden: The studios all passed for the same reason. They said, "The Dan Gallagher character is a bad guy. How can we root for a guy who cheats on his wife?" We would defend the story by saying, "It may be wrong, but it happens all of the time. Half of your audience has been in that situation and half your audience is worrying about that situation." The studios that passed felt the audience would not be able to relate to Michael Douglas' character. You would think he was a child molester. But, he was just an ordinary guy who had a one-night stand with a crazy woman who would not leave him alone.

Hirschberg: When you think about the Dan Gallagher and Alex Forrest characters, what is the fine line that makes them heroes, villains, or both?

Dearden: By the time the film was released, there was a debate raging about women becoming successful in a man's world on their own terms and having to sacrifice their personal lives to get there. So, a lot of feminists saw the Alex Forrest character as a representative for everything they were fighting for. Unfortunately, they also felt the film was saying she was a psycho and had to be killed. In that context, Alex can be viewed as the villain. For Dan, I see him as an everyman who is caught up in a situation that has spiraled out of his control. The story is about losing control. He begins with this perfect life, meets this strange woman, and it's a Pandora's Box. Suddenly, the genie is out of the bottle and everything is unraveling. One could argue that Dan's wife, Beth, while not quite the hero of the story, captures the bulk of the audience's sympathy and admiration when she kills Alex in the scene's climax.

Hirschberg: How do you approach creating authentic dialogue?

Dearden: You need to develop your ear. With most of the characters I create, I hear them talking inside my head. Hopefully, they are talking in believable voices. As you get more experienced, you get better at avoiding the traps of being overly explanatory. Most new writers tend to overwrite dialogue – their characters explain too much. The key is to keep it simple and keep it natural.

Hirschberg: The Alex Forrest character has been called a monster. Is that a fair characterization?

Dearden: No. I don't think she's a monster at all. I see her as a woman who has had quite a few affairs with single and married men – none of whom treated her very well. She's a sad, unhinged woman. She's unbalanced and has been tipped over the edge. As we know, when people are scorned in love, they can become a little bit crazy.

Hirschberg: The ending for the film was famous in that it was completely changed after negative reactions from test screen audiences. What happened?

Dearden: The original ending of the film had Alex cutting her throat while listening to *Madame Butterfly* in her apartment. The knife she used had Dan Gallagher's fingerprints on it from a previous scene. Then, we see Dan, his wife Beth, and their daughter outside their home. The cops arrive and arrest Dan for Alex's murder. After all, he was seen leaving the apartment, his fingerprints were on the knife, and she's dead on the bathroom floor. They also shot a final scene, which was not in my original script, that showed Beth playing a tape previously recorded by Alex in which she says she was going to kill herself. The idea being that Dan will be set free. The reason that final scene was not in my original script was because I conceived the piece as a film noir – the hero is flawed and he usually ends badly, like Fred MacMurray in *Double Indemnity.*

Hirschberg: As a writer, what was it like experiencing the success of the film?

Dearden: For the first couple of months, I was blissfully unaware of its success, as I was working on another film in Greece. I did get calls from Sherry Lansing, touting the film's box office performance. The movie was "platformed," meaning it opened in relatively few theaters and built week after week. The positive word of mouth kept the film going. When I got back to England, I was interviewed on national television. It was surreal – and a little uncomfortable, due to the perceived anti-feminism of the movie. In some cases, I was verbally attacked on TV as some sort of male chauvinist devil.

Hirschberg: Why is this film as relevant today as it was in 1987?

Dearden: It's a simple story about human nature and would be just as relevant in Biblical times. The reason the Bible is still a good read is because it's filled with good stories. People haven't changed much in the last two thousand years and they certainly haven't changed much since 1987. I also think that in most marriages, there is an unspoken fear in one or both of the partners that manifests itself with questions like, "Have you had an affair?" "Will you have an affair?" "Are you having an affair?" The movie is not about a specific time – the landscape is more or less what it is today and that's why I think the film is still relevant.

Hirschberg: What are some films you would recommend that feature memorable heroes and villains?

Dearden: I think the most memorable film villain of all time is Orson Welles in *The Third Man*. He's one of the most charismatic characters you'll ever meet. The Kirk Douglas character in *Paths of Glory* is a great heroic figure. It's a film that really illustrates the nobleness in the human soul. Humphrey Bogart in *Casablanca* is also a wonderful heroic figure, especially at the end when he lets the love of his life go – a great act of self-sacrifice. I love when a tough hero shows a human side. Russell Crowe in *Gladiator* is a memorable hero. He's the incredibly tough guy who has a soft side. He's the guy we would all love to be – the guy who takes on the bully in the playground and saves the kid from getting beaten up. He's the sort of character we would follow to the end of the Earth.

Hirschberg: What is your advice to a writer trying to sell a script in the marketplace?

Dearden: First of all, you have to be prepared for a lot of disappointment and make sure this is what you really want to do. I do believe, however, that if you are talented, at some point something will break. But, it can take an awfully long time. The key is to write a great screenplay and get it to that one person who can do something with it.

chapter 6

Creating Your Own
Memorable Heroes and Villains

So, you want to create a villain with the mind of Hannibal Lecter or a hero with the soul of Indiana Jones? Are you itching to invent a scene-stealer like the Joker or a courageous leader like Ellen Ripley?

I just might have the tool for you.

Throughout my years of screenwriting, I have developed a process that greatly facilitates the creation of memorable, three-dimensional heroes and villains who will help you better connect with your audience. I have also found this tool to be incredibly effective in helping writers discover the heroes and villains who lay dormant in their minds.

The tool in question, which asks the writer to thoughtfully complete thirty-seven questions, is affectionately named, "The Hero-Villain Persona." If used properly, it will help you construct the types of characters who will jump off the page and onto the screen.

Table 3: The Hero-Villain Persona

1. Name:
2. Age:
3. Physical Description/Dress:
4. Marital Status:
5. Childhood/Nuclear Family:
6. Current Occupation:
7. Job History:
8. Education:

Table 3: The Hero-Villain Persona (continued)

9. How much does he/she earn a year? How much in savings? Debt?
10. Hobbies:
11. Biggest regret in life:
12. How many sexual partners?
13. Favorite Book/Movie/Album:
14. Magazine Subscriptions:
15. Describe a typical Saturday night for the character:
16. Does the character have a credo? Words to live by?
17. Whom or what does the character fear?
18. Whom or what does the character hate?
19. Whom or what does the character love?
20. What is the character's goal?
21. What is the character's motivation?
22. Is the character's goal compelling enough to move us through three acts?
23. Is the character active or passive in achieving the goal?
24. Who or what prevents the character from achieving the goal?
25. What is the character's fatal flaw?
26. What is the transformation arc of the character?
27. Who or what helps the character change?
28. What is the character's purpose in the overall story?
29. How does the character speak?
30. What is the first image of the character?
31. Does the character have conflicting personality traits?
32. What happened in the character's childhood that has affected him/her?
33. How does culture affect the character's actions?
34. What happens if the character does not achieve his/her goal?
35. What is the character's secret?
36. What is the character missing in his/her life?
37. Who is the character's mentor?

Since younger writers (like many of my students) often have limited life experiences, it is frequently the case that characters in their scripts are either consciously or subconsciously based on films or television programs they have seen. For the reader (and the viewer), the result is a familiar, predictive feeling of knowing what a character is going to say or do before the character speaks or acts. The Persona helps avoid this all-too-familiar phenomenon by aiding writers in transforming what are typically one-dimensional, underdeveloped characters into three-dimensional, inspired characters.

That is not to say experienced writers and development executives cannot benefit from the Persona. How many times have you sat in a movie theater (watching a film that has been vetted by an entire Hollywood establishment), only to cringe at the believability, or lack thereof, of the main characters? If you're like me, you lost count at *Gigli*.

As you can imagine, properly answering all thirty-seven questions for your main characters results in a lengthy document – filled with a plethora of information, much of which will never overtly make it to the script. The key is the word "overtly," as most of your answers will covertly infuse themselves in everything your characters say and do. Still, it is an emotionally difficult document to complete. Most writers – I include myself in this group – desperately want to type FADE IN and get to the good stuff. Unfortunately, the good stuff must be based on a foundation and that foundation takes the form of a Hero-Villain Persona.

The Persona is critical for writers not only to know their characters, but also to *be* their characters. Anything less will result in tired, familiar characters wrought with clichés.

The greatest benefit in completing The Persona is that the document becomes a reference you can utilize throughout the scriptwriting process. On countless occasions I have referred to completed Personas when the curse of writer's block has struck. Think of it as a complement to your story outline or treatment.

In fact, I would argue you should complete a Hero-Villain Persona for your main characters before you tackle an outline because the shape your characters take will influence the structure of your screenplay. If used properly, this exercise also will help you differentiate characters from one another while creating an enjoyable experience for the reader.

Finally, I recommend you complete a Persona for each of the principal characters in your story – not just the hero and the villain. The more your hero and villain are supported by an assemblage of fresh and unique characters, the more compelling and original your story will be to your audience.

A Persona in Progress: *The Samsons*

I thought it would be helpful to include a draft of two Hero-Villain Personas for a screenplay I am currently writing entitled, *The Samsons*. Because this script is an ensemble comedy (or, "comedy-drama," whatever that means), it is important to for me to create characters who are:

- Unique
- Distinctive in their point-of-view
- Likeable/sympathetic (or have at least a few likeable/sympathetic traits)
- Different from one another
- Attractive for actors to portray

Not an easy mountain to climb. But these are the mountains all of us writers must be ready, willing, and able to ascend. Below, you will find Personas for the two main characters in the script.

The Samsons' *Hero-Villain Personas*

Roger Samson

ROGER SAMSON is an obsessive-compulsive Professor of Biology.

1. *Name:* Roger Samson (George Clooney type)

2. *Age:* 44

3. *Physical Description/Dress:* George Clooney with a tweed jacket. Indiana Jones in *Raiders of the Lost Ark*.

4. *Marital Status:* Separated, en route to a divorce.

5. *Childhood/Nuclear Family:* Grew up in Cambridge, Massachusetts. Father: Arthur; Mother: Helen; Sister: Julie (also a Harvard grad and the youngest National Security Advisor in the history of the U.S., under President Reagan. Missing since 1998. Rumors include she: 1) changed genders and is now in Congress; 2) committed suicide with a cult; 3) is living in the woods and was most recently romantically linked to The Zodiac killer). Roger grew up in a very liberal, academically-oriented family. No TV. No radio. No record player. Just books. And lots of them. Unfortunately, Roger's parents were more interested in reading than spending time with their kids. The result was that Roger and his sister basically had to raise themselves.

6. *Current Occupation:* Professor of Biology, Harvard University. Roger is also a well-known researcher, with a specialty in the human genome (he was the only member of his research team who did not win a Nobel Prize, which is a constant source of bitterness – the winners of the Nobel Prize in 2002 were Sydney Brenner, H. Robert Horvitz, and John E. Sulston.) Roger is more comfortable conducting research, often by himself, than teaching.

7. *Job History:* B.A., Harvard; PhD, Harvard; Brief stint as a researcher at Merck, where he did not get credit for developing a billion dollar cholesterol-lowering drug (which resulted in more bitterness). Full Professor of Biology at Harvard ever since.

8. *Education:* See above.

9. *How much does he/she earn a year? How much in savings? Debt?* About $175,000 per year, plus another $50,000 for lectures/consulting. Has a good pension. Some savings, but he'll never be rich – and that bothers him. Roger has several friends who have made millions in stock at biotech firms. He had plenty of offers to be involved in such companies when they were starting, but he never had the guts to leave the security of academia. He could have been worth millions.

10. *Hobbies:* Roger was on the first table tennis Olympic team in 1988 (Ping-Pong). This was the first year table tennis was an Olympic sport – in Seoul. He missed getting a medal by one point. The story of his life (even more bitterness).

11. *Biggest regret in life:* Not taking a chance in the private sector, where he believes he would have made millions with a drug company. He sometimes regrets marrying Judy, but realizes he has always and will always love her.

12. *How many sexual partners?* Ten (including six prostitutes).

13. *Favorite Book/Movie/Album: One Flew Over the Cuckoo's Nest. One Flew Over the Cuckoo's Nest.* The Soundtrack to *One Flew Over the Cuckoo's Nest.*

14. *Magazine Subscriptions:* Biology trade magazines. *Forbes* (so he can read about all of his colleagues who are making tons of money). *Penthouse* (Roger has a mild to moderate addiction to porn).

15. *Describe a typical Saturday night for the character.* After trying to get his soon-to-be ex-wife to go out with him (and she typically says, "no"), spending the night with a high-priced Cambridge prostitute. He uses three condoms and makes her wear latex gloves and a surgical mask. If he cannot obtain a prostitute, he will sit home alone in his study, reading – and brooding.

16. *Does the character have a credo? Words to live by?* "I hate everyone." Actually, there's a large element of self-loathing with Roger. Having said that, he is a misanthrope through and through.

17. *Whom or what does the character fear?* Arthur, his father. Judy, his wife. God (even though, like his father, he is also an atheist). Anything threatening his OCD. Roger is the master of phobias, rituals, and the like. Loves to wash hands, always stays away from germs. Has an unnatural fear of bugs (was stung by a bee while playing soccer when he was five and it was all downhill from there). Bottom line is his OCD controls aspects of his life and he has never been able to adequately control the disease.

18. *Whom or what does the character hate?* His sister, for abandoning the family and leaving all of the emotional/physical/financial dealings of the family to him. She was able to focus on her career and he resents her lack of familial involvement.

19. *Whom or what does the character love?* His wife, Judy, with whom he desperately wants to reconcile. Judy is Roger's one and only true love and it is his goal to have that sentiment reciprocated.

20. *What is the character's goal?* Two goals: 1) To reconcile with his wife; and 2) to find out who killed his father and why. These goals are equally important and both carry significant emotional weight for Roger, as they both revolve around sustaining his family. Roger's hope is that searching for answers regarding his father's death will lead to the family coming back together and, most importantly, his reunion with Judy.

21. *What is the character's motivation?* He loves his wife (and believes they are soul mates) and he loved his father and wants to ensure he did not die in vain.

22. *Is the character's goal compelling enough to move us through three acts?* Yes. Finding out who killed his father and why will take Roger through a journey of self-discovery – one that will ultimately bring his family back together. This journey will also be the catalyst for Roger and Judy reuniting (or not... you'll have to read the screenplay).

23. *Is the character active or passive in achieving the goal?* Very active. Roger brings the family together for the first time while searching for the truth regarding Arthur's mysterious death. In doing so, he is also active in pursuing a reunion with Judy. These two goals work on parallel paths.

24. *Who or what prevents the character from achieving his/her goal?* The president of Harvard – William Miller – and The Secret Society. They will do anything to protect their secret and their reputations. While William and The Secret Society are the primary villains of this story, Roger's insecurities are also a villain in the story, in that they are obstacles for him in achieving his goals.

25. *What is the character's fatal flaw?* The OCD is a big flaw. Roger's addiction to prostitutes is another flaw. Also, the fact he has not been a good father and role model to his children is a major flaw because it makes it much more difficult to bring the family together for a common cause – namely, finding out who killed Grandpa and why.

26. *What is the transformation arc of the character?* He goes from someone who is not willing to do anything to keep the family together (he has essentially given up), to a man on a mission – needing to find the murderer of his father and, at the same time, finding newfound strength to bring the family back together. Roger also begins our story as someone who is a prisoner of his OCD and other dysfunctions. By the end of the movie, he has learned to deal with his demons.

27. *Who or what helps the character change?* His wife, Judy. His kids. His daughter gets pregnant, which goes a long way toward transforming him. "Maybe," Roger rationalizes, "I can be a better grandfather than a father. This is my second chance. My Act Two."

28. *What is the character's purpose in the overall story?* 1) To find out who killed his father and why; 2) to bring the family back together; and 3) to reconcile with his wife, Judy.

29. *How does the character speak?* Very fast. New York City affect (even though he's from Cambridge). Anxiety-ridden. Type-A. OCD. Impatient. Loves to say, "Are you done?" Typically, makes the other people uncomfortable as he can be socially awkward.

30. *What is the first image of the character?* Something OCD-related, but something relating to the illness we have not seen before. Not washing hands. Maybe he wakes up in the middle of the night to make sure the oven is off. Then he does it again, and again, and again....

31. *Does the character have conflicting personality traits?* He is an academic scholar, yet he yearns for more money... more material goods... more stuff... As a professor in a highly-respected university, he is supposed to shun material goods. Yet, he can't help being bitter about all of the times in his life he has had the opportunity to make millions but has blown it.

32. *What happened in the character's childhood that has affected him/her?* The incident at Merck... The Olympics story... Always the smartest kid in the class – always misunderstood. Incidents as a child when Roger desperately wanted the affection of his parents and they were more interested in burying themselves in books.

33. *How does culture affect the character's actions?* Harvard has a typical academic, stuffy, and bureaucratic culture and that sometimes impedes Roger's ability to find out who killed his father and why.

34. *What happens if the character does not achieve his/her goal?* His life will be meaningless, he will never have love, and his father will have died in vain.

35. *What is the character's secret?* He is obsessed with paying for sex.

36. *What is the character missing in his/her life?* A loving family. An accomplishment fitting of his intellect.

37. *Who is the character's mentor?* His father, Arthur, although Roger would never admit it to him.

Judy Samson

Roger's wife, JUDY SAMSON (they're separated), is an English professor who lusts after her female students.

1. *Name:* Judy Samson (Catherine Zeta-Jones type)

2. *Age:* 38 (although the rumor is that she might be 42)

3. *Physical Description/Dress:* Very pretty. You would never think she is a professor at Harvard. Always wearing the latest fashions, although she really can't afford it. Looks great in glasses. Sexy.

4. *Marital Status:* Married to Roger Samson. Separated – on the road to divorce.

5. *Childhood/Nuclear Family:* Maiden name: Judy Blumenthal. Jewish/ Conservative. From Short Hills, New Jersey. Father is the former CEO of Merck (he got Roger his job there). High-powered corporate executive. Very wealthy family. Very well-connected family. Mother is an alcoholic who basically drank herself to death when Judy was young. Two brothers – one is a corrupt U.S. congressman; the other a more corrupt U.S. senator. Parents were distant with their children – much more concerned with themselves. When the kids were upset about something, the parents would buy them something expensive with the hope the feelings would go away.

6. *Current Occupation:* Professor and Chair of the English Department at Harvard.

7. *Job History:* Former model (she ran away from home at eighteen to NYC and became a highly-paid fashion model). Got caught up in drugs and became a heroin addict (sort of like, Gia in *Gia*). Then, she straightened herself out and enrolled in Columbia, where she stayed for eight years and earned her bachelor's, master's, and PhD. She taught at Cornell for a few years (that's where she met Roger), then saw him compete at a Ping-Pong tournament, and fell for him immediately. She would later say that watching Roger play table tennis would give her an orgasm.

8. *Education:* See above.

9. *How much does he/she earn a year? How much in savings? Debt?* Same as Roger. Except she does still occasionally buy and take drugs, which cuts into her savings. She has also bought drugs for some of her students, which further cuts into her savings.

10. *Hobbies:* Reading. Writing. Pot. Cocaine. She's also a semipro puppeteer (a part-time job she developed to combine her love of costumes and her love of theater).

11. *Biggest regret in life:* Not coming out of the closet when she realized she was bisexual, which was in college. So, she regrets ever getting married and having kids. She is not maternal and never gave her kids the love they deserved. Marriage and motherhood were a mistake, at least at the beginning of our story.

12. *How many sexual partners?* Dozens – mostly other women (and a few male teaching assistants) while she was married to Roger.

13. *Favorite Book/Movie/Album: Fear of Flying. Double Indemnity.* Anything by Stevie Nicks.

14. *Magazine Subscriptions: Cosmo, Elle* – all of the high-end fashion magazines. She rarely immerses herself in academic publications, although she is an expert on Shakespeare and reads him regularly (she is also fluent in Greek and Latin).

15. *Describe a typical Saturday night for the character.* She still lives in the same house with Roger, mostly for financial reasons (as stated, she "blows" a lot of money on drugs. Pun intended). They have this fabulous brownstone in Cambridge and neither wants to be the one who moves into a one-bedroom apartment. At the beginning of our story, the two are estranged, but Roger does not know Judy is bisexual. That will come out later. While Roger usually stays home on Saturday nights – alone reading – Judy is quite the party animal, going to clubs, bars, and restaurants she can't afford.

16. *Does the character have a credo? Words to live by?* "Life is short – way too short." She discovers this when she finds out she has cancer. She must make a decision on how she will live the rest of her life.

17. *Whom or what does the character fear?* Her father – in a big way. Since her diagnosis, she is also very afraid of her own mortality. Going public with her sexual orientation – she's bisexual. Judy is afraid of alienating her family and most importantly, her four children. So, she keeps her sexual orientation a secret as long as she can.

18. *Whom or what does the character hate?* Her father – in a big way – for never paying attention to her.

19. *Whom or what does the character love?* On some level, she still loves Roger and is torn about leaving him. She loves her four children. But most of all, she is falling madly in love with Cindy, one of her graduate students. One of Judy's problems is she has never really known how to love. She blames it on her childhood, where there was very little love in the home. Just a lot of narcissism on the part of her parents.

20. *What is the character's goal?* To be true to herself… finally. To move on with her life. To be a couple – with Cindy. To reconnect with her children and possibly be the mother she never had. To remain friends with Roger without being his wife. To help Roger find out who killed her father-in-law and why.

21. *What is the character's motivation?* That she has been living a lie her entire life. It is time to be truthful about her sexuality – a secret she

has kept hidden forever. When she is diagnosed with cancer, she is motivated to finally tell the truth. Getting diagnosed is her primary motivation for taking her life to the next act.

22. *Is the character's goal compelling enough to move us through three acts?* Yes, because she does join Roger on his journey of finding his father's murderer, but more importantly, she grows as a character throughout the story – learning how to be true to herself.

23. *Is the character active or passive in achieving the goal?* First passive, then, after the diagnosis, she becomes more active. The diagnosis acts as a catalyst for her to change her life.

24. *Who or what prevents the character from achieving his/her goal?* Society and her father. The fact she followed societal norms and had a big family without ever communicating she was bisexual. The more time goes on, the more difficult it is for Judy to "come out of the closet." She knows she will be shunned by society and her father will most likely never speak with her again (probably a good thing).

25. *What is the character's fatal flaw?* She has sex with her students – usually graduate students and teaching assistants, but students nonetheless. And, she is very insecure about her looks and believe it or not, about her brains – she never thought she was deserving of her academic achievements. She is also a perfectionist and never able to live up to her own expectations. She gets this insecurity from her father.

26. *What is the transformation arc of the character?* She begins as the bored mother and the bored housewife. She becomes selfish, but in a good way. In the end, she has a better relationship with her husband and her kids than in the beginning of the story because she is finally honest about who she is.

27. *Who or what helps the character change?* The diagnosis certainly helps inspire her to change. Cindy helps her change for the better. Roger, in his own way, helps her change. Her kids saying they will always accept her unconditionally also helps her change.

28. *What is the character's purpose in the overall story?* To help Roger find the truth about Arthur's death. Even though she shows outward animosity toward Arthur, we later learn he was more of a father figure to Judy than her own father. She loved him (although she always hid the emotion) and is therefore also motivated to find out who killed him and why. She also partners with Roger as a driving force in getting the family to reconcile all of their differences with one another.

29. *How does the character speak?* She speaks in a patronizing tone. Loves metaphors (she is a master of English literature). Loves quoting authors – it makes her look smarter (don't forget she is insecure). It annoys most of the people around her. She loves throwing out a quote and saying, "Quick – who said that?" Cindy is her only equal in this arena.

30. *What is the first image of the character?* She is in the women's bathroom of a hip, young, underground nightclub in Boston snorting crystal meth with a hot girl twenty years her junior (turns out the girl is a grad student in Judy's English class – "This is some great shit, Professor..."). We're not quite sure what to make of this character.

31. *Does the character have conflicting personality traits?* Married mother of four vs. bisexual and living the life of a college student. She and Roger never had a good marriage and they kept having babies as a way to try to solve their marital problems. This, of course, never worked.

32. *What happened in the character's childhood that has affected him/her?* The first time she was with a woman. The first time she was with a man (Roger) after his Ping-Pong tournament. Her discovering in therapy that her father sexually abused her when she was eight years old.

33. *How does culture affect the character's actions?* Culture has made her play the role of a happy, heterosexual mother of four. Society has prevented her from freeing herself from the lie she has lived.

34. *What happens if the character does not achieve his/her goal?* She will probably commit suicide if she has to live the rest of her life in a lie. It is that bad. She will also be very depressed if she does not find out who killed Arthur and why.

35. *What is the character's secret?* She's bisexual. And a Marxist.

36. *What is the character missing in his/her life?* A loving family. Confidence to be herself – no matter the consequences.

37. *Who is the character's mentor?* Heidi Klum, with whom she did some modeling in the 1990s. Also Professor D. Andrew Ring of Cornell, the world's preeminent Shakespeare scholar (she's had a crush on him for years).

As you can see, fully completing Hero-Villain Personas for the principal characters in your script can be a daunting task – especially given that a vast amount of the information will not make it to your screenplay. Don't worry. The answers to your Personas round out your characters – making them three-dimensional and fresh enough to avoid clichés.

The more you utilize the information in the Personas, the richer your characters will be – which translates to an enjoyable reading and (hopefully) viewing experience.

Before you embark on the Persona, here are some tips to keep in mind:

1. *Try to write each Persona in one sitting.* Set aside at least an hour to get through all of the questions and don't overanalyze. Free association will give you the richest character traits. Write without stopping. You can always rewrite them at a later date.

2. *The more Personas, the better.* Always write a Persona for your primary hero and villain, but if you are able to craft Personas for a few of your supporting characters, your script will be filled with even more rich dialogue and interesting people.

3. *Have an actor/actress in mind.* It is always helpful to visualize an actor/actress while you are completing a Persona, even if your screenplay never lands on said actor's/actress' desk.

4. *Always keep your Personas by your side.* Just as your treatment is your story blueprint, your Personas are your character blueprints. Keep them with you throughout the writing process. Refer to them often. Respect their power.

5. *Write a Persona for an existing memorable character.* Choose a successful film similar to the one you are writing and craft an abbreviated Persona for the hero or the villain. See how much information you can glean from what you see and what you don't see.

chapter 7

The Hero and Villain
Treks in Three Acts

For much of this book, I have focused on what makes heroes and villains tick and their motivations ("Why do they do what they do?"). By dissecting three films — *Die Hard*, *Raiders of the Lost Ark*, and *Spider-Man* — this chapter will focus on how the hero and villain treks fit within a classic three-act structure.

Now, I suspect many of you already have books on "How to Write a Screenplay." My goal is not for you to disregard these texts; rather to view this information as a supplement to what you already have learned with regard to structure. The hero and villain treks will ultimately drive your story forward and keep your audiences (readers and moviegoers alike) giddy with anticipation of their next moves.

The Protagonist vs. The Antagonist

It is prudent to begin this section with a discussion of protagonists and antagonists and how these two terms coincide with heroes and villains. One of the definitions used by *The American Heritage Dictionary of the English Language* for a protagonist is, "In ancient Greek drama, the first actor to engage in dialogue with the chorus." This dictionary defines an antagonist as "The principal character in opposition to the protagonist."

With these definitions in mind, let's also reprise a quote from my interview with Steven E. de Souza (Chapter Five):

> "In film, the protagonist is the character who gets the
> ball rolling. In *Jaws*, the protagonist is the shark. In *Die
> Hard*, it's Hans Gruber. In most cases, the hero cannot do

anything until something else happens – and it's almost always the protagonist who inspires the hero to act. After that, it's a chess game – the protagonist (who is often the villain) makes a move, then the antagonist (who is often the hero), makes a counter-move. To be clear, nine times out of ten, the protagonist is the villain in genre movies."

While this line of thought may seem counterintuitive (our instincts tell us the protagonist and the hero are the same person), de Souza's appraisal is absolutely on the mark – protagonists make the first move and antagonists counter. After all, if Darth Vader and the Empire never threatened to take over the Galaxy, there would be no reason for Skywalker and the Rebels to thwart them, right? The Empire constructs the Death Star, which motivates the Rebels to destroy it. With no Death Star or evil intentions on the part of the Empire, the Rebels simply have nothing to do. The Jedis would just stay at home and watch TV (or whatever home entertainment available in a galaxy far, far away).

It is important to note de Souza's disclaimer: These definitions typically hold true in "genre" movies. These are types of films that are easily classified by Hollywood (e.g., comedy, romantic comedy, drama, thriller, horror, Western, and the like). For the sake of this discussion, I will assume you are writing a genre picture.

The Hero and Villain Treks in *Die Hard*

Speaking of genre pictures, let's analyze one of the most important action films in the last twenty-five years – one that has spawned endless inferior copies and countless pitches beginning with, "It's *Die Hard* in a ...."

We have already discussed this film's memorable villain, Hans Gruber. Now let's delve into the film's structure to figure out how this "chess game" begins and how it is expertly played throughout the story with Gruber and the movie's hero, John McClane.

Act One

When the film begins, we meet New York City police officer John McClane – who is visiting his wife Holly Gennaro McClane at her company's Christmas party in Los Angeles. As we would in any worthy Act One, we meet most of the major characters we are going to care about in the first twenty-five minutes or so of the film. It is established that their marriage has been strained by Gennaro's move to Los Angeles with their two children and the resulting geographical handicap the two have had to endure. Still, one gets the sense they love each other and want to make the union succeed.

But this is not a movie about a couple working out their differences. There will be no time to delve into the sources of their marital difficulties. Why? Because before we know it, McClane hears bullets being fired at the party and he knows all is not well. Being a prudent hero, he escapes to another floor and tries to call the police. Thankfully, the phone doesn't work – for if he was able to get through, *Die Hard* would have lasted about thirty minutes.

Now, I know what you are saying: "McClane is the protagonist because he is actively trying to call for help." Not so fast. Remember we are defining the protagonist as the one who makes the first move – the character who gets the ball rolling. In this case, it is Gruber – because if Gruber and his associates do not take over Nakatomi Plaza, there is no movie. Like so many popular Hollywood films, heroes are introduced with little or nothing to do until someone – or something – comes along and commits an act the hero is compelled to counter.

So, the first chess move belongs to Gruber, who has infiltrated Gennaro's Christmas party with enough firepower to conquer a small country. The next move is McClane's, who must figure out how to save his wife and the other hostages. McClane is the hero-antagonist who will try to defeat the plans of Gruber, the villain-protagonist, by the end of the film. Sound simple enough? *Die Hard* is actually a very simple story that never loses sight of its hero and villain and their respective roles in the film. The genius of the movie is how the chess game works so seamlessly, naturally, and with suspense at every turn. As any writer will hear innumerable times from producers and studio executives, it is all in the execution.

So, let's summarize Act One of the film:

1. We meet John McClane – the meat and potatoes, tough-as-nails New York City police officer who has just landed in Los Angeles to meet his estranged wife.

2. We meet Holly Gennaro McClane – the equally tough-as nails corporate executive at Nakatomi Corporation who is interested in reconciling with McClane.

3. We meet Hans Gruber and his band of thugs, who want to steal $640 million in bearer bonds from the Nakatomi vault. Gruber is an educated, stylish villain who seems like he would be just as comfortable presenting to a board of directors as he is taking a few dozen innocent people hostage.

4. Gruber and Co. effectively take over Nakatomi Plaza (all of the floors are empty, except for the Christmas party).

5. McClane escapes the chaos and finds temporary solace on another floor, where he unsuccessfully tries to contact the police.

At this point (twenty-nine minutes into the film), we understand our hero (McClane), our villain (Gruber), the villain's goal (to steal $640 million), the hero's goal (to save his wife and the other hostages, while thwarting the plans of the villain), and the stakes, or "What happens if the hero does not achieve his goal?" (the villain gets away with $640 million, but more importantly, he may kill some or all of the hostages – including Gennaro). We also have a grasp on the tone of the film and its genre.

Let's not take all of this valuable information for granted. How many times have you sat in a movie theater and were unable to answer these questions after the Act One conclusion? Too many to count.

So, hats off to the filmmakers – they have taken Billy Wilder's famous advice when he was asked for his top ten screenwriting tips; namely, "Grab 'em by the throat and never let 'em go." We are sufficiently "grabbed by the throat" by the end of Act One of *Die Hard* and ready to travel down the long and winding road of Act Two.

Act Two

Now that we have the basics of the story in hand, the chess game continues with vigor. Gruber executes Takagi when the CEO refuses to reveal the code to the vault that houses the bonds (thank goodness, for if he did reveal the code, the movie would once again be over and McClane would have nothing left to do). Interestingly, after McClane witnesses the execution, his instinct is not to storm the bad guys and pick them off one by one. Instead, he says to himself, "Argyle [McClane's limo driver, who is in the garage of the building], tell me you heard the shots and you're calling the police right now." McClane is the reluctant hero who is content to let the authorities handle this incident. As we move deeper into the story, however, he will have no choice but to step up and take matters into his own heroic hands.

But, not before he tries to involve the authorities again. McClane notices a fire alarm on the floor and pulls it. But in this game of chess, the bad guys call the authorities at the last moment and tell them it is a false alarm.

The next move belongs to Gruber, who sends one of his henchmen to the floor where the fire alarm was pulled. We all know a lower-level lieutenant in Gruber's Army is not about to stop our hero, so McClane quickly and efficiently does away with his adversary (showing a bit of the other side of his "shadow") and boldly displays his lifeless body for all the bad guys to see.

McClane then makes his way to the roof, where he calls the police from a radio. Interestingly, he is still pleading for help instead of taking on Gruber and gang by himself. That is what makes *Die Hard* so memorable – this hero is not a reincarnation of the Schwarzenegger or Stallone action heroes made popular in the 1980s. Rather, he is a real person who does what most rationale people would do – try to get the authorities involved. The difference between McClane and us, however, is that when the police fail to rectify the situation, McClane transforms into the hero we all have dreamed we could be.

And while we're on the subject, let's briefly discuss what I believe to be *Die Hard's* minor flaw – the involvement of the police and FBI. Never have I seen a more inept group of law enforcement officials mishandle a major crime scene. I recognize the importance of not making them too competent – for if they were, John McClane would have nothing to do but sit back and let the cops save the day. And we all know we didn't pay for tickets, popcorn, Goobers, and a soda to watch a team of anonymous officers defeat Gruber and his assemblage of international thugs. We paid for McClane to save the day. So, we don't want the police and FBI to be too competent.

We do, however, expect a modicum of realism. I should disclose that I have never personally experienced a high-stakes hostage situation, so my thoughts on this matter can be construed as conjecture. However, as a literate moviegoer, I do expect some level of professionalism on the part of the authorities – something between the Green Berets and the Keystone Cops.

Their involvement serves as an unorthodox midpoint for the story. As we have discussed, the midpoint often signifies a moment when the stakes are raised for the hero – effectively splitting Act Two into two parts. One would think police involvement would lower the stakes for McClane, since they can now handle the brunt of the hostage situation. But, that would have been too easy. This midpoint works because the ineffectiveness of the police and FBI actually makes it more difficult for McClane to achieve his goal – thus raising the stakes for our hero.

Even with the above in mind, the ineptitude of the police and unrealistic bravado of the FBI are not enough to disengage us emotionally from this film. By the time they arrive in force (about fifty-eight minutes into the movie), we are already so invested in the McClane-Gruber chess match that nothing is going to stop us from staying on this ride until the bitter end.

At an hour into the movie, McClane and Gruber speak for the first time via walkie-talkies (they'll meet later). At this point, our hero has the upper hand because he knows more about our villain than the villain knows about him. Additionally, McClane has eliminated a few members of the villainous crew while confiscating their firearms (including an all-important batch of detonators). As a viewer, we like this shift in power… even if we know it is not going to last.

As we have seen with some of the films discussed in this book, many heroes have sidekicks to help them achieve their goals. *Die Hard* is no different. In the middle of Act Two, it is quite possible the filmmakers felt audiences would grow tired of McClane talking to himself. So, they gave him a buddy in the form of Sergeant Al Powell. Powell is the first cop on the scene, playing the voice of reason. When incompetence runs amok, he speaks on behalf of the audience's frustration. And when McClane needs a break in between shooting bad guys, their conversations provide all-important respites in an otherwise chaotic display of firepower.

At one hour and thirty minutes, the hero and villain treks collide as the two men come face to face for the first time. As discussed in Chapter Four, Gruber pretends to be an American hostage and McClane pretends he believes him. A mini chess game of wits commences, then predictably ends with another bullet fest between our hero and villain.

At the end of Act Two (which usually occurs anywhere from five to twenty minutes before the end of the film), the hero is usually furthest away from his goal. It is the "all is lost" moment when the audience scratches its collective head and says, "How in the world is he going to get what he wants?" In *Die Hard*, a bruised and bloodied McClane calls down to Powell.

> McCLANE
> Listen man, I'm starting to get a
> bad feeling up here. I want you
> to do something for me. I want
> you to find my wife. Don't ask me
> how — by then, you'll know how.
> I want you to tell her something.
> I want you to tell her that… tell
> her that it took me a while to
> figure out what a jerk I've been.
> But, that when things started to
> pan out for her, I should've been
> more supportive. And, I should've
> been behind her more. Tell her
> (MORE)

```
                McCLANE (CONT'D)
        that she's the best thing that
        ever happened to a bum like me.
        She's heard me say "I love you"
        a thousand times. She never heard
        me say, "I'm sorry." And I want
        you to tell her that, Al, and I
        want you to tell her that John
        said that he was sorry. Okay, you
        got that, man?
```

Suddenly, our hero doesn't sound very heroic — and that's the point. He sounds like he is a step away from death and has all but given up his attempt to trounce Gruber and save those poor hostages. Still, there is something worth noting in his speech — McClane has changed. It may have taken a treacherous journey for him to become self-reflective but he nonetheless has gone from being unappreciative of his marriage to appreciating everything about his wife. A rare classic character arc fulfilled, set against the backdrop of a shoot-'em-up action flick.

And what about Gruber? Well, we don't expect a murderous villain to suddenly become self-actualized, so he has essentially the same views of the world at the beginning of the film as he does at its conclusion. And in the case of Gruber, it makes sense. We wouldn't believe it if he suddenly realized kidnapping, murder, and grand larceny were reprehensible in nature and he is now committed to saving the planet, right?

To make matters worse for our hero, Gruber's IT guy has just successfully opened the vault (a project he has been working on throughout the movie), so the $640 million in bearer bonds are now Gruber's for the taking. Is it possible this chess game has ended with Gruber victorious? Don't fret. Things rarely look good for the hero at the end of Act Two and *Die Hard* is no exception.

So, let's summarize the second act of the film:

1. McClane and Gruber have been playing a chess game that, up until the end of Act Two, has been fairly even.

2. McClane has killed several of Gruber's lower-level henchmen.

3. Gruber has shown a sense of humanity in dealing with the hostages.

4. The police and FBI arrive and prove to be more of a hindrance and than a source of assistance.

5. McClane meets a buddy, Sergeant Powell, with whom he takes a break and shares his innermost thoughts in between gun battles.

6. McClane has an epiphany, sensing he may not make it. So, he asks his friend Powell to tell his wife he's sorry for the way he has acted in their marriage.

Act Three

At this point, we are eighteen minutes from the rolling credits, so our hero and villain treks better wrap up quickly. No more time for relationship building or character development. This is the end of the chess game and each move must be taken quickly and efficiently.

The audience can sense when a film enters Act Three and appropriately becomes a bit antsy. Fortunately for us, the *Die Hard* filmmakers understand how to deal with an antsy audience – continue to "Grab 'em by the throat and never let 'em go."

As Act Three takes shape, McClane's journey finally intersects with Gruber's top lieutenant, Karl (McClane killed Karl's brother in Act One, so we all know this skirmish is simply a matter of time), while at the same time, Gruber discovers Gennaro is McClane's wife. McClane does away with Karl (it is quite common in these types of films that the lower-level bad guys are killed first, then the villain's right-hand men, and finally the villain himself), then figures out the bad guys intend on blowing up the roof of the building with the hostages on it. Uh oh.

McClane appropriately gets the hostages off the roof and our hero and villain meet a second (and final) time. It is McClane, of course, who shoots Gruber but in typical Hollywood form, that bullet doesn't quite do it.

Gruber needs to die in a spectacular way fitting for a villain of his stature – falling thirty floors to his demise does the trick.

While McClane and Gennaro's relationship is on the rocks at the beginning of the film, it is his three-act trek as hero that changes him, defeats Gruber, and saves his marriage.

Checkmate.

The Hero and Villain Treks in *Raiders of the Lost Ark*

In Chapter Three, we discussed Indiana Jones as both a hero who is incomplete and one who plays both sides of the "shadow." In this section, we will follow the precarious treks of Jones and the film's primary villain, Belloq.

Act One

But first, another word about protagonists and antagonists. As mentioned, the protagonist is the character (although it could be a tornado, shark, earthquake, spaceship, or the like), who makes the first move – the one who gets the ball rolling. You can always ask yourself: "If character X does not achieve goal Y, will there still be a movie?" In most cases, if the protagonist does not make the first move, you might as well pack up your box of Raisinets and go home.

In *Raiders of the Lost Ark*, there are essentially two protagonists: the Nazis and Belloq. As the story begins, we learn that the Nazis are digging in Tanis with the hope of finding the famous Ark of the Lost Covenant. Jones' job is to find it first. As stated in Chapter Three, it is Jones' colleague, Marcus Brody, who perfectly summarizes the stakes of the story by exclaiming, "An army which carries the Ark before it is invincible."

Without the Nazis-Belloq combo pursuing the Ark, Jones would have nothing to do but teach at his university and occasionally seek out relics from antiquity – not a very intriguing movie. So, Jones is the hero and antagonist and the Nazis and Belloq are the villains and protagonists. And, since "the Nazis" is a difficult character to follow (villains don't usually work well as groups, with some alien films as notable

204

exceptions), we will follow Belloq as the primary villain – the character with whom Jones will consistently interact throughout the film.

The film wastes little time for the two characters to meet. Ten minutes into the movie, after Jones completes a perilous journey through a cave filled with every gimmick imaginable to kill its guests, he is confronted by Belloq and a few dozen Hovitos brandishing spears and arrows. "Dr. Jones," Belloq says with utter confidence, "again we see there is nothing you can possess which I cannot take away. And you thought I had given up." Jones gives Belloq the idol he has just risked life and limb to obtain and our chess match between hero and villain officially has commenced.

Back at home, Brody informs Jones that representatives from Army Intelligence want to see him. As discussed, this critical meeting of cleverly communicated story exposition establishes the villains and the stakes for our hero (the Nazis, as protagonists, have already started digging for the Ark in Tanis). But, there is little mention of Belloq with regard to this situation. Not yet.

It is also important to note that at this point in the film, we have a sense of Jones' opinion toward the occult and supernatural occurrences. While explaining the perceived power of the Ark of the Covenant, Jones says it supposedly contains "the actual Ten Commandments. The original stone tablets Moses brought down out of Mount Horeb and smashed – if you believe in that sort of thing." And when he shows the others a picture of the Ark with yellow bands of light emanating from it, he dismissingly describes the setting as "Lightning. Fire. The power of God, or something."

In the next scene, Brody warns Jones about the potential power of the Ark and the danger Jones might encounter. Jones, however, remains the skeptic.

> BRODY
> ... For nearly three thousand years,
> man has been searching for the
> Lost Ark. Not something to be
> taken lightly. No one knows its
> secrets. It's like nothing you've
> ever gone after before.

```
                    INDIANA JONES
            Marcus, what are you trying to do,
            scare me? You sound like my
            mother. We've known each other
            for a long time. I don't believe
            in magic — a lot of superstitious
            hocus-pocus. I'm going after a
            find of incredible historical
            significance and you're talking
            about the Boogey Man.
```

So, we are now convinced that Jones, while passionate about archeology, does not believe in the tales that accompany the pieces of antiquity he covets. But, will his heroic trek through three acts change him? Tune in.

At twenty-three minutes into the film, Jones boards a plane to begin his adventure — which brings us to the end of Act One.

Let's summarize what we have learned in the first act:

1. We meet Indiana Jones — the heroic and tough archeology professor who just so happens to be courageous, adventurous, and great with a whip.

2. We meet Marcus Brody, Jones' colleague — the one who helps facilitate Jones' trek to find the Lost Ark of the Covenant.

3. We meet Belloq, who is a rival archeologist and bent on defeating Jones. He also has no qualms about killing Jones in the process.

4. We understand Jones' goal — to find the Ark before the Nazis and bring it home.

5. We understand the stakes (i.e., What happens if Jones does not achieve his goal?). Namely, that if the Nazis get to the Ark before Jones, they may become "invincible." These stakes are high, as most of us have trouble using the words "Nazis" and "invincible" in the same sentence.

Now Jones will enter Act Two of his heroic trek. As for our villain, Belloq, don't be concerned, for we will meet him again soon.

Act Two

Jones' next stop is Nepal, where we are introduced to Marion Ravenwood (Karen Allen) – his love interest... sort of. Apparently, Jones and Ravenwood were quite the item several years ago and it ended badly, with Jones walking out on her. But, he's not there to reminisce about old times. He wants a circular bronze medallion that will help him find the Ark. She tells Jones to come back tomorrow and he exits, just in time for us to meet another villain in the story, the sinister SS officer, Major Toht (Ronald Lacey). Jones' unique brand of heroism is at work again as he takes out Toht's thugs (of course, Toht gets away – high level cinematic bad guys don't usually die until the end of movies) and saves Ravenwood from certain demise.

Jones' trek continues with Ravenwood to Cairo, where they meet his old friend, Sallah. During their meeting – thirty-five minutes into the film – Sallah informs Jones that the Nazis are progressing with their archeological dig and, more importantly, that Belloq is an integral part of the team. So, we now know Belloq is working with the Nazis, which means it cannot be long until the treks of this hero and villain again intersect.

After the Nazis commence a wild chase through the labyrinth that is Cairo, Jones and Ravenwood find themselves separated. She ends up in a truck filled with munitions – which inadvertently ignites. The truck explodes and Jones is heartbroken. Clearly, this is a low point in our hero's trek. Just as he reconnects with his lost love, she is gone (Or is she? More on that later).

The following scene is key in that it reunites Jones with Belloq. We haven't seen them together since the opening of the film and their treks now have taken them from South America to Cairo – this time, pursuing the same goal. In a café, the two enemies sit across from one another and Belloq attempts to rationalize their similarities. This is the moment Belloq makes the case that Jones and he are really "shadowy reflections" of each other.

```
             BELLOQ
     You and I are very much alike.
     Archeology is our religion, yet
     we have both fallen from the pure
     faith. Our methods have not
     differed as much as you pretend.
     I am a shadowy reflection of you.
     It would take only a nudge to make
     you like me. To push you out of
     the light.
```

It is true our hero has killed during his trek, but Jones (and the audience) feels his actions are, for the most part, justifiable. Belloq, on the other hand, has a different agenda and a bankrupt conscience. While Jones wants to obtain the Ark so it can be displayed in a museum, Belloq's intentions are far more fiendish.

```
             BELLOQ
     ... Jones, do you realize what the
     Ark is? It's a transmitter. It's
     a radio for speaking to God. And,
     it's within my reach.
```

These are two complex, three-dimensional characters who have sometimes been pushed "out of the light." Their "shadows" are alive and well.

So, at this point in our story, Jones and Belloq are actively pursuing the same goal – but for different reasons. In addition, while Belloq has dozens of Nazis and great financial resources at his disposal, Jones must rely mostly on his wits. Considering the formidability of our hero, this is an even match.

Fifty-five minutes into the film, Jones stumbles upon Ravenwood, who is very much alive. This subplot is a nice sleight of hand by the filmmakers, as they made us believe Jones lost his true love. She is now back, better than ever, and ready to help. But, not before our hero and villain treks intersect once again – this time, on a personal level. When Belloq enters the tent where Ravenwood is being held captive, he tries to seduce her with food, drink, and a new dress. You can tell Ravenwood has little interest in a romantic rendezvous with Belloq, but that doesn't stop Belloq from trying. Even considering the lack of participation on Ravenwood's part, you can add "love triangle" to the integrated treks of our hero and villain – parallel paths of the professional and the personal.

So, when Belloq previously warns Jones, "Again we see there is nothing you can possess which I cannot take away," he is not kidding. Stealing the fruits of Jones' archeological labor is not enough – Belloq must have Jones' girlfriend too. A true full-service villain.

As it turns out, Jones does find the Ark before Belloq. The problem is getting it home. Belloq and the Nazis find out about Jones' discovery, summarily take the Ark as if it were theirs, then load it on a truck en route to Cairo.

In the next sequence, Jones earns his title as one of the great heroes in cinematic history. There are no less than fourteen heavily armed Nazis accompanying the Ark on its journey and you're going to tell me a lone archeologist on a horse is going to outsmart them all? Yes, that is precisely what I am going to tell you. Belloq and his buddies seem helpless as Jones offs them one by one. At an hour and thirty-one minutes into the movie, Jones, Ravenwood, and the Ark set sail. They have won; the Nazis have lost; all is well with the universe. But, hold on a second. This story is not yet over – and neither are the treks of our hero and villain.

In true chess game fashion, the Nazis commandeer Jones' boat, take possession of the Ark, and Jones and Ravenwood end up on board the Nazi vessel as it makes its way to a remote island. There, the Ark finally will be opened. In a long procession headed by Belloq, the Ark is brought to its presumed resting place, where all involved will witness "the power of God."

But, before they reach their destination, Jones threatens to destroy the Ark – with his only demand being that he'll walk away if they release Ravenwood. Interestingly, our villain refuses, thus re-prising the unorthodox "love triangle" between Jones, Ravenwood, and Belloq. Jones reluctantly gives up and the Nazis take him and Ravenwood as prisoners.

Like any end of Act Two worth its weight in gold, *Raiders of the Lost Ark* does not disappoint. Jones has never been further from achieving his goals (to bring the Ark home and to be with Ravenwood) and we are left scratching our heads wondering, "How in the world is he going to get out of this one?"

A perfect feeling for us to experience and a perfect transition into Act Three.

But first, let's briefly summarize what we learned in Act Two:

1. Jones and Ravenwood had a relationship many years ago and it ended badly, with Jones initiating the separation. Still, there is a chemistry between the two that has not dissipated.

2. Jones meets up with his old friend, Sallah, in Cairo, who will help him find the Ark.

3. Belloq shows considerable interest in Ravenwood, thus establishing somewhat of a quirky "love triangle."

4. Jones and Sallah discover the Ark before the Nazis; the Nazis steal it; Jones takes it back; and the Nazis steal it once again.

5. The Second Act ends with Jones and Ravenwood taken as prisoners of the Nazis, just as Belloq and Co. prepare to open the Ark.

Act Three

This is one of those abbreviated third acts – about five minutes in duration. That's okay, because the entire film has been building to this very moment – the instant the contents of the Ark will be revealed.

In the dead of the night, the Nazis bring the Ark to a secret area where Belloq is waiting to oversee a religious ceremony. In the back are Jones and Ravenwood, who are tied to a post (of course, they could have done away with Jones, but there is an aspect of Belloq that wants his greatest competitor to experience this "radio for speaking to God"). So, after an international battle for possession of the Ark, the treks of our hero and villain have ended at the same venue, with both of them eagerly waiting to view what's inside.

As the ceremony begins, the top of the Ark is removed – and something unexpected happens. Belloq reaches inside, only to reveal a handful of sand. Toht emits a maniacal guffaw (as if to say, "I told you this wouldn't be worth the effort"), and the expression on Belloq's face is one of utter shock and disappointment.

But, that doesn't last very long.

Without warning, the electrical equipment in the area fails, a white smoke creeps along the ground, and spirits arise from the Ark. To be sure, it is a spooky scene and no one seems to know what will happen next. Except Jones.

It is at this moment when he changes. No longer is Jones the same person who said, "I don't believe in magic – a lot of superstitious hocus-pocus." After witnessing the manifestation of the Ark's powers, a look of despair comes across his face as he turns to Ravenwood.

```
            INDIANA JONES
      Marion, don't look at it. Shut
      your eyes, Marion. Don't look at
      it. No matter what happens.
```

Jones' trek has changed him to the core. These are no longer the words of a cynical archeologist – they are the words of a hero who has newfound respect for the antiquities he studies. As he should. Belloq and his gang of ruffians do not have the sense to close their eyes and thus pay the ultimate price as the spirits from the Ark destroy all who witness their power.

God has spoken… and it has taken a treacherous trek for Indiana Jones to finally listen.

The Hero and Villain Treks in *Spider-Man*

As discussed in Chapter Three, Peter Parker is riddled with guilt and looks to his alter ego to help him conquer his demons and feel complete. And as we have seen throughout the *Spider-Man* trilogy, he is also a character wrestling with his "shadow" – that delicate line between good and evil. In this section, we will explore the treks of this eternal hero and his arch nemesis, the Green Goblin. As you will see, their journeys are filled with many of the emotions that make films memorable – love, hate, jealousy, and honor... just to name a few.

Act One

While the film quickly establishes Peter Parker as a hapless soul scorned by his classmates and ignored by the love of his life, Mary Jane Watson, his trek as hero does not begin until ten minutes into the movie – the moment he is bitten by a radioactive spider (as an aside: we are never told what happens to the infamous spider (it just scampers away) and I have always wondered if there could be a movie about the other people it may have bitten).

So, the bite has transpired and we must now experience its ramifications. Even when Parker sees the bite has caused a significant lesion on his hand, does he seek medical attention? Of course not. Heroes – even unlikely heroes like Parker – tend to take matters into their own hands. And from an audience perspective, do you really want to sit through a ten-minute sequence of Parker going through a battery of tests at New York Hospital? I think not. We want to see him deal with this on his own, which he does when he returns home to his Uncle Ben and Aunt May.

At fourteen minutes into the film, Peter goes through a psychedelic trip that would make Timothy Leary green with envy. He finally passes out, going to sleep as mild-mannered Peter Parker and awakening as someone very different indeed.

The next scene begins our villain's trek, as Norman Osborn tests his controversial performance-enhancer drug on himself. Of course, the substance is not ready for human trials but just as we're not interested in Parker going to the doctor, we are also less than enamored of the prospect of Osborn conducting a series of double-blind studies on rats before he takes matters into his own hands. So, he instructs his subordinate to inject the controversial green-colored serum into his body and instantly undergoes a metamorphosis that transforms him into a sadistic villain of unparalleled strength.

So, within eighteen minutes our hero and villain have come into being. Their treks have commenced, they are traveling on parallel paths, and there is no turning back to their former selves. Now the fun begins.

In the superhero genre, all heroes need to take their newfound powers for a test drive – it is part of the job and the rules they all must follow. *Spider-Man* is no exception. So, when Parker inadvertently embarrasses Flash Thompson (Joe Manganiello) – the biggest bully in school – Thompson starts a fight with him that the entire school is certain will end very badly for Parker. But sometimes the masses are wrong. Sometimes they underestimate the will of a burgeoning hero.

To his own amazement, Parker effortlessly does away with the hulky Thompson, then embarks on a journey of discovering the extent of his newfound abilities. He climbs up a wall, jumps from rooftop to rooftop, and experiments with his organic webbing (a change from the web cartridges used in the comic book). We must assume Norman Osborn – aka, the Green Goblin – is also going through a similar montage of self-discovery, but the filmmakers make the prudent decision of focusing our attention on the hero.

So, at twenty-seven minutes into the film, we have reached the end of Act One. What did we learn?

1. We meet our hero, Peter Parker: a smart, nerdy, high school student who yearns to be with the love of his life, Mary Jane Watson.

2. We meet Harry Osborn, Peter's best friend and a key player in Act Two and Act Three.

3. Parker is bitten by a radioactive spider and acquires great powers.

4. We meet our villain, Norman Osborn, who has been altered into something potentially green and definitely villainous.

Act Two

As we transition into Act Two of *Spider-Man*, we must not forget Parker's voice over at the beginning of the film: "… but let me assure you – this, like any story worth telling, is all about a girl. That girl. The girl next door. Mary Jane Watson. The woman I've loved since before I even liked girls."

Since the core of this film is about a boy vying for the affection of a girl, Parker decides to use his pristine powers to impress Watson. Banking on the anonymity of a makeshift superhero costume, Parker gets in a steel cage match with a professional wrestler with the hope of winning three thousand dollars. Parker's plan is to use the winnings to buy a car he assumes would be appealing to Watson. So, the match not only becomes a test of Parker's super abilities, but a mechanism to bring him closer to the woman he loves.

Too bad life in superhero land is never quite that easy.

Yes, he easily beats the wrestler, but is also shortchanged by the promoter. To make matters worse, Parker lets a robber exit the premises with the promoter's money. This is the very same robber who ultimately kills Uncle Ben. And therein lies the most critical moment in this hero's trek – namely, he will forever fight for justice because of guilt (I do argue in Chapter Three that Parker is also an incomplete character and thus fights crime to feel complete, but for the purposes of this discussion I will also argue – as David Koepp does in Chapter Five – that guilt is also a particularly strong motivator for Parker).

As Parker's trek transitions him to a life of heroism, Norman Osborn's trek quickly becomes one of villainy. Interestingly, the two men intersect as Parker and Osborn long before they intersect as Spider-Man and the Green Goblin. At Parker's graduation, Norman Osborn says to Parker, "Commencement. The end of one thing. The start of something new." While Osborn is clearly referring to Parker's high school graduation and his plans for the future, the audience knows better. We understand this "start of something new" is all about the treks these two men will embark on for the rest of the film. They are high-speed trains racing toward one another – and the first crash is about to occur.

Appropriately, it is the film's midpoint (at an hour and six minutes into the movie) when the Green Goblin appears on his glider at the World Unity Festival – a celebration of thousands on the streets of Manhattan. This is the first time Parker and Norman Osborn meet one another not as teenager and father to his best friend, but as superhero and super villain – and it is a battle that does not let us down. In true midpoint fashion, the stakes have been raised for our hero.

Without warning, the Green Goblin causes massive destruction throughout the festival, and explosions abound. Parker swiftly makes the change into Spider-Man and the two brawl until the Green Goblin is forced to retreat. And upon said retreat, he calls out a warning to our hero: "We'll meet again, Spider-Man!" And meet again they shall.

At the end of the sequence, Spider-Man saves Mary Jane Watson and she is understandably smitten by her savior. In a way, Spider-Man slowly is achieving the one goal Parker cannot – to be with Watson.

As Norman Osborn struggles with his alter ego (in some memorable schizophrenic sequences), Parker comes to terms with the fact that he is the only one capable of stopping the malevolent Goblin from wreaking havoc throughout the streets of New York City and beyond. When Harry Osborn asks Parker, "What was that thing?" in reference to the Goblin's exploits at the World Unity Festival, Parker confidently responds by saying, "I don't know. Whatever it is, somebody has to stop it."

The two meet again as the Green Goblin puts forth a proposal to Spider-Man. As discussed in Chapter Three, the Goblin asks our hero to join forces, thus becoming the ultimate power couple. Of course, Spider-Man declines, which further motivates the Goblin to get rid of our hero, as he sees him as his sole obstacle to the Goblin obtaining ultimate power. (While the film leaves it up to the audience as to the Goblin's definition of "power," it is safe to assume he is not interested in founding a nonprofit organization.)

As a follow-up to saving Watson at the World Unity Festival, Spider-Man once again comes to her aid as he beats the living day-lights out of a gang of thugs with ill intentions toward her. He and Watson kiss and it is clear she's falling for her masked rescuer – yet Parker can only wish he could elicit the same emotions without the costume. While he is making great strides toward his goal of being with Watson, he is only doing so as Spider-Man, which makes Parker's trek much more emotionally hazardous.

Speaking of hazardous, Parker and Norman Osborn's treks collide again at a Thanksgiving dinner, with Watson, Harry Osborn, and Aunt May also in attendance. It is during this vital scene when Norman Osborn notices that a cut on Parker's arm is exactly the same as a slash suffered by Spider-Man in their last tête-à-tête. His eyes narrow, his brow furrows, and he politely excuses himself from dinner. If this were a tennis match, the score would be "Advantage, Norman Osborn," as he now knows Peter Parker and Spider-Man are one and the same – which means he also knows the way to defeat his arch nemesis is to hurt the people closest to Parker's heart.

The Green Goblin wastes little time executing this new strategy by attacking Aunt May, who subsequently ends up in the hospital. When Parker rushes to her side, she can only exclaim, "Those eyes! Those horrible yellow eyes!" At this point, Parker understands that the Green Goblin knows who he is – why else would the Goblin attack an innocent old woman at home? Still, Parker does not know the identity of the Green Goblin, which is why this tennis match is still "Advantage, Goblin."

The Green Goblin's trek toward eliminating Spider-Man and becoming all-powerful continues on its merry way when Norman Osborn discovers Parker's intense affection for Watson. You can see the wheels spinning in Osborn's head as he must be thinking, "Watson shall be my next victim."

And the next victim, she is.

At one hour and thirty-nine minutes into the film, Watson finds herself at the top of a bridge near a gondola filled with children hanging high above the raging seas. With this torrential tableau presented to Spider-Man, we are officially shepherded into Act Three.

Before we delve into who will win match point during this final convergence of hero and villain treks, let's briefly summarize what we learned in Act Two:

1. Parker allows a robber to get away and the robber ends up killing Parker's Uncle Ben, thus injecting Parker with enough guilt to use his "great powers" with "great responsibility" for the rest of his life.

2. Spider-Man and the Green Goblin battle several times, discovering they are worthy adversaries.

3. While not discussed in this analysis, there is a love triangle between Parker, Watson, and Harry Osborn that continues to grow more complicated with higher emotional stakes.

4. Norman Osborn discovers that Peter Parker and Spider-Man are one and the same and he will punish those whom Parker loves.

5. After being rescued by Spider-Man on two occasions, Watson tells Parker she is in love with the masked hero, not knowing she is really in love with Parker.

Act Three

In keeping with the tennis metaphor, it is the final round of the U.S. Open, fifth set tiebreaker – and Spider-Man and the Green Goblin are fighting it out for the championship.

As mentioned in Chapter Three, the Green Goblin sets up a seemingly impossible scenario, where he holds Watson with one hand and a wire connected to a gondola filled with children in the other hand. This moment is not about the Green Goblin finding pleasure in causing the death of innocent people – it is all about the Goblin punishing Spider-Man for embarking on the trek of a hero.

Predictably, the Green Goblin lets go of Watson and the wire – forcing Spider-Man to make a choice. Since this story, "like any story worth telling, is all about a girl. That girl. The girl next door. Mary Jane Watson," there is little doubt as to whom he will save first. That said, Spider-Man is not the type of superhero who is about to allow a group of kids to perish. So, he miraculously saves them too.

Advantage, Spider-Man.

Although this match is not yet over, the multifarious treks of our hero and villain are about to come to an end in the form of a good old-fashioned fistfight in a dilapidated, dingy area filled with vacant buildings. Like any respectable climactic movie moment, the fight keeps us on the edge of our seats until Parker discovers the Green Goblin is none other than Norman Osborn and we are left with the hero standing over the pathetic image of a once powerful villain, now pleading for help.

                    GREEN GOBLIN
        Peter, stop, stop, it's me!

                    SPIDER-MAN
        Mr. Osborn.

                    GREEN GOBLIN
        Peter, thank God for you.

                    SPIDER-MAN
        You killed those people on that
        balcony.

                    GREEN GOBLIN
        The Goblin killed. I had nothing
        to do with it. Don't let him take
        me again. I beg you, protect me.

                    SPIDER-MAN
        You tried to kill Aunt May, you
        tried to kill Mary Jane.

                    GREEN GOBLIN
        But, not you. I tried to stop it. I
        couldn't stop it. I would never
        hurt you. I knew from the beginning.
        If anything ever happened to me,
        it was you that I could count on,
        you Peter Parker would save me
        and so you have. Thank God for you.
        Give me your hand. Believe in me,
        as I believed in you. I've been
        like a father to you. Be a son
        to me now.

                    SPIDER-MAN
        I have a father. His name was
        Ben Parker.

GREEN GOBLIN
Godspeed, Spider-Man.

And with that, the Green Goblin devilishly watches as his deadly glider races toward Spider-Man. At the last moment, Spider-Man evades the flying weapon, allowing it to pierce through the Green Goblin's abdomen. The Green Goblin, once an unstoppable force of ill will, makes a final request to Spider-Man ("Peter, don't tell Harry"), then expires.

Game, set, and match to: You guessed it.

While our villain's trek has come to an unfortunate ending (Do villains ever experience fortunate endings?), our hero has a couple of more important moments to experience. First, guilt once again gets the best of Spider-Man as he delivers a deceased Osborn back to his penthouse. Unfortunately, Harry Osborn walks in at that exact moment and assumes Spider-Man killed his father. Not good for Spider-Man, but a brilliant setup for a Spidey revenge-laden sequel.

Second, in the film's final scene – the funeral of Norman Osborn – Parker shares an emotional and poetic moment with Watson. She declares her devotion for Parker, professing her love. Ironically, while this is the very goal Parker set out to achieve at the beginning of the movie, he rejects Watson's overture – telling her he will always be there for her... but as a friend. Parker's selfless response is explained in his voice over.

PETER (V.O.)
No matter what I do. No matter
how hard I try. The ones I love
will always be the ones who pay.

It is a touching, bittersweet, and tragic moment, as we want this hero to conclude his trek by achieving the goal closest to his heart. But, this is no ordinary hero – his love for Watson transcends the standards we place on the run-of-mill cinematic good guy. In the end, he will heed the words of the writer Richard Bach: "If you love someone, set them free."

summary

Think of the journeys your hero and villain take. Obviously, they must begin somewhere and end someplace else. At some points, they will be parallel – at other points, they will intersect. More often than not, your hero's and villain's treks will come to the same focal point at the end of your script, culminating in the climax we have been waiting for since the first frame of the film. As we have seen in *Die Hard*, *Raiders of the Lost Ark*, and *Spider-Man*, the treks of these heroes and villains constitute the dramatic spines of these stories, helping make them enjoyable viewing upon viewing.

After you have crafted a logline for your screenplay (a statement summarizing your movie idea in about thirty words or less) and have tackled the prerequisite Personas, try mapping out the treks of your hero and villain.

1. *Where will your treks begin?* In most cases, you won't show these characters from the time they are born. Rather, since a movie is essentially a snapshot of a character's life (e.g., a week, a month, a year), you must decide when their journeys begin and when they will intersect. Take two pieces of paper – one for your hero and one for your villain – and draw a timeline for each. Give each character at least four milestones they will achieve during the screenplay.

2. *Be aware of three-act structure.* As I have discussed, the objective of this book is not to teach you structure (for that, I recommend *Save the Cat!*, by Blake Snyder). So, your challenge is to fit your hero and villain treks within three acts. You will find that an understanding of these treks will help guide you through your treatment and screenplay.

3. *Rewatch three successful films similar to the one you are writing.* Map out the treks of the heroes and villains on a piece of paper and compare their major milestones with those of the characters in your screenplay. Analyze the journeys in these successful films and ask yourself, "Why do they work?" The goal is to discover trends that take place at the end of Act One, the midpoint, the end of Act Two, and the end of Act Three.

chapter 8

Jeff's Eleven "Laws" of Great Storytelling

Throughout my eighteen years of screenwriting I have read and analyzed thousands of scripts from writers of all levels, including screenplays
from my students at Buffalo State College, Cornell University, Syracuse
University's Newhouse School, and R.I.T.'s School of Film and
Animation.

During this time, I discovered Eleven "Laws" of Great Storytelling – trends that tend to exist in many of the most memorable
stories of all time. Of course, creating unforgettable heroes and villains
is an integral part of all the "Laws" and should always be in the forefront
of your mind as a writer.

I use the word "Laws" with humility, as I am all too aware that a
great story is most certainly in the eye of the reader or the moviegoer.
If writing were mathematics, crafting a memorable screenplay would
be as easy as solving a rudimentary geometry equation. But, alas, we
have chosen a discipline requiring us to make hundreds of creative
decisions over the course of each script – with each choice having a
unique and often profound impact on the efficacy of the story.

So while it is impossible to have a foolproof objective formula
for a great story, I have learned that if certain principles are followed,
the probability of your story achieving a modicum of greatness increases
dramatically.

With this disclaimer firmly in place, here goes:

1. Assume everyone has ADD.
2. Spend most of your time on the first ten pages of your script.
3. Write roles to attract movie stars.
4. Write economically.

5. Make sure every character has a unique voice.
6. Understand your audience.
7. Know your three-act structure.
8. Be aware of theme, and keep it consistent throughout the script.
9. Watch and rewatch successful movies similar to your story.
10. Know what your hero wants (the goal), what happens if he doesn't achieve his goal (the stakes), and who/what is preventing him from getting what he wants (the villain).
11. Leave them wanting more.

Now, let's take a closer look at these "Laws" to see how you can apply them as a screenwriter.

1) Assume everyone has ADD.

There has never been a greater truism in Hollywood. While I am once again guilty of playing dime store psychologist, one does not need a PhD in Clinical Psychology to conclude that audiences (that means us) tend to have short attention spans.

Now, we can argue there are certain external factors contributing to a population of diminishing attention spans (MTV, video games, text messaging, IM, and the Internet to name a few possible culprits), but it is safe to say that the attentiveness (or lack thereof) of the audience is directly related to its ability to make a successful emotional connection – and that connection must be made quickly, or you will lose your audience even more quickly.

Before we delve further into this subject, a word about "audience." As a screenwriter you may believe your audience is the paying public, but you are wrong. Your initial audience is typically an entry-level reader for an agency, management company, production company, television/cable network, or Hollywood studio. These are the folks who determine if your screenplay lives to see another day (i.e., the script will be read by the reader's boss), or if it will die a quick death.

Readers, like moviegoers, need to be entertained very quickly.

And they are trained to say, "No."

When a reader submits his or her coverage (a brief synopsis and analysis of your script), it is accompanied by a one-word assessment:

"Pass," "Consider," or "Recommend." The problem is that if the reader selects "Recommend," he or she is, in a sense, putting his or her professional reputation on the line – for if his or her boss disagrees, the boss may question the reader's subsequent opinions.

It is therefore easier (and safer for those readers who are concerned about keeping their jobs) to gravitate towards a "Pass" rating or on fewer occasions, a "Consider" rating.

Which brings us back to the attention span of readers.

Ultimately, it is not their fault.

Put yourself in their shoes: They're underpaid, overworked, and often unappreciated. They may read twenty or more screenplays per week and are expected to provide a thoughtful analysis on each and every one of them. And, oh, most of the scripts are bad. Really bad. Just ask any reader.

So, if you can walk a mile in their shoes, it might help you write a script that effectively battles against their short attention spans. And the only antidote to this malady is to craft a page-turner from the moment you write: FADE IN.

More on this tactic in the next "Law" – "Spend most of your time on the first ten pages of your script."

But, before we transition to the next "Law," think about some films we have discussed that would be a good match for a reader's ADD. In *Raiders of the Lost Ark*, we are captivated the moment the Paramount Pictures logo dissolves into a similar-sized mountain in South America. For the next twelve minutes or so, we follow Indiana Jones through a precarious labyrinth filled with potentially fatal hazards at every turn.

While we know he's not going to kick the bucket right after the opening credits, we remain on the edge of our seats – an objective sought after by most filmmakers, yet so frequently achieved in execution. Ultimately, it is the relentless pace of the film that keeps even the shortest attention span brimming with excitement.

Casablanca is another film that understands the importance of pace. While *Raiders of the Lost Ark* relies more on wall-to-wall action, *Casablanca's* genius is in its free-flowing, quick-witted, character-revealing dialogue – a dream for any reader with an abbreviated attention span.

Because films like *Casablanca* were produced before the Motion Picture Association of America's ratings system (founded in 1968), filmmakers had to be much more adroit with their use of the written word. With no sex, violence, or "adult" language allowed, screenwriters and directors had to utilize witty repartee and innuendo to keep the audience interested.

Another example of uncompromising dialogue is *All About Eve* (written by Joseph L. Mankiewicz), which I highly recommend to any filmmaker or film enthusiast.

So, what have we learned about readers and their real or imagined ADD? From a medical standpoint, absolutely nothing. But, from a practical standpoint, it is important for you to understand and empathize with your initial audience – the one that can make or break your screenplay. Since the worst emotion you can emit from a reader is boredom, you must always be cognizant of your responsibility to create a pleasantly expeditious pace that will keep the reader engaged and entertained from FADE IN to FADE OUT.

2) Spend most of your time on the first ten pages of your script.

Speaking of page turners, this next "Law" – which is a cousin to "Assume everyone has ADD" – is critical for said reader to actually finish your screenplay.

A former student of mine who reads for a major Hollywood production company told me his marching orders were, "If you're not completely engaged with the script by page twenty-five, give it a 'Pass' and move on to the next screenplay." For the purposes of this discussion, I suggest you do not wait until page twenty-five to engage your reader. Take the Billy Wilder approach and "Grab 'em by the throat and never let 'em go" from the beginning.

If we agree with the premise that each page of a screenplay equals about a minute of screen time, let's look at the first ten minutes of some memorable films to see if they pass the "first ten pages" test.

As discussed, *Raiders of the Lost Ark* passes with flying colors. So does *Casablanca*. What about *Gladiator*? We are immediately engaged as we are introduced to our hero – General Maximus – and the respect he commands from the Roman army. Add an action-packed, bloody opening battle to the mix, and we are sold. We will give the filmmakers the next two hours of our lives in exchange for the experience of a masterfully told story.

In *Annie Hall*, we are laughing from the moment Alvy Singer mutters his first line of dialogue – a prudent reminder that if you are writing a comedy, it is a good idea for the script to actually be funny from the onset.

In *Pulp Fiction*, the first ten pages of the script feature a restaurant robbery and the prophetic musings of two unforgettable hit men. The dialogue is fresh, imaginative, and unrelenting in its pace and originality. If you are a reader perusing the screenplay, you undoubtedly want to continue turning the page.

In *American Beauty*, we meet Lester Burnham and are told that within the year, he'll be dead. The first ten pages not only communicate his eventual demise (which begs the questions, "How does he die and why?"), but we also are introduced to a cast of dysfunctional characters we can't wait to meet again.

Tootsie's first ten minutes brilliantly establish Michael Dorsey as an incredibly difficult yet gifted actor who will do anything to obtain a role – a perfect foundation for the moment he transforms into a woman to land a part on a soap opera. We immediately sympathize with Dorsey and gladly join him for his journey. And like *Annie Hall*, it is funny from its inception – never something we should take for granted in a comedy.

In *Fargo*, Joel and Ethan Coen waste no time setting up their comedic murder mystery. In the film's first scene, Jerry Lundegaard hires hit men Carl Showalter and Gaear Grimsrud to kidnap his wife so they can split the ransom. While there are no heroes to root for in the movie's opening moments (we'll meet Police Chief Marge Gunderson later), the first ten pages of the screenplay nonetheless capture our attention and compel us to read onward.

While there are many scripts that easily pass the "first ten page" test, it is also useful to examine memorable screenplays that do not necessarily engage the audience during those precious initial pages.

Yes, there are great films that defy this "Law." These examples are not offered to refute the "Law." Rather, they demonstrate that sometimes greatness takes more than ten minutes to unfold.

The Godfather, arguably the best film to ever come out of Hollywood, does not open with a murder, heated argument, or other memorable dramatic encounter. It begins with a wedding juxtaposed with visitors to Don Corleone's home office. While the beginning does illustrate Corleone's power and commitment to family, one has to wonder if the screenplay would elicit a "Recommend" rating from a twenty-first century, entry-level reader. Imagine a world where *The Godfather* was eradicated at the script stage. An unthinkable scenario for all of us.

As discussed in Chapter Three, *To Kill a Mockingbird* has a very slow, deliberate start. It takes about seventeen minutes before we learn Finch is being appointed to defend an accused rapist – an awfully long time for a reader to understand the direction a story is heading. While it is worth the wait, one must acknowledge the film was made in a time (1962) when audiences probably had a longer attention span than the "immediate gratification" world of today.

The Wizard of Oz – another timeless American classic – also does not bring us to the edge of our seats during the first ten minutes. Sure, we are gently amused by the provincial antics of Dorothy, Hunk, Zeke, Hickory, Uncle Henry, and Auntie Em, but let's face it, the beginning of the script does not give us any hint of the brilliance that is yet to come. While the setup is critical to Dorothy's journey, a new reader of the screenplay could easily miss the references and stamp a "Pass" rating before our heroine takes a solitary step onto the yellow brick road.

Finally, imagine you are a reader and your boss hands you a script entitled *Rocky*, by an unknown screenwriter/actor named Sylvester Stallone. As we discussed in Chapter Three, the beginning of the film is devoted to showing the audience Rocky Balboa's world. The problem is that it is not exactly intriguing. The movie commences with a mediocre bout between Balboa and a forgettable opponent. Then, we transition to Balboa's cramped apartment, a mundane introduction of his love interest, and a bland taste of the streets of Philadelphia. While we all know these sequences set the tone for the rest of the film, a reader might not be so willing to turn to page eleven. No page eleven, no Bill Conti score to blast during your morning run, and no *Rocky*.

Unfortunately, there have been countless scripts like *Rocky*, *The Wizard of Oz*, *To Kill a Mockingbird*, and *The Godfather* that never have made it past the desks of the powerful readers who inhabit Hollywood. So, your objective as a writer (writing for readers and studio executives) or a director (directing films for moviegoers) is to make the first ten minutes of your story as captivating as possible. How do you do it? Following the Eleven "Laws" of Great Storytelling is a noble start.

Here's another tip. When you are finished with your script, give the first ten pages to a group of friends or family you trust. Then ask each of them one simple question: "Do you want to read more?" If the overwhelming response is in the affirmative, you are on the right road to writing a memorable screenplay. If not, listen to what your readers have to say (taking constructive criticism is an important skill for any writer), look for commonalities in their responses, and write another draft of the first ten pages until you get it right.

3) Write roles to attract movie stars.

Create a memorable hero or villain and chances are you just might attract a movie star to your script. Why? Because characters like the heroes and villains featured in this book are unique, intelligent, and intriguing people with magnetism to spare. Who wouldn't want to play Hans Gruber, Norma Rae Webster, Hannibal Lecter, Ellen Ripley, or Gordon Gekko?

A producer friend of mine once told me he would only submit a screenplay to a studio if an "A-List" actor or actress (Read: movie star) was attached – no matter how much he liked the script. His reasoning was simple: With the average Hollywood film costing over $100 million (including prints and advertising), studios want to do everything possible to mitigate their risks. Much of that risk reduction comes in the form of making films with movie stars attached to their scripts – the rationale being that "A-List" actors and actresses have their own global brands with their own "pre-sold audiences" (i.e., millions of fans around the world who will go to a movie simply because a certain movie star is in it).

While there are plenty of examples of films with movie stars that underperformed (have you ever seen *Family Business* with Sean Connery, Dustin Hoffman, and Matthew Broderick?), there is also an abundance of evidence suggesting movie stars still earn their moniker by starring in films that generate profits far more often than losses.

Another way studios minimize risk is by making movies with stories that have "pre-sold audiences" (i.e., movies emanating from comic books, novels, television shows, plays, older movies, and the like). As a screenwriter there is not much you can do about this phenomenon, except hope a studio calls you someday to write a screenplay based on one of these stories.

For the sake of this discussion, let's assume your intention is to write a screenplay that will garner the attention from an "A-List" actor. Where do you begin?

As a start, let's take a look at the fifty Academy Award nominees and winners for Actor in a Leading Role in the last ten years. Below is a list of the nominees from 1998 – 2007 (an asterisk is next to each year's winner):

ACTOR IN A LEADING ROLE

1998: ★Roberto Benigni – *Life Is Beautiful* {"Guido"}
Tom Hanks – *Saving Private Ryan* {"Captain Miller"}
Ian McKellen – *Gods and Monsters* {"James Whale"}
Nick Nolte – *Affliction* {"Wade Whitehouse"}
Edward Norton – *American History X* {"Derek"}

1999: Russell Crowe – *The Insider* {"Jeffrey Wigand"}
Richard Farnsworth – *The Straight Story* {"Alvin Straight"}
Sean Penn – *Sweet and Lowdown* {"Emmet Ray"}
★Kevin Spacey – *American Beauty* {"Lester Burnham"}
Denzel Washington – *The Hurricane* {"Rubin 'Hurricane' Carter"}

2000: Javier Bardem – *Before Night Falls* {"Reinaldo Arenas"}
★Russell Crowe – *Gladiator* {"Maximus Decimus Meridius"}
Tom Hanks – *Cast Away* {"Chuck Noland"}
Ed Harris – *Pollock* {"Jackson Pollock"}
Geoffrey Rush – *Quills* {"The Marquis de Sade"}

2001:   Russell Crowe – *A Beautiful Mind* {"John Nash"}
Sean Penn – *I Am Sam* {"Sam Dawson"}
Will Smith – *Ali* {"Muhammad Ali"}
★Denzel Washington – *Training Day* {"Alonzo"}
Tom Wilkinson – *In the Bedroom* {"Matt Fowler"}

2002: ★Adrien Brody – *The Pianist* {"Wladyslaw Szpilman"}
Nicolas Cage – *Adaptation* {"Charlie Kaufman & Donald Kaufman"}
Michael Caine – *The Quiet American* {"Thomas Fowler"}
Daniel Day-Lewis – *Gangs of New York* {"Bill 'The Butcher' Cutting"}
Jack Nicholson – *About Schmidt* {"Warren Schmidt"}

2003:   Johnny Depp – *Pirates of the Caribbean: The Curse of the Black Pearl*
              {"Jack Sparrow"}
Ben Kingsley – *House of Sand and Fog* {"Behrani"}
Jude Law – *Cold Mountain* {"Inman"}
Bill Murray – *Lost in Translation* {"Bob Harris"}
★Sean Penn – *Mystic River* {"Jimmy Markum"}

2004:   Don Cheadle – *Hotel Rwanda* {"Paul Rusesabagina"}
Johnny Depp – *Finding Neverland* {"Sir James Matthew Barrie"}
Leonardo DiCaprio – *The Aviator* {"Howard Hughes"}
Clint Eastwood – *Million Dollar Baby* {"Frankie Dunn"}
★Jamie Foxx – *Ray* {"Ray Charles"}

2005: ★Philip Seymour Hoffman – *Capote* {"Truman Capote"}
Terrence Howard – *Hustle & Flow* {"DJay"}
Heath Ledger – *Brokeback Mountain* {"Ennis Del Mar"}
Joaquin Phoenix – *Walk the Line* {"John R. Cash"}
David Strathairn – *Good Night, and Good Luck* {"Edward R. Murrow"}

2006:   Leonardo DiCaprio – *Blood Diamond* {"Danny Archer"}
Ryan Gosling – *Half Nelson* {"Dan Dunne"}
Peter O'Toole – *Venus* {"Maurice"}
Will Smith – *The Pursuit of Happyness* {"Chris Gardner"}
★Forest Whitaker – *The Last King of Scotland* {"Idi Amin"}

2007:   George Clooney – *Michael Clayton* {"Michael Clayton"}
★Daniel Day-Lewis – *There Will Be Blood* {"Daniel Plainview"}
Johnny Depp – *Sweeney Todd the Demon Barber of Fleet Street*
              {"Sweeney Todd"}
Tommy Lee Jones – *In the Valley of Elah* {"Hank Deerfield"}
Viggo Mortensen – *Eastern Promises* {"Nikolai"}

Now, you may ask yourself, "What does this list have to do with my screenplay?" Plenty. Movie stars can buy anything from Porsches to Picassos; they have adoring fans throughout the world who will wait for hours to get a glimpse of them; and they are told by sycophantic agents, managers, attorneys, studio executives, PR professionals, writers, producers, and directors that they are nothing less than the great Da Vinci reincarnated.

But, they cannot buy the respect an Academy Award affords them (for a moment, leave your cynical hats at the door and maintain that these awards cannot be bought). So, if you can write a juicy role that will attract the attention of one or more movie stars, you just might find yourself in the midst of a studio bidding war.

Let's take a closer look at some of the winners for Best Actor in a Leading Role to see if there are any trends we can glean that could have a positive impact on your scripts.

Roberto Benigni (*Life Is Beautiful*):
Funny, resourceful, paternal, and selfless

Kevin Spacey (*American Beauty*):
Funny, self-deprecating, acerbic, and sarcastic

Russell Crowe (*Gladiator*):
Heroic, dutiful, loyal, paternal, and honest

Denzel Washington (*Training Day*):
Intimidating, forceful, brutal, and confident

Jamie Foxx (*Ray*):
Honest, brilliant, resourceful, and sympathetic

Daniel Day-Lewis (*There Will Be Blood*):
Intimidating, selfish, greedy, and dictatorial

The above characteristics should be in the forefront of your mind when crafting your Hero and Villain Personas (Chapter Six), as these traits can help you better understand the types of characters who will not only enrich your screenplay, but are more likely to attract the type of actors and actresses who have the power to get your script sold and greenlit. More importantly, it is a good idea to watch (or rewatch) these films and study what makes these characters memorable.

4) Write economically.

Throughout my years of writing and reading screenplays, one of the most common mistakes I have experienced is "overwriting." This phenomenon often falls into two categories: 1) verbose stage direction; and 2) "on the nose" dialogue.

Verbose Stage Direction

It is important to keep in mind you are writing a screenplay – not a book and not a play. And since you are writing a screenplay and hopefully aspire to craft one hundred-plus pages that will captivate the most cynical of readers, it is critical for you to read great screenplays. While it is difficult to obtain the shooting scripts of motion pictures (they are typically only available through the studios), I would suggest purchasing your favorites online, as many screenplays have been released in book format. In addition, many DVDs now include the shooting scripts as special features. So, your first task is to read as many great screenplays as possible. You will begin to see trends that exist, like economical stage direction.

A friend of mine who worked at one of the major talent agencies in Los Angeles once told me if she sees an excessive amount of stage direction in a script, she scans down the center of each page – only reading the dialogue. As a writer, I cannot think of a more egregious statement. Here I am, painstakingly selecting every solitary word of stage direction – ensuring my characters' actions jump off the page – only to discover that readers pass through my precious descriptions at lightning speed.

Ah, but with every unnerving comment from a Hollywood executive, there is a lesson to be learned. In this case, keep your stage direction short (I recommend trying to keep each paragraph to less than five lines) and to the point. That does not mean to write drab direction that simply and stoically describes what your characters are doing at the moment. Never forget you are writing a piece of entertainment, and stage direction should entertain as much as it informs us as to the comings and going of your characters.

Remember that lone reader with twenty screenplays to get through over the weekend? Put yourself in her shoes. She doesn't want to view your screenplay as a chore to plow through because it is her job to do so. She wants to be entertained. And she doesn't want to be distracted by too many words. "The more white space, the better" an agent once exclaimed to me, referring to the notion that the more dialogue and the less stage direction, the better.

If you think this tactic is related to "Assume everyone has ADD," you're right. So, keep your stage direction brief, to the point, and above all, entertaining.

"On the Nose" Dialogue

Several years ago, I sent a script to my manager and received notes including quite a few pieces of dialogue circled with the comment, "OTN." I was perplexed and asked him to explain. He said these were several instances where my dialogue was too "on the nose." In other words, the exposition was too overt. For instance, consider the following conversation:

                    BOB
          How do you feel, Gloria?

                    GLORIA
          I'm your wife, Bob. How do you
          think I feel?

                    BOB
          It's funny. You were always happy
          when we had the money to jet all
          over the world with our three
          kids. But now that we have nothing,
          you're miserable.

```
        GLORIA
It's not about the money. It's
about your extracurricular
activities, Bob. You know, all
of the affairs you had.


        BOB
I was forced to stray — because
you never gave me the emotional
support I needed. And it didn't
help that I never saw you without
a glass of vodka in your hand,
Gloria.
```

You get the point. All of the information communicated in this scene is about as subtle as a giant anvil falling onto the audience. Think about it. In this brief exchange, we are told:

1. Bob and Gloria are married.
2. They used to have money; now they don't.
3. They have three kids.
4. Bob has a history of cheating on Gloria.
5. Gloria has a drinking problem.
6. They are fond of saying each other's names in conversation.

While this is a lot of information for a short scene (a good thing), this is not how real people talk (a bad thing) and it comes off as patronizing to the audience (a worse thing). The scene reeks of amateur "on the nose" exposition and illustrates a common problem with many scripts and unmemorable movies.

The point is to make the audience work a bit for the information – not too much (we don't want to frustrate them) – but enough for them to feel emotionally involved in your story.

Put simply, we don't want to be told every single iota of information about each character. It is far more interesting for us to discover the complexities of your story on our own.

5) Make sure every character has a unique voice.

Think about going out to dinner with your three oldest friends. Chances are you have similar educational, professional, and socioeconomic backgrounds. Chances are you tend to speak alike and have similar views on the world. While that's great for a night out with your best buddies, it doesn't make for a compelling story. Movies work most effectively when they are populated with characters who are unique from one another. Sound easy? It isn't. Just take a look at any film currently playing in your local multiplex. Chances are many of them are filled with characters who look and sound alike.

So, if you agree with the premise that a homogeneous cast of characters does not usually result in a memorable film, what are some rules you can follow to help make your characters unique? Consider the following rules as an adjunct to the Hero and Villain Persona discussed in Chapter Six. Combining these two tools will undoubtedly breathe life into your screenplay and help assure a cast of original, three-dimensional characters.

Avoid stereotypes.

One of the problems I see over and over again with new writers is the depiction of characters who feel familiar and stereotypical. With younger writers, I believe this occurs because of their lack of life experience and tendency to mimic characters they have seen on television and film.

The key is to go against stereotypes, thus providing your audience with the refreshing read they crave. For example, in *Pulp Fiction*, who would think two hit men would be so prophetic and self-reflective? The fact that Vincent and Jules muse about a litany of subjects from fast food in Amsterdam to foot massages to the meaning of life is not what we would expect from hired assassins – and that's exactly the point. Give your readers characters that defy stereotypes and they'll keep turning the page.

Surprise us with quirks and unusual traits.

Every once in a while, I'll be sitting in a movie theater and suddenly I'll discover something fresh and unusual about one of the main characters. It is that feeling of surprise we all desire and unfortunately, those moments are few and far between. What's a screenwriter to do? Consider giving your main characters quirks or unusual traits that will help engage the audience.

Alvy Singer is a hapless neurotic in *Annie Hall*; Marge Gunderson is a pregnant police chief in *Fargo*; Indiana Jones suffers from ophiophobia (fear of snakes) in *Raiders of the Lost Ark*; Dr. Hannibal Lecter is a cannibal in *The Silence of the Lambs*; Sonny Wortzik is a gay bank robber in *Dog Day Afternoon*; Chance is a simpleminded gardener mistaken for a genius in *Being There*; and Dr. Emmett Brown is the definition of quirky in *Back to the Future*.

The point is these qualities humanize your characters – making them more three-dimensional – and help you avoid turning your script into a cast of clichés.

Create someone an actor will love to play.

Earlier in this chapter, we discussed some of the Academy Award nominees and winners for Actor in a Leading Role in the last ten years. Let's take a look at some of the Academy Award nominees and winners for Actress in a Leading Role over the same time period to see why these roles garnered the attention of many of the industry's most talented actresses.

As an actress, who can resist the Bard? Not Gwyneth Paltrow, who played Viola De Lesseps in 1998 in *Shakespeare in Love*. Clearly, this was a juicy role for its language (screenplay by Marc Norman and Tom Stoppard) and subject matter. A strong female character plus Shakespearean dialogue plus a memorable love story equaled an Oscar.

One can only imagine Julie Roberts' reaction when she read the script for *Erin Brockovich*. It is simply not the typical role afforded to actresses in Hollywood. The hero of the film is a quintessentially strong character any actress would love to play. She is confident, bold, sympathetic, and has plenty of memorable monologues. It is a classic underdog story resulting in Roberts winning the Oscar in 2000.

In 2003, Charlize Theron transformed herself into the complex Aileen Wuornos in *Monster* and the role earned her an Oscar. Like so many memorable roles that have received critical raves and awards, actors love to go through a metamorphosis to play a juicy part. Now, since you don't know who will be portraying your main characters when you are drudging through your screenplay, it is still a good idea to analyze movies like the ones above and ask yourself, "Am I writing a role an actor would love to play?"

Transform him/her over your story.

As discussed in Chapter One, Rick Blaine in *Casablanca* is a great example of a hero transforming over the course of the story. At the beginning of the film he confidently states his mantra, "I stick my neck out for nobody." But, at the end of the film, he does just that – sticking his neck out for the woman he loves.

In my interview with David Koepp (Chapter Five), he states, "The classic model of character change in American cinema is Michael Corleone in *The Godfather*. He went from, 'That's my family – that's not me' to 'I am my family.'" It is this specific transformation that is the main driver through the entire *Godfather* series. With your screenplay, ask yourself, "Does my hero change?"

Make everything about his/her journey difficult.

We love watching our heroes struggle. What would *Raiders of the Lost Ark* be if Indiana Jones immediately stumbled upon the Ark of the Covenant and brought it back to America? What if John McClane burst into the Nakatomi Christmas party and took out Hans Gruber and all of his henchmen in one momentous moment? And, what if Ellen Ripley easily discovered the Alien's whereabouts as well as a surefire way to destroy the monster?

These would all make for excessively boring movies that would never be remembered past their opening weekends. But, your story is different. You will place every obstacle imaginable in front of your hero to ensure he has the toughest time possible in achieving his goal. And at times, you will make us feel his goal is insurmountable and unachievable. You will do all of this because you understand it is the struggle that creates conflict – the dramatic underpinning of any great story. And a great story you shall write.

6) Understand your audience.

When you are writing a screenplay, there are two audiences you should consider: 1) the readers, agents, managers, producers, and studio executives who will be reading your screenplay (aka, the buyers); and 2) the demographic you believe will be most interested in seeing your movie (let's be overly optimistic and assume your script will someday be depicted on the silver screen).

In the first two "Laws" of this chapter, we discussed the mindset of the folks who are required to devour dozens of scripts on a weekly basis. It is worth restating the importance of empathizing with these crucial gatekeepers of the entertainment industry. They are paid to find the next *Harry Potter*, *Wedding Crashers*, or *Juno*.

And, it is your job to entertain them.

If your script is a comedy, it must be funny. If you are writing a horror script, it must be scary. Sounds like common sense? It isn't. Talk to a professional reader and ask her how many comedy and horror scripts she has read of late that are actually funny and scary. "The comedy scripts are scary and the horror scripts are funny," is the answer you just might receive.

The fact that so many readers are bombarded with substandard product should present itself as an opportunity for you. While it is true there is no shortage of screenplays in the marketplace, it should give you hope that most of the scripts in the universe are simply not that good. Again, any reader, agent, manager, producer, or studio executive will echo this sentiment.

And while I hope your screenplay will be that diamond in the rough, you must never forget that every time a reader stamps "Recommend" on a script, he places a small amount of his reputation on the line, hoping his boss will agree with his assessment.

Now that you have a better understanding of the folks who will read your script, let's take a moment to discuss demographics. It is important for you to know the intended audience for your film, as it can impact the fundamentals of your screenplay.

Hollywood studios like to categorize the world into four simple compartments, typically referred to as quadrants: 1) Male under 25; 2) Male over 25; 3) Female under 25; and 4) Female over 25. If you ever wondered why every Pixar film seems to make a billion dollars in worldwide gross and ancillary revenues, it is because the company excels at making Four Quadrant movies – films that appeal equally to males and females under 25 and over 25 (in other words, everyone). The Four Quadrant film is the ultimate box office generator, simply because it appeals to most moviegoers.

If you were to peruse the list of the top box office films of all time, you would see it filled with these demographic grand slams. It should be no surprise movies like *Titanic*, the *Harry Potter* films, the *Spider-Man* films, the *Star Wars* films, *E.T.*, and *Finding Nemo* occupy the list. These are big pictures with universal themes that attract audiences of all ages across the globe.

That is not to say, however, your script must appeal to all ages. *Sex and the City* was a hit with its target audience – females over 25. *The Saw* series of films enjoyed considerable success targeting males and females under 25.

The point is to know for whom you are writing.

While no one will ask you to craft a marketing plan for your script, it is always a good idea to be able to articulate your intended audience. Why? Because it is more likely your well-crafted screenplay will result in meetings with producers and studio executives than be released on four thousand screens in North America. I have taken several such meetings and in many instances the person sitting on the other side of the table has asked, "What motivated you to write this script?" This is a good opportunity to mention the type of audience you wanted to engage.

These types of meetings are essential to building relationships and we all know this is a business of relationships. Buyers in the industry (as a screenwriter, you are a seller) will get to know you and your scripts – which someday may result in work for you.

7) Know your three-act structure.

Like it or not, Hollywood has a language all its own. One of the most used (and abused) concepts by buyers is anything and everything related to three-act structure. While Aristotle is usually credited for creating the concept that all stories must have a beginning, middle, and end, you may be hard pressed to find a buyer in Hollywood familiar with the Greek philosopher. Still, the notion of the three-act structure is alive and well in modern day filmmaking.

Here is what buyers expect from your script:

1. By page ten, they want to be introduced to your hero, what he wants (his goal), and the genre of the story you are telling. As stated, if you are writing a comedy, it must be funny at the onset or your script might find itself in a trash bin or worse, with the word "Pass" plastered across its cover. Also, readers will quickly appraise you as a writer during these first critical ten pages. Are you a natural storyteller? Do you have a good ear for dialogue? Do you understand conflict? Can you create interesting characters? Is this clearly a first-time writer or someone who knows how to craft an entertaining screenplay?

2. By the end of Act One (page twenty-five or so), readers want to know exactly where this story is going. The stakes (What happens if the hero does not achieve his goal?) and the villain (The person, place, or thing preventing the hero from achieving his goal) are the two other main elements that must be addressed in Act One.

3. By the midpoint (the middle of Act Two, page fifty-five or so), readers like to feel that the stakes for the hero have been raised in some fashion. Maybe a new character has been introduced. Maybe a new obstacle or villain has reared its head. Maybe the hero has experienced a distinct character transformation (e.g., going from reactive to proactive). My experience is that this plot point is often the hardest to define and attain. But, it is worth sweating it out during the treatment phase to create a midpoint that effectively breaks your script into two equal halves.

4. By the end of Act Two (page ninety or so), readers presume your hero will be in a heap of trouble. Up until now, the hero may have been steadily moving toward achieving his goal. But at the end of Act Two, things have changed. He has suddenly been put in a corner and the audience is asking itself, "How in the world is he going to get out of this one?" This is one of the most predictable plot points in

classic Hollywood three-act structure – namely, at the end of Act Two (about five to twenty minutes from the end of the film), the hero is usually furthest from his goal. Watch any studio picture and you will be amazed at how consistently this phenomenon occurs.

5. In Act Three, readers want your hero to somehow devise a new plan and escape from the mess that has presented itself at the end of Act Two. This is the big finish. The climax. The series of quick-paced scenes concluding with the defeat of our villain and the success of our hero. Whether it is obtaining the Ark of the Covenant, destroying the Death Star, mobilizing a company to form a union, going the distance with the heavyweight champion of the world, or saving hundreds of Jews from certain death, we are finally fulfilled. Our hero has proactively solved the problem presented to him in Act One and we can now go back to our mundane lives.

In addition to being conversant in traditional three-act structure, it is also imperative to understand some basic principles that should go into every scene you write. For instance, every scene should:

Advance your story
Even if you love a particular scene, if it doesn't move your story forward, delete it.

Contain conflict
Conflict is what keeps readers turning the page.

Reveal character/motivations
We should never be scratching our head and asking, "Why did he just do that?" All motivations must be clear.

Explore and/or expand upon your theme
Your theme should be clearly and consistently woven throughout your script.

Begin as late as possible
Always delete superfluous action and dialogue at the beginning of a scene. Get to the point.

End as early as possible
Always delete superfluous action and dialogue at the end of a scene. After you have made your point, move on to the next scene.

8) Be aware of theme, and keep it consistent throughout the script.

Norma Rae is a journey of self-discovery – a woman realizing her capabilities as a leader. *Wall Street* is about the seduction of greed. *Spider-Man* is about a young man learning that with great power comes great responsibility.

Theme is a tough nut to crack. When I ask my students the theme of *Die Hard*, they often restate the film's core concept (or, in Hollywood terms, the "logline"), saying something like, "It's about a cop thwarting a group of international terrorists while saving his wife and a bunch of innocent people." While this is true, it doesn't quite touch on theme. I then dig deeper, suggesting *Die Hard* is really about a man trying to reconnect with his wife. True, this reconnection takes place amidst the backdrop of an action-packed heist, but at its core, this is a story about John McClane discovering the importance of family and the love and appreciation he has for his wife, Holly.

You need proof? Let's reprise the scene we discussed in Chapter Seven between McClane and Sergeant Al Powell:

                    McCLANE
        Listen man, I'm starting to get a
        bad feeling up here. I want you
        to do something for me. I want
        you to find my wife. Don't ask me
        how — by then, you'll know how.
        I want you to tell her something.
        I want you to tell her that... tell
        her that it took me a while to
        figure out what a jerk I've been.
        But, that when things started to
        pan out for her, I should've been
        more supportive. And, I should've
                    (MORE)

243

```
                McCLANE  (CONT'D)
      been  behind  her  more.  Tell  her
      that  she's  the  best  thing  that
      ever  happened  to  a  bum  like  me.
      She's  heard  me  say  'I  love  you'  a
      thousand  times.  She  never  heard
      me  say,  'I'm  sorry.'  And  I  want
      you  to  tell  her  that,  Al,  and  I
      want  you  to  tell  her  that  John
      said  that  he  was  sorry.  Okay,  you
      got  that,  man?
```

This monologue, which takes place at the end of Act Two, is all about theme. It is about McClane coming to the conclusion that his wife is far more important than he ever realized. It takes a life-and-death ordeal for him to come to this conclusion, but nevertheless, he now appreciates his wife in a way unthinkable at the beginning of the film.

Time and time again, I find writers struggling with the concept of theme, but one cannot overstate the importance of knowing the theme of your script. Ask yourself, "What am I trying to say?" If you can answer that question, you are on your way to conceptualizing a theme. And once you have a deep understanding of the theme of your script, it is your duty to ensure this theme is effectively woven throughout your entire story. Your readers (and ultimately, the audience) will love you for it.

Here are some tips on how to approach theme for your story:

1. Devise a theme that best summarizes the point of your story. The theme should start with the sentence, "This story is about…" and be a cousin to your logline.
2. Infuse your theme through as many scenes as possible. Keep in mind that themes are often tied to the lessons your hero learns throughout the story.
3. Consider creating "B" or "C" plots that will help bolster your theme. Since it is often difficult to completely immerse a singular theme into a full-length screenplay, it is sometimes

necessary (and dramatically appropriate) to create subplots that will help your story move along and reinforce its theme.

4. Reread some classics you may have read in high school. They are classics for a reason – and it is often because these books deal with universal and timeless themes. Which of these themes can you apply to your story?

9) Watch and re-watch successful movies similar to your story.

There is an old adage in Hollywood: They want the same, but different. A Catch-22 for any writer, yet these are words that should be heeded. As discussed, because the average studio picture costs over $100 million to produce and market, studios are in the risk aversion business every bit as much as they are in the movie business. The impact on you is that these buyers of product tend to gravitate toward the familiar – stories they think will have the best chance at attracting a global audience.

To be sure, these are not the times of the studio system when moguls like Louis B. Mayer made any picture they fancied. Today, studios are part of international, publicly-traded conglomerates that have intense profit demands on their entertainment subsidiaries. Which means the executives who buy, develop, and greenlight screenplays have the same financial pressures on them as their corporate parents. So, at least we have a basic understanding as to a buyer's motivation in the modern era.

With this in mind, it is prudent to watch and re-watch successful movies similar to your script. Not to plagiarize, of course, but to help you answer the all-important question, "Why do these films work?" Study the way they set up their characters – especially their heroes and villains; study their structure; and study their dialogue. If you can determine why these films work, you may be able to utilize the lessons learned to improve your screenplay and make it more attractive to the marketplace.

Since you know how your script should be structured (see "Know your three-act structure"), study how a successful film deals with hitting the major plot points. For instance, let's take a high-level look at *Fatal Attraction*:

1. By page ten, we are introduced to our hero (family man Dan Gallagher), what he wants (single woman Alex Forrest), and the genre (drama).

2. By the end of Act One (page twenty-five or so), we know Forrest (the villain) is unstable and wants to have a relationship with Gallagher, who clearly wants a clean break. We also know the stakes – if Gallagher's wife (Beth) finds out about the affair, his family may be ruined. So far, so good.

3. By the midpoint (the middle of Act Two, page fifty-five or so), the stakes are raised when Forrest tells Gallagher she is pregnant. Moreover, she is intent on keeping the baby. Now, Gallagher and Forrest are indelibly tied together. What's an adulterer to do?

4. By the end of Act Two (page ninety or so), there is a sequence of "all is lost" moments leading up to the end of the act: Gallagher tells Beth about the affair, she kicks him out of the house, Forrest kidnaps their daughter, and Beth gets into a car accident.

5. In Act Three, there is a tension-filled, suspenseful climax, as Forrest attacks Beth at home, a battle ensues, Gallagher comes to the rescue, and Beth heroically shoots Forrest dead.

Now that you have a better idea of how three-act structure works within an established film, what are the benefits of studying films similar to your script?

Let's say you are writing a raunchy, R-rated comedy. I would suggest watching *Wedding Crashers*, *The 40-Year-Old Virgin*, and *Superbad*. These are all critically acclaimed, financially successful films still fresh in the minds of Hollywood executives. Since we know there is no lack of short attention spans in the entertainment industry, don't attempt to devise a panacea to cure the TV/film business of this ailment (an impossible task) – you are better off working within the constraints presented to you. In this case, that means associating your screenplay with successful movies familiar to today's buyers.

A quick, cynical comment on "today's buyers": We already know they are under intense profit pressures from their corporate bosses, but you should also know there are many buyers of product in Hollywood who are not as film literate as you may think. Sure, they are likely to have an encyclopedic knowledge of the domestic box office champs over the last several weeks, but be careful comparing your script to a film more than twenty-five years old.

True story: I once pitched a feature film idea to a friend who was a literary agent at one of the major talent agencies. "It's a Billy Wilder-type comedy," I said enthusiastically. "Like *Some Like it Hot.*" He furrowed his brow and replied, "Who is Billy Wilder?"

I'm not saying there aren't plenty of executives who are not only familiar with Billy Wilder, but are fanatical fans of his catalogue of films. There are many. The point is that when pitching a movie idea to an executive, you can never go wrong referring to hit films produced in the not-so-distant past.

Let's say you have a college comedy with a horror twist. Say, *Old School* meets *Scream*. Okay, maybe that's a bit ridiculous, but you get the point. No one has time to read a script that takes thirty minutes to explain. And, the reader plowing through your screenplay doesn't have thirty minutes to pitch your script to his boss. He has more like thirty seconds.

So, the easier your script is to pitch – and the more it is similar in tone to successful films – the better chance you and your painstaking work have of climbing up the development ladder to someone who can actually say, "Yes." And, that is the screenwriter's most cherished word in the English language.

10) Know what your hero wants (the goal), what happens if he doesn't get what he wants (the stakes), and who/what is preventing him from getting what he wants (the villain).

You may look at this "Law" and say, "Duh. Every movie answers these questions." Not so fast. Go to your local multiplex this weekend, take in a new release or two, and let me know if the three questions listed above are adequately answered to your liking. You can reach me at: *jeff@threeact.com* with your thoughts.

Think about some films you haven't loved. I bet one of the reasons there was no love connection was because they failed to answer the questions above. Before we fall into another abyss of cynicism, let's take a positive approach and look at a few films that do answer these pivotal questions with brilliant efficiency and clarity.

In *Toy Story 2*, Buzz Lightyear is the primary hero whose goal is to lead a group of toys to save Woody from being sent to a museum in Japan. The primary villain of the story is Al (of "Al's Toy Barn" fame) and the stakes are simple: If our hero and his team do not achieve their goal, they will never see Woody again. While you can argue that The Prospector is a secondary villain and Woody is a secondary hero, the film still quickly and succinctly establishes its primary goal, stakes, hero, and villain. The result is a brilliant script that can focus on its ensemble cast of characters because the film's foundation is clear and perfectly executed.

Jaws is another movie that quickly answers our burning questions. By the end of Act One, we know Police Chief Martin Brody (with the support of Quint and Hooper) is our hero, his goal is to kill the shark, the villain is the shark itself, and the stakes are: If Brody does not achieve his goal, more residents of Amity will die. Simple? Yes. Easy to achieve? Of course not.

In *The Shawshank Redemption*, everyman Andy Dufresne is our hero, his goal is to break out of prison and gain his freedom, the villain is the Shawshank Prison (and to a lesser extent, Warden Norton), and the stakes are: If he doesn't break free, he will forever be stripped of his freedom and subjected to the cruelties of prison life.

One of my favorite examples of a film concisely communicating the goal of its hero, stakes, and villain is *Finding Nemo* – which amazingly has the goal of the movie in its title. Marlin needs to find his son, Nemo, who is lost in the seas; the villain is the ocean itself; and the stakes couldn't be more grave – if Marlin doesn't achieve his goal, he will never see his only son again. A perfect story, perfectly executed.

Now that we have seen some examples of films that answer these critical questions, why do so many films fail to do the same? The reason is that it is very difficult to stay focused on these simple queries and very easy to go off on tangents. Many scripts begin with the best of intentions but end up mired in B and C plots that have little to do with the spine of the story. Other scripts include multiple goals and/or multiple villains that end up muddying the final product.

While teaching a class at Cornell, I had the pleasure of interviewing John Cleese as part of my screenwriting course. He was as funny and insightful as we had hoped. When I asked him the key to creating a memorable hero, his answer was simple and succinct: "We have to know what he is after," he said with utter confidence.

So, once we know what our hero "is after" (his goal), the villain (Who/what is preventing him from achieving his goal?), and the stakes (What happens if he doesn't achieve his goal?), your story will fall into place.

These are all questions that ideally should be answered by the end of Act One of your screenplay (usually about twenty-five pages into the script). Since a properly formatted page of a script typically equals about a minute of screen time, we should know the hero, his goal, the villain and the stakes no later than about twenty-five minutes into a film. Go rewatch a few of your favorites and you'll find this concept is right more often than not.

11) Leave them wanting more.

This "Law" seems to be as ancient as showbiz itself. Yet, it is just as relevant today as it was at the turn of the twentieth century. The "Law" is really about crafting a memorable, climactic ending that will forever be satisfying to your audience. An outstanding ending can often save a mediocre film while a mediocre ending can often ruin an otherwise outstanding story. Why? Because the ending is the last taste we are left with in our emotional palette – it is the part of the story we will best remember and are most likely to discuss with friends.

So, does your climax…

1. Feel like a big, fulfilling finish?
2. Reveal a significant character trait of your hero or villain?
3. Resolve the central problem established in Act One?
4. Contain a satisfying surprise?
5. Appear five to twenty minutes or so before the end of the film?

If your story accomplishes the above, you are on your way to crafting a memorable conclusion to your script. Speaking of memorable conclusions, consider the "leave them wanting more" endings of the following films:

Martin Brody kills the shark in **Jaws.**

It is the last moments of this classic thriller and Brody and his boat are readily sinking. He has just thrown a combustible tank into the Great White's mouth and has one round left in his shotgun to blow this underwater villain to bits. The shark speeds toward Brody, opens his mouth wide, and our hero takes aim. There's not a moment to spare when he pulls the trigger and bellows, "Smile, you son of a... " Then Ka-Boom! The shark explodes into millions of peaceful pieces – and we can finally go back into the water again.

Luke Skywalker destroys the Death Star in **Star Wars.**

The entire film chronicles the personal growth of this unforgettable farm boy from "a long time ago in a galaxy far, far away." So, when a group of Rebel Alliance pilots take off with the objective of destroying the Death Star, we know it is only a matter of time until every single one of them succumbs to the enemy, leaving Skywalker alone with his inexperience and insecurities. Like Brody, Skywalker conquers his inner demons and, at the last possible moment, blows the Death Star into space – creating an eruption of movie patron cheers I have never experienced since.

Michael Corleone executes all of his enemies in **The Godfather.**

In one of the most mimicked sequences in modern film, we watch in awe as we witness the baptism of Corleone's nephew juxtaposed with the brutal execution of all of the family's enemies. We have seen ironic endings before, but nothing like this. Later, when Michael tells his soon-to-be-dead brother-in-law, Carlo, "Today, I settled all family business," we don't doubt him for a solitary moment.

Dorothy Gale discovers she can go home in **The Wizard of Oz.**

While one can argue the Land of Oz may be a more appealing place to live than the Land of Kansas, we feel Dorothy's pain throughout the movie as she longs to be back with her family and friends.

So, when she taps her heels together at the end of her journey and is magically transported back home, we smile with grand gratification – because there's no film like *The Wizard of Oz*.

Rick Blaine lets Ilsa Lund get on a plane without him in Casablanca.

There has not been a more selfless act in American film than Rick Blaine letting the love of his life board a plane for her own safety – knowing they will never see each other again. "Here's looking at you kid," he says right before she despairingly disappears into the fog. Watching the final scene of this unforgettable film left me reflecting, "I think this is the end of a beautiful movie."

Ben thwarts Elaine's wedding and they end up together on a bus in The Graduate.

Who could forget Benjamin Braddock's frantic flight to stop Elaine Robinson's wedding at the conclusion of *The Graduate*? He confronts a number of obstacles along the way until he is forced to run the last leg of the trip to the church. Mayhem ensues, he steals Robinson from the ceremony, and they end up on a bus – apparently free from their respective familial pressures. But, it is that final furtive glance between Braddock and Robinson that leaves us wanting more and ultimately wondering what will happen when they arrive at their destination.

Michael reveals himself to be a woman in Tootsie.

The fact that Dorothy Michaels is really Michael Dorsey is the running gag that has just about everyone fooled in the movie – except the audience. That's why we can't wait until the end of Act Two moment when he tears off his wig on live television. And we are not let down. The movie concludes with Dorsey succinctly stating the film's theme by telling his love, Julie Nichols, "... I was a better man with you, as a woman, than I ever was with a woman, as a man." Sure, it takes us a minute to process the sentiment, but when we do, there are few films more rewarding.

Phil's nightmare of living the same day over and over finally comes to end when Rita falls in love with him in **Groundhog Day.**

Even we are tired of hearing "I Got You Babe" every single morning. We can only imagine how Phil Connors feels – living the same mundane day over and over. That is, until he figures out there just may be an opportunity to win Rita's heart. The scheme goes sour until he learns to be himself rather than what he thinks she wants him to be. It is a touching final scene – when they not only fall asleep together, but wake up together the next morning. The curse has been broken and we couldn't be happier for our own Punxsutawney Phil.

Marty and Doc Brown execute a complex plan to travel to the future via a clock tower, a Delorean, and an expected bolt of lightning in **Back to the Future.**

In one of the most exciting and memorable action movie endings you are apt to see, Marty McFly must race his dilapidated Delorean sports car to eighty-eight miles per hour and trip an electrical wire the moment lightning strikes a clock tower or he and his family will cease to exist in the future. Sound impossible? That's exactly what director Robert Zemeckis wants you to think. But, in a heart-stopping, nail-biting, unrelenting sequence, McFly and Brown pull off the impossible and we are left happily scratching our heads as to how they made it all work.

At the disappointment of anyone who ever watched the film, E.T. goes back home in **E.T.: The Extra-Terrestrial.**

By the end of the movie, we all love E.T. After all, who wouldn't want a little guy around the house who can levitate objects, make limp plants come alive, and even get inebriated? So, in the film's swelling final minutes, we just want E.T. to stay with Elliot for eternity and beyond. But, we also realize E.T. wants to go home. What's an audience to do? We hope both of them get what they want – and that's precisely what happens. E.T. reunites with his family, but not without gently pointing toward his best friend's heart and tenderly saying, "I'll be right here." The moment leaves us completely content, knowing these two special friends will forever be connected and someday meet again.

chapter 9

Conclusion

First of all, congratulations. You have successfully read – and hopefully somewhat retained – over 75,000 words on memorable heroes and villains and information on creating your own timeless stories and characters. I am, of course, making the leap that you actually perused the entire book and are not simply flipping to the end to see how it turns out (a la Harry Burns in *When Harry Met Sally…*).

Now that you know the commonalities of memorable heroes and villains and tools to create your very own unforgettable stories, it is worth noting some hero and villain traits you may want to avoid – clichés that will be sensed by any Hollywood executive – resulting in a Pavlovian response to politely "Pass" on your project.

Unlike the proceeding "Laws," these are overused story elements I have seen ad infinitum throughout my years as a writer, professor, and script consultant. If you avoid them, you will surely enhance the quality of your main characters and thus, your entire story. While there are certainly exceptions to these guidelines, they remain prudent rules to keep in mind.

Hero Don'ts

1. Don't let your hero's buddies save the day at the end of your story.

As we have discussed, memorable heroes are most successful when they do it themselves. Sure, they often have mentors who help them throughout their journeys, but when it comes to Act Three climaxes, they prefer to go it all alone. Just ask Special Agent Clarice Starling or Luke Skywalker.

2. Don't make anything too easy for your hero.

We love watching our heroes struggle to achieve their goals. And the more they resemble David to a villainous Goliath, the better. Watch *Rocky* for inspiration.

3. Don't create heroes who are emotionally flawless.

As we have discussed, memorable heroes typically have a shadowy counterpart. The more imperfect they are, the more we root for them throughout every stage of their journeys. For example, Indiana Jones does not negotiate to get what he wants – he sometimes is forced to act in a traditionally non-heroic manner. That's a nice way of saying he kills people when he has to – and we forgive him.

4. Don't make your hero too cocky.

Hubris does not typically equate to likeability – not in real life and not in the movies. So, it is always a good idea to create a hero who can make fun of himself without losing his innate heroic qualities. For example, John McClane has that perfect balance of self-deprecation and confidence in *Die Hard* – as does Aaron Altman in *Broadcast News*.

5. Don't have your hero come from a privileged background.

Sure, there are examples of wealthy heroes (Tony Stark in *Iron Man* comes to mind), but let's face it: It is usually much more interesting to experience a hero go from nothing to something (Peter Parker in *Spider-Man*), even if his transformation does not necessarily include becoming rich (once again, Peter Parker in *Spider-Man*).

Villain Don'ts

1. Don't give your villain a maniacal laugh.

We'll give Belloq a pass with his brief guffaw at the end of the first sequence in *Raiders of the Lost Ark* – mostly because he is so brilliant in the rest of the film. But for your villain, we will only laugh at him instead of with him – which is probably not the response you desire.

2. Don't make your villain impervious to pain.

It is comforting to know that even the Green Goblin can get the daylights beaten out of him. And don't forget pain can be physical or emotional. For example, Amon Goeth in *Schindler's List* is hopelessly in love with his Jewish servant, Helen Hirsch. It is, of course, an impossible love that strives to humanize this murderous villain.

3. Don't create a villain without family or friends.

Who would have predicted Darth Vader was a dad? You get the point.

4. Don't conceive dumb villains.

Would Hannibal Lecter be nearly as interesting if he were a high school dropout who never picked up a book? I don't think so.

5. Don't have your villain trap your hero, place him in an elaborate concoction designed to kill him, then leave so your hero can invent a creative way to escape.

How many times have we seen this scenario? Too many to chronicle.

Now that we have some "don'ts" to add to our list of "do's," where do you go from here? The short – and frustrating – answer is, "It depends."

If you are a burgeoning writer of television, film, novels, or the Internet, my simple advice is to write. A lot. Every day. And get in the habit of consistently showing your work to others for constructive criticism.

Also, don't try to follow trends of the entertainment industry. For example, if studios are producing an inordinate number of horror films in a given year, it doesn't make a lot of sense to write a horror film with the hope of a studio blindly snatching it up.

Why? Because if you are lucky enough to have your screenplay optioned or bought, it could take years before the script is rewritten, cast, and placed into production (assuming you are lucky enough to have your screenplay greenlit). By then, the studios will have moved on to their next genre du jour.

Think about what makes you unique and you may just discover the next hero (and possible villain) for your next script. If you have been playing piano since you were a kid, maybe you should write a romantic comedy set against the backdrop of a Julliard-type school. If your uncle was a police officer, maybe you should write a procedural drama set in your hometown. Any chance you lived in a fraternity or sorority? Maybe a college comedy is up your alley. The point is (Warning: Cliché Alert), write what you know.

While this is one of the most overused and abused tenets in Hollywood, there is more than a degree of truth to the adage. Namely, the more "real" your script feels, the more it will jump off the page and be an entertaining experience for a reader (and we know how fickle they can be).

If you are a film enthusiast, my advice is to watch (or rewatch) as many of the films featured in this book as possible – viewing them with a judicious eye toward their heroes and villains. And feel free to apply "Jeff's Eleven 'Laws' of Great Storytelling" whenever the need arises.

Most importantly, I hope this book gives you permission to be more critical of films and have more fun with the moviegoing experience.

So now that you're done reading about the movies, it is probably a good time to get up and actually go to the movies.

Enjoy the show.

References

Academy of Motion Picture Arts and Sciences. 2008. Awards Database. Retrieved October 10, 2008. *www.awardsdatabase.oscars.org.*

Antagonist. (n.d.). *The American Heritage® Dictionary of the English Language, Fourth Edition.* Retrieved September 8, 2008, from Dictionary.com website: *dictionary.reference.com/browse/antagonist*

American Film Institute. 2003. *100 Years... 100 Heroes & Villains.* Retrieved October 1, 2006. *www.afi.com.*

Arsenault, Raymond. 1998. "Wall Street (1987): The Stockbroker's Son and the Decade of Greed." *Film & History.* 28.1/2: 16-27.

Burke, Ken. 1990. "Heroes and Villains in American Film." *International Journal of Instructional Media.* 17.1: 63-72.

Campbell, Joseph. 1972. *The Hero With a Thousand Faces.* Princeton, NJ: Princeton University Press.

Crowe, Cameron. 2001. *Conversations With Wilder.* New York: Alfred A. Knopf.

Fischoff, Stuart. 1987. *Fatal Attraction* DVD "Social Attraction." [Motion picture]. USA: Paramount Pictures.

Henderson, J. L. 1964. *Ancient Myths and Modern Man.* In Jung, C.G. (Ed.), *Man and His Symbols* (101). New York: Dell.

Hirschberg, Jeffrey. 2007. "The Incomplete Hero: Rick Blaine to Rocky Balboa." *Feedback* 48.3: 4-15.

The Internet Movie Database. 2008. *www.imdb.com.*

Joshel, Sandra. 1992. "Fatal Liaisons and Dangerous Attraction: The Destruction of Feminist Voices." *Journal of Popular Culture.* 26.3: 59-70.

Mackey-Kallis, S. 2001. *The Hero and the Perennial Journey Home in American Film.* Philadelphia: University of Pennsylvania Press.

Meyer, Michaela. 2003. "Utilizing Mythic Criticism in Contemporary Narrative Culture: Examining the 'Present-Absence' of Shadow Archetypes in *Spider-Man.*" *Communication Quarterly.* 51.4: 518-529.

Norden, Martin. 2000. "The Changing Face of Evil in Film and Television." *Journal of Popular Film and Television.* 28.2: 50-53.

Pratt, Ray. 2001. *Conspiratorial Visions in American Film: Projecting Paranoia.* Lawrence, KS: University Press of Kansas, 2001.

Protagonist. (n.d.). *The American Heritage® Dictionary of the English Language, Fourth Edition*. Retrieved September 8, 2008, from Dictionary.com website: *dictionary.reference.com/browse/protagonist*

Rushing, J. H. & Frentz, T. S. 1995. *Projecting the Shadow: The Cyborg Hero in American Film*. Chicago: The University of Chicago Press.

Salamon, Linda. 2000. "Postmodern Villainy in *Richard III* and *Scarface*." *Journal of Popular Film and Television*. 28.2: 54-64.

Stone, John. 2000. "Evil in the Early Cinema of Oliver Stone: *Platoon* and *Wall Street* as Modern Morality Plays." *Journal of Popular Film and Television*. 28.2: 80-87.

Vogler, Christopher. 2007. *The Writer's Journey: Mythic Structure for Writers*. (3rd ed.). Studio City, CA: Michael Wiese Productions.

Wee, Valerie. 2006. "Resurrecting and Updating the Teen Slasher." *Journal of Popular Film and Television*. 34.2: 50-61.

Wells, S. & Taylor, G. (Ed.). 1988. *William Shakespeare: The Complete Works* (Hamlet: II, ii, 606). Oxford: Clarendon Press.

"Weekend Box Office." EDI FilmSource. *Fatal Attraction* and *Wall Street*. 1 July 2007. <*www.variety.com*>.

Excerpts from the following scripts have been reproduced in this book:

Gladiator. Screenplay by David Franzoni, John Logan, and William Nicholson, based on a story by David Franzoni. ©2000. DreamWorks Pictures and Universal Pictures. All Rights Reserved.

Misery. Screenplay by William Goldman, based on the book by Stephen King. ©1990. Castle Rock Entertainment and 20th Century-Fox. All Rights Reserved.

Mommie Dearest. Screenplay by Robert Getchell, Tracy Hotchner, Frank Perry, and Frank Yablans, based on the book by Christina Crawford. ©1981. Paramount Pictures. All Rights Reserved.

Norma Rae. Screenplay by Harriet Frank Jr. and Irving Ravetch. ©1979. 20th Century-Fox. All Rights Reserved.

One Flew Over the Cuckoo's Nest. Screenplay by Lawrence Hauben and Bo Goldman, based on a novel by Ken Kesey. ©1975. United Artists. All Rights Reserved.

Raiders of the Lost Ark. Screenplay by Lawrence Kasdan, based on a story by George Lucas and Philip Kaufman. ©1981. Paramount Pictures and Lucasfilm. All Rights Reserved.

Return of the Jedi. Screenplay by Lawrence Kasdan and George Lucas, based on a story by George Lucas. ©1983. 20th Century-Fox and Lucasfilm. All Rights Reserved.

Rocky. Screenplay by Sylvester Stallone. ©1976. United Artists. All Rights Reserved.

Schindler's List. Screenplay by Steven Zaillian, based on a book by Thomas Keneally. ©1993. Universal Pictures and Amblin Entertainment. All Rights Reserved.

The Silence of the Lambs. Screenplay by Ted Tally, based on a novel by Thomas Harris. ©1991. Orion Pictures. All Rights Reserved.

Spider-Man. Screenplay by David Koepp, based on the Marvel comic book by Stan Lee and Steve Ditko. ©2002. Columbia Pictures. All Rights Reserved.

Star Wars. Screenplay by George Lucas. ©1977. 20th Century-Fox and Lucasfilm. All Rights Reserved.

To Kill a Mockingbird. Screenplay by Horton Foote, based on a novel by Harper Lee. ©1962. Universal Pictures. All Rights Reserved.

Wall Street. Screenplay by Stanley Weiser & Oliver Stone. ©1987. 20th Century-Fox. All Rights Reserved.

The Wizard of Oz. Screenplay by Noel Langley, Florence Ryerson, and Edgar Allan Woolf – adapted by Noel Langley, based on a novel by L. Frank Baum. ©1939. Metro-Goldwyn-Mayer. All Rights Reserved.

About the Author:

Photo by Bruce Fox. Buffalo State College

JEFFREY HIRSCHBERG is an Assistant Professor and Director of the Television and Film Arts Program at Buffalo State College. He has been a professional screenwriter for eighteen years and has written sixteen feature-length screenplays and numerous television scripts.

A member of the Writers Guild of America and judge for the WGA Awards, Jeffrey has had screenplays optioned by Hollywood production companies and has written and/or created shows for Showtime Networks, Lifetime Television, and ABC. He has worked at NBC, Warner Bros., and Viacom and has taught at Cornell University, Syracuse University's Newhouse School, and R.I.T.'s School of Film and Animation.

In addition to his writing and professorial duties, Jeffrey is an active screenplay consultant via his ThreeAct script consulting service (*www.ThreeAct.com*).

Prior to founding ThreeAct, Jeffrey held numerous executive marketing and advertising positions in New York City. He holds a bachelor's degree from Cornell University and a master's degree in TV-Radio-Film from Syracuse University's Newhouse School.

Jeffrey lives with his wife and three sons in upstate New York.

Email: *jeff@threeact.com*
Website: *www.ThreeAct.com*

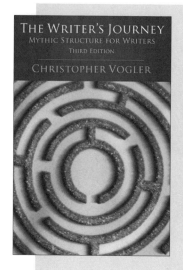

THE WRITER'S JOURNEY – 3RD EDITION
MYTHIC STRUCTURE FOR WRITERS

CHRISTOPHER VOGLER

BEST SELLER
OVER 180,000 COPIES SOLD!

See why this book has become an international best seller and a true classic. *The Writer's Journey* explores the powerful relationship between mythology and storytelling in a clear, concise style that's made it required reading for movie executives, screenwriters, playwrights, scholars, and fans of pop culture all over the world.

Both fiction and nonfiction writers will discover a set of useful myth-inspired storytelling paradigms (i.e., "The Hero's Journey") and step-by-step guidelines to plot and character development. Based on the work of Joseph Campbell, *The Writer's Journey* is a must for all writers interested in further developing their craft.

The updated and revised third edition provides new insights and observations from Vogler's ongoing work on mythology's influence on stories, movies, and man himself.

"This book is like having the smartest person in the story meeting come home with you and whisper what to do in your ear as you write a screenplay. Insight for insight, step for step, Chris Vogler takes us through the process of connecting theme to story and making a script come alive."
> – Lynda Obst, Producer, *Sleepless in Seattle, How to Lose a Guy in 10 Days*;
> Author, *Hello, He Lied*

"This is a book about the stories we write, and perhaps more importantly, the stories we live. It is the most influential work I have yet encountered on the art, nature, and the very purpose of storytelling."
> – Bruce Joel Rubin, Screenwriter, *Stuart Little 2, Deep Impact,*
> *Ghost, Jacob's Ladder*

CHRISTOPHER VOGLER is a veteran story consultant for major Hollywood film companies and a respected teacher of filmmakers and writers around the globe. He has influenced the stories of movies from *The Lion King* to *Fight Club* to *The Thin Red Line* and most recently wrote the first installment of *Ravenskull*, a Japanese-style manga or graphic novel. He is the executive producer of the feature film *P.S. Your Cat is Dead* and writer of the animated feature *Jester Till*.

$26.95 · 448 PAGES · ORDER NUMBER 76RLS · ISBN: 9781932907360

THE POWER OF THE DARK SIDE
CREATING GREAT VILLAINS
AND DANGEROUS SITUATIONS

PAMELA JAYE SMITH

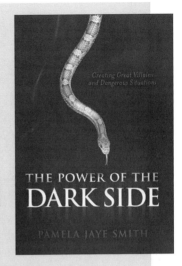

Who doesn't love the Dark Side? Darth Vader, Cruella De Vil, Tony Soprano — everybody loves a great villain. And every story needs dramatic conflict — internal and external — to really resonate. This comprehensive, accessible book gives you tools to craft the most despicable villains in your stories.

Conflict is the very heart and soul of drama. Mythologist Pamela Jaye Smith's latest book explores character conflict and a multitude of ways to achieve it:

· Defining the Dark Side helps you select and clarify the worldview that influences your characters' actions.

· The Three Levels of the Dark Side — personal, impersonal, and supra-personal — offer layers of interweaving conflict.

· A roll-call of Villains includes Profiles and Suggestions for creating your own versions of reader's bad-to-the-bone favorites.

· Learn to match Antagonists to Protagonists, and to use the Sliding Scale of Evil.

"The Power of the Dark Side *is an incredible exploration of the different dimensions of Evil. Pamela Jaye Smith demonstrates once again that she is one of the world's experts, not only on multicultural mythology but also on the application of the ideas of archetype, symbol, and cognitive science. While she's written this book with the writer in mind, her exploration of the ideas of evil will be of great value to teachers, therapists, and anyone who deals with people, education, motivation, or persuasion. For writers, it opens up a world of ideas that will help in building more complex antagonists. To have a great hero, you need a great villain. Dark Side delivers far more than you'd expect from one book."*
>   — Rob Kall, publisher of *OpEdNews.com* and founder, Storycon Summit
>   Meeting on the Art, Science and Application of Story

PAMELA JAYE SMITH is an international speaker, consultant, writer, award-winning producer-director, and founder of MYTHWORKS www.mythworks.net. Credits include Microsoft, Paramount, Disney, Universal, GM, Boeing, the FBI and US Army. Smith has authored the MWP book, *Inner Drives*. She has taught writers, directors, and actors at USC, UCLA, American Film Institute, RAI-TV Rome, Denmark, France, New Zealand, Brazil, and many other venues.

$22.95 · 266 PAGES · ORDER NUMBER 82RLS · ISBN 13: 9781932907438

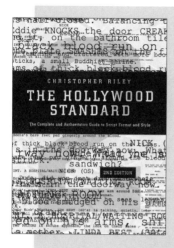

THE HOLLYWOOD STANDARD
2ND EDITION
THE COMPLETE AND AUTHORITATIVE GUIDE TO SCRIPT FORMAT AND STYLE

CHRISTOPHER RILEY

This is the book screenwriter Antwone Fisher (*Antwone Fisher, Tales from the Script*) insists his writing students at UCLA read. This book convinced John August (*Big Fish, Charlie and the Chocolate Factory*) to stop dispensing formatting advice on his popular writing website. His new advice: Consult *The Hollywood Standard*. The book working and aspiring writers keep beside their keyboards and rely on every day. Written by a professional screenwriter whose day job was running the vaunted script shop at Warner Bros., this book is used at USC's School of Cinema, UCLA, and the acclaimed Act One Writing Program in Hollywood, and in screenwriting programs around the world. It is the definitive guide to script format.

The Hollywood Standard describes in clear, vivid prose and hundreds of examples how to format every element of a screenplay or television script. A reference for everyone who writes for the screen, from the novice to the veteran, this is the dictionary of script format, with instructions for formatting everything from the simplest master scene heading to the most complex and challenging musical underwater dream sequence. This new edition includes a quick start guide, plus new chapters on avoiding a dozen deadly formatting mistakes, clarifying the difference between a spec script and production script, and mastering the vital art of proofreading. For the first time, readers will find instructions for formatting instant messages, text messages, email exchanges and caller ID.

"*Aspiring writers sometimes wonder why people don't want to read their scripts. Sometimes it's not their story. Sometimes the format distracts. To write a screenplay, you need to learn the science. And this is the best, simplest, easiest to read book to teach you that science. It's the one I recommend to my students at UCLA.*"

— Antwone Fisher, from the foreword

CHRISTOPHER RILEY is a professional screenwriter working in Hollywood with his wife and writing partner, Kathleen Riley. Together they wrote the 1999 theatrical feature *After the Truth*, a multiple-award-winning German language courtroom thriller. Since then, the husband-wife team has written scripts ranging from legal and political thrillers to action-romances for Touchstone Pictures, Paramount Pictures, Mandalay Television Pictures and Sean Connery's Fountainbridge Films.

In addition to writing, the Rileys train aspiring screenwriters for work in Hollywood and have taught in Los Angeles, Chicago, Washington D.C., New York, and Paris. From 2005 to 2008, the author directed the acclaimed Act One Writing Program in Hollywood.

$24.95 · 208 PAGES · ORDER NUMBER 130RLS · ISBN: 9781932907636

CINEMATIC STORYTELLING
THE 100 MOST POWERFUL FILM CONVENTIONS
EVERY FILMMAKER MUST KNOW

JENNIFER VAN SIJLL

BEST SELLER

How do directors use screen direction to suggest conflict? How do screenwriters exploit film space to show change? How does editing style determine emotional response?

Many first-time writers and directors do not ask these questions. They forego the huge creative resource of the film medium, defaulting to dialog to tell their screen story. Yet most movies are carried by sound and picture. The industry's most successful writers and directors have mastered the cinematic conventions specific to the medium. They have harnessed non-dialog techniques to create some of the most cinematic moments in movie history.

This book is intended to help writers and directors more fully exploit the medium's inherent storytelling devices. It contains 100 non-dialog techniques that have been used by the industry's top writers and directors. From *Metropolis* and *Citizen Kane* to *Dead Man* and *Kill Bill*, the book illustrates — through 500 frame grabs and 75 script excerpts — how the inherent storytelling devices specific to film were exploited.

You will learn:
· How non-dialog film techniques can advance story.
· How master screenwriters exploit cinematic conventions to create powerful scenarios.

"Cinematic Storytelling *scores a direct hit in terms of concise information and perfectly chosen visuals, and it also searches out... and finds... an emotional core that many books of this nature either miss or are afraid of.*"
— Kirsten Sheridan, Director, *Disco Pigs*; Co-writer, *In America*

"*Here is a uniquely fresh, accessible, and truly original contribution to the field. Jennifer van Sijll takes her readers in a wholly new direction, integrating aspects of screenwriting with all the film crafts in a way I've never before seen. It is essential reading not only for screenwriters but also for filmmakers of every stripe.*"
— Prof. Richard Walter, UCLA Screenwriting Chairman

JENNIFER VAN SIJLL has taught film production, film history, and screenwriting. She is currently on the faculty at San Francisco State's Department of Cinema.

$24.95 · 230 PAGES · ORDER NUMBER 35RLS · ISBN: 9781932907056

SAVE THE CAT!® GOES TO THE MOVIES
THE SCREENWRITER'S GUIDE
TO EVERY STORY EVER TOLD

BLAKE SNYDER

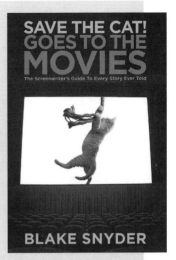

In the long-awaited sequel to his surprise bestseller, *Save the Cat!*, author and screenwriter Blake Snyder returns to form in a fast-paced follow-up that proves why his is the most talked-about approach to screenwriting in years. In the perfect companion piece to his first book, Snyder delivers even more insider's information gleaned from a 20-year track record as "one of Hollywood's most successful spec screenwriters," giving you the clues to write *your* movie.

Designed for screenwriters, novelists, and movie fans, this book gives readers the key breakdowns of the 50 most instructional movies from the past 30 years. From *M*A*S*H* to *Crash*, from *Alien* to *Saw*, from *10* to *Eternal Sunshine of the Spotless Mind*, Snyder reveals how screenwriters who came before you tackled the same challenges you are facing with the film you want to write – or the one you are currently working on.

Writing a "rom-com"? Check out the "Buddy Love" chapter for a "beat for beat" dissection of *When Harry Met Sally...* plus references to 10 other great romantic comedies that will make your story sing.

Want to execute a great mystery? Go to the "Whydunit" section and learn about the "dark turn" that's essential to the heroes of *All the President's Men*, *Blade Runner*, *Fargo* and hip noir *Brick* – and see why ALL good stories, whether a Hollywood blockbuster or a Sundance award winner, follow the same rules of structure outlined in Snyder's breakthrough method.

If you want to sell your script and create a movie that pleases most audiences most of the time, the odds increase if you reference Snyder's checklists and see what makes 50 films tick. After all, both executives and audiences respond to the same elements good writers seek to master. They want to know the type of story they signed on for, and whether it's structured in a way that satisfies everyone. It's what they're looking for. And now, it's what you can deliver.

BLAKE SNYDER, besides selling million-dollar scripts to both Disney and Spielberg, is still "one of Hollywood's most successful spec screenwriters," having made another spec sale in 2006. An in-demand scriptcoach and seminar and workshop leader, Snyder provides information for writers through his website, *www.blakesnyder.com*.

$24.95 · 270 PAGES · ORDER NUMBER 75RLS · ISBN: 9781932907353

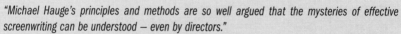

Our books are all about helping you create memorable films that will move audiences for generations to come.

Since 1981, we've published over 100 books on all aspects of filmmaking which are used in more than 600 film schools around the world. Many of today's most productive filmmakers and writers got started with our books.

According to a recent Nielsen BookScan analysis, as a publisher we've had more best-selling books in our subject category than our closest competitor — and they are backed by a multi-billion dollar corporation! This is evidence that as an independent — filmmaker or publisher — you can create the projects you have always dreamed of and earn a livelihood.

To help you accomplish your goals, we've expanded our information to the web. Here you can receive a 25% discount on all our books, buy the newest releases before they hit the bookstores, and sign up for a newsletter which provides all kinds of new information, tips, seminars, and more. You'll also find a Virtual Film School loaded with articles and websites from our top authors, teacher's guides, video streamed content, free budget formats, and a ton of free valuable information.

We encourage you to visit www.mwp.com. Sign up and become part of a wider creative community.

Onward and upward,
Michael Wiese
Publisher, Filmmaker

If you'd like to receive a free MWP Newsletter,
click on www.mwp.com to register.

FILM & VIDEO BOOKS

SCREENWRITING | WRITING

And the Best Screenplay Goes to... | Dr. Linda Seger | $26.95
Archetypes for Writers | Jennifer Van Bergen | $22.95
Cinematic Storytelling | Jennifer Van Sijll | $24.95
Could It Be a Movie? | Christina Hamlett | $26.95
Creating Characters | Marisa D'Vari | $26.95
Crime Writer's Reference Guide, The | Martin Roth | $20.95
Deep Cinema | Mary Trainor-Brigham | $19.95
Elephant Bucks | Sheldon Bull | $24.95
Fast, Cheap & Written That Way | John Gaspard | $26.95
Hollywood Standard, The | Christopher Riley | $18.95
I Could've Written a Better Movie than That! | Derek Rydall | $26.95
Inner Drives | Pamela Jaye Smith | $26.95
Joe Leydon's Guide to Essential Movies You Must See | Joe Leydon | $24.95
Moral Premise, The | Stanley D. Williams, Ph.D. | $24.95
Myth and the Movies | Stuart Voytilla | $26.95
Power of the Dark Side, The | Pamela Jaye Smith | $22.95
Psychology for Screenwriters | William Indick, Ph.D. | $26.95
Rewrite | Paul Chitlik | $16.95
Romancing the A-List | Christopher Keane | $18.95
Save the Cat! | Blake Snyder | $19.95
Save the Cat! Goes to the Movies | Blake Snyder | $24.95
Screenwriting 101 | Neill D. Hicks | $16.95
Screenwriting for Teens | Christina Hamlett | $18.95
Script-Selling Game, The | Kathie Fong Yoneda | $16.95
Stealing Fire From the Gods, 2nd Edition | James Bonnet | $26.95
Way of Story, The | Catherine Ann Jones | $22.95
What Are You Laughing At? | Brad Schreiber | $19.95
Writer's Journey, – 3rd Edition, The | Christopher Vogler | $26.95
Writer's Partner, The | Martin Roth | $24.95
Writing the Action Adventure Film | Neill D. Hicks | $14.95
Writing the Comedy Film | Stuart Voytilla & Scott Petri | $14.95
Writing the Killer Treatment | Michael Halperin | $14.95
Writing the Second Act | Michael Halperin | $19.95
Writing the Thriller Film | Neill D. Hicks | $14.95
Writing the TV Drama Series – 2nd Edition | Pamela Douglas | $26.95
Your Screenplay Sucks! | William M. Akers | $19.95

FILMMAKING

Film School | Richard D. Pepperman | $24.95
Power of Film, The | Howard Suber | $27.95

PITCHING

Perfect Pitch – 2nd Edition, The | Ken Rotcop | $19.95
Selling Your Story in 60 Seconds | Michael Hauge | $12.95

SHORTS

Filmmaking for Teens | Troy Lanier & Clay Nichols | $18.95
Ultimate Filmmaker's Guide to Short Films, The | Kim Adelman | $16.95

BUDGET | PRODUCTION MGMT

Film & Video Budgets, 4th Updated Edition | Deke Simon & Michael Wiese | $26.95
Film Production Management 101 | Deborah S. Patz | $39.95

DIRECTING | VISUALIZATION

Animation Unleashed | Ellen Besen | $26.95
Citizen Kane Crash Course in Cinematography | David Worth | $19.95
Directing Actors | Judith Weston | $26.95
Directing Feature Films | Mark Travis | $26.95
Fast, Cheap & Under Control | John Gaspard | $26.95
Film Directing: Cinematic Motion, 2nd Edition | Steven D. Katz | $27.95
Film Directing: Shot by Shot | Steven D. Katz | $27.95
Film Director's Intuition, The | Judith Weston | $26.95
First Time Director | Gil Bettman | $27.95
From Word to Image | Marcie Begleiter | $26.95
I'll Be in My Trailer! | John Badham & Craig Modderno | $26.95
Master Shots | Christopher Kenworthy | $24.95
Setting Up Your Scenes | Richard D. Pepperman | $24.95
Setting Up Your Shots, 2nd Edition | Jeremy Vineyard | $22.95
Working Director, The | Charles Wilkinson | $22.95

DIGITAL | DOCUMENTARY | SPECIAL

Digital Filmmaking 101, 2nd Edition | Dale Newton & John Gaspard | $26.95
Digital Moviemaking 3.0 | Scott Billups | $24.95
Digital Video Secrets | Tony Levelle | $26.95
Greenscreen Made Easy | Jeremy Hanke & Michele Yamazaki | $19.95
Producing with Passion | Dorothy Fadiman & Tony Levelle | $22.95
Special Effects | Michael Slone | $31.95

EDITING

Cut by Cut | Gael Chandler | $35.95
Cut to the Chase | Bobbie O'Steen | $24.95
Eye is Quicker, The | Richard D. Pepperman | $27.95
Invisible Cut, The | Bobbie O'Steen | $28.95

SOUND | DVD | CAREER

Complete DVD Book, The | Chris Gore & Paul J. Salamoff | $26.95
Costume Design 101 | Richard La Motte | $19.95
Hitting Your Mark – 2nd Edition | Steve Carlson | $22.95
Sound Design | David Sonnenschein | $19.95
Sound Effects Bible, The | Ric Viers | $26.95
Storyboarding 101 | James Fraioli | $19.95
There's No Business Like Soul Business | Derek Rydall | $22.95

FINANCE | MARKETING | FUNDING

Art of Film Funding, The | Carole Lee Dean | $26.95
Complete Independent Movie Marketing Handbook, The | Mark Steven Bosko | $39.95
Independent Film and Videomakers Guide – 2nd Edition, The | Michael Wiese | $29.95
Independent Film Distribution | Phil Hall | $26.95
Shaking the Money Tree, 2nd Edition | Morrie Warshawski | $26.95

OUR FILMS

Dolphin Adventures: DVD | Michael Wiese and Hardy Jones | $24.95
On the Edge of a Dream | Michael Wiese | $16.95
Sacred Sites of the Dalai Lamas– DVD, The | Documentary by Michael Wiese | $24.95
Hardware Wars: DVD | Written and Directed by Ernie Fosselius | $14.95